This Day

...

DIARIES
from American Women

This Day

...

DIARIES
from American Women

...

Compiled and Edited by
Joni B. Cole, Rebecca Joffrey, and B. K. Rakhra

BEYOND
WORDS
Publishing
I N C

Beyond Words Publishing, Inc.
20827 N.W. Cornell Road, Suite 500
Hillsboro, Oregon 97124-9808
503-531-8700

The views expressed by each day diarist are her own. The statements of any day diarist
do not necessarily reflect the views of any other contributor, or any of the organizations
of which the day diarist may be a part; nor do they necessarily reflect the views of the
book's editors, Joni B. Cole, Rebecca Joffrey, and B. K. Rakhra, or the publisher.

Note: The Collective Glimpses survey was completed by 493 (out of 529) day diarists.
The yes-or-no questions in the survey referred exclusively to October 15, 2002, and all
responses were anonymous.

Editor: Jenefer Angell
Managing editor: Julie Steigerwaldt
Copyeditor/proofreader: David Abel
Design: Angela Lavespere and Dorral Lukas
Cover photograph: Henders Haggerty
Composition: William H. Brunson Typography Services

Printed in the United States of America
Distributed to the book trade by Publishers Group West

Library of Congress Cataloging-in-Publication Data
This day : diaries from American women / compiled and edited by Joni B. Cole,
Rebecca Joffrey, and B.K. Rakhra.
    p. cm.
  ISBN 1-58270-102-4
  1. Women—United States—Diaries. 2. Women—United States—Biography.
I. Cole, Joni B. II. Joffrey, Rebecca. III. Rakhra, B. K. IV. Title.
HQ1412.T453 2003
305.4'092'273—dc22

                                                              2003014316

The corporate mission of Beyond Words Publishing, Inc.:
  Inspire to Integrity

For Stephen, Esme, and Thea,
who put the "home" in home office; and for my parents
Joni B. Cole

• • •

For Elizabeth Susan Joffrey, born November 21, 2002,
into the company of great women (and her father, Alan!)
Rebecca Joffrey

• • •

To my family for their love and support, which allowed me
to take a chance on writing
(and without whom I'd still be working nine to five)
B. K. Rakhra

Contents

Introduction

About two years ago, I was in the throes of a serious self-pity party. My dad had recently suffered a massive stroke, leaving me and my family shell-shocked as we struggled to adjust to the new reality of ICUs and long-term care. At the same time, my husband and I were hit with an enormous tax bill—one we couldn't possibly pay without getting loans on top of our loans. As I sat at my desk in my home office (a door laid across two filing cabinets in a corner of my bedroom), the springtime view out my Vermont window showed snow mixed with freezing rain, and my stomach remained in knots over the morning's major battle with my four-year-old daughter over socks. ("If you don't put something on your feet *this second*, I'm going to throw every sock you own out the window!")

As noon came and went, I found myself still wearing my Queen Bee flannel pajamas, since I hadn't the energy to shower or dress—and who was I trying to impress anyway, the dog? What's more, the idea of my home office seemed like a bad joke, since my most recent writing assignment (a polyp-prevention newsletter, if you must know the truth) was long gone, with no new job prospects in sight. Despite this sad fact, both my daughters (one sockless; one aged two) had been consigned to our three-day-a-week daycare provider, a saint who made play-dough and tomato soup from scratch, and who, even at this very moment, probably was usurping my rightful place in my children's hearts.

Hunched at my desk, eating lunch out of a microwavable cardboard box, I wondered if anybody else I knew was feeling this miserable. I started imagining what my friends might be doing while I sulked in my pajamas. Likely, they were on assignment (I've always loved that term—"on assignment"—I think it was the sole reason I went into journalism), or helping their preschoolers self-actualize before kindergarten, or bonding with other women over luncheons (yes, luncheons!) at restaurants with linen tablecloths and salt cellars. In this frame of mind, I decided to e-mail a few women from different circles of my life, and ask what a day in their life was actually like.

The responses they sent back were illuminating. Part itinerary, part journal, these "day diaries" revealed their lives from the inside out—showing not only how they spent their time, but what was in their heads and hearts as they went through those twenty-four hours. As I read these day diaries—experiencing each woman's day from her point of view—my own misconceptions and judgments about their lives quickly faded in the face of reality. I understood these women in a way that I never had before.

The day diaries also helped me gain a better perspective on my own life. Surprising points of connection emerged between me and these other women—not necessarily in our specific work or family situations, but on a more human level. Just like me, they worried, goofed off, rose above, gave up, succeeded, got by, lost it with their spouses and kids, and then lavished those very same family members with attention and love—all in the multitude of moments that make up any given day. Reading each one of these day diaries, I felt a little more connected, enlightened—even normal. In essence, I felt like I was in good company—the company of women—and that's when the idea for the book hit me. What is "a day in the life" really like for any woman—a CEO, a single mom, a TV celebrity, an inmate, a woman with disabilities? Intrigued by details, and infinitely curious about other people's lives, I couldn't imagine anyone whose day diary I wouldn't be interested in reading. And so the concept for *This Day: Diaries from American Women* was born.

I and my two partners in this book project—Rebecca Joffrey and Bindi Rakhra—spent three months inviting women from across the United States and from all walks of life to create a day diary on a single Tuesday in October. We chose a Tuesday because it seemed like the most "ordinary" day of the week. We chose October 15 because it was a window in the American calendar, unencumbered with holidays or national significance. All the participants in this book project created their day diaries on the same day, whether those twenty-four hours proved typical or atypical, and regardless of what was going on in the outside world.

Our goal was to recruit as diverse a group of American women as possible—reaching across experiential, cultural, geographic, and socioeconomic boundaries. To that end, we made countless cold calls, and sent e-mails to our friends, alumni networks, business associates, and anyone else we could think of who might be able to close the distance between Vermont and the rest of the country. We enlisted the help of organizations, from the Guide Dog Foundation for the Blind, to Habitat for Humanity, to the United States Polo Association. We approached clerks at mall kiosks, and accosted our women seatmates on planes and trains. Becky even tried to recruit the MCI telemarketer who called her about switching her phone service. (The woman ultimately declined, but we did end up with better long distance rates.)

We also asked our newly recruited participants: Whose day diary would *you* like to read? In response, they connected us with their own mentors, mothers, clients, "weird" cousins, and personal heroines. When we saw a gap in our recruitment efforts ("North Dakota! We don't have any day diarists from North Dakota!") they scrambled for us, posting the project on listservs and bulletin boards, and helping us tap into demographic groups and ethnic communities we never would have reached without their efforts.

All told, 529 women contributed day diaries to this book project. Every day diarist participated as an unpaid volunteer and was well aware that her contribution might never be published, since the book could only accommodate thirty-five complete day diaries, as well as excerpts from the remaining pool. Regardless, the participants directed a magnitude of positive energy and effort toward this project.

As day diaries jammed our post office box in White River Junction—and as we moved from the "project" to the "book" phase—our most difficult task became choosing the contributions for this collection. As we read hundreds of day diaries, we were transported to corporate board rooms, concert halls, play groups, maternity and cancer wards, soup kitchens, classrooms, fashion shows, prison cells, television studios, and hundreds of households across the United States.

We discovered what women love (and don't love!) about their families, their jobs, and their lives. We noticed common themes—from our too-hectic lifestyles ("Rush! Rush! Rush!"—the refrain of countless day diaries); to our shared craving for chocolate (one of the basic food groups, according to one of our physician day diarists); to the astounding prevalence of e-advertisements touting the benefits of Viagra. We learned what women are actually thinking about in meetings, in the shower, and while changing diapers. We saw how women run the world . . . and how they sometimes get in their own way. (Ladies, do we *really* need to iron our shower curtains before going to bed?)

The more day diaries we read, the more addicted we became to reading them, with each contribution lending yet another voice to the mix. Both individually and collectively, the day diaries revealed an important truth. Homemaker. Celebrity. Lesbian. New Yorker. Clinically Depressed. Trucker. Native American—while the labels we assign ourselves, or society assigns to us, may be accurate, they are also inadequate. They may describe a woman's circumstances, or skin color, or "type." Yet, as one day diarist wrote: "I am not a typical woman. There is no such thing as typical. I am just me." By sharing the perspective of another woman—if only for one day—readers may see a truer glimpse of the individual behind the stereotype; the person behind the label.

The thirty-five day diaries presented in this collection represent a diversity of American women—young and old, rich and poor, well-known and ordinary citizens. We chose these particular women because we found their day diaries sincere, intimate, funny, intriguing, and compelling. No doubt, our own life experiences and personality quirks influenced the selection process; no doubt, we could have featured a completely different selection of women with equally compelling results.

In the first months of working on this project, my partners and I wondered if women would be willing to participate in a project that asked them to share the details of their professional and personal lives with the reading public. After all, it is one thing to keep a private diary or journal tucked in a bedside drawer—it is quite another to see your seatmate in 22A chuckling over your husband's unhealthy predilection for computer chess. As the project unfolded and October 15 came and went, many of our participants shared their reactions and insights about the day diary experience. In one e-mail, a day diarist used the salutation "Dear friends," explaining, "I have to use that word because you now know things about me that only my therapist knew before." The day diarists believed in the value of this project enough to entrust the details of their lives and their private thoughts to anyone who might pick up a copy of this book, including total strangers, their mothers-in-law, and their supervisors at work. ("Really, I was only kidding about hating my job, really.") Their generosity in sharing their days energized our own faith in this project, and confirmed our belief that this is what matters—these moments both funny and serious, quiet and dramatic, that occur throughout any given day, and illuminate who we really are as individuals, as women, and as Americans.

One of our favorite descriptions of the book project came from a fifty-one-year-old nurse's aide and mother of four grown children, who suggested, "This is the biggest movement since women burned their bras." Yet, rippling through this sea of enthusiasm was an undercurrent of hesitancy among some participants. Several women we approached, or who approached us, expressed doubts about whether their day diaries would be "good enough" to merit inclusion. "Not too many times in your life do people want to know about you, especially if you're a woman," commented one sixty-two-year-old retired secretary and artist.

In their feedback about the day diary experience, participants shared some amusing—and some not-so-amusing—stories. One came from a forty-year-old mom who was feeling a bit of the empty nest syndrome, since her only child had recently started kindergarten. She happened to have an appointment with her chiropractor that morning, and told him how she was chronicling a single day in her life for a book. His response: "Well . . . but who would want to buy it?" Lying face down, her cheeks wedged between the crinkly paper-covered bumpers, she was confronted with yet another suggestion that her life was trivial and her perspective irrelevant. A similar story came from a forty-four-year-old mother, marathon runner, and library worker, who explained to her husband over breakfast that she was writing in her day diary, to which he replied, "Why would they be interested in anything you have to say? They're only interested in lawyers and playwrights." While we appreciate the man's curious juxtaposition of livelihoods, it doesn't change the fact that he was wrong.

A few weeks before October 15, Becky's husband, Alan, attended the funeral of an uncle outside Chicago. After the service, family and friends returned to his parents' house. Several women at the gathering happened to be participants in the book project, or they knew about it through Alan's mother, who had told her Mah Jongg friends, who had told other Mah Jongg friends, and so on and so on. Circled around the deli platter from Max and Benny's, the women started speculating about who among them might "get in" the book. One woman had actually brought a writing sample with her to the funeral—a story she had published in a local newspaper. She offered the article to Alan, in the hopes he might pass it along to us for consideration of her writing skills.

The woman is indeed a fine writer—but that's not the value of her day diary. Neither writing skill nor public acclaim were prerequisites for participation in *This Day*. Each and every one of our 529 day diarists enhanced this book project and informed the pages you see here, because they all lent a unique voice to the project. And that is why their contributions matter, because each woman offers readers a perspective from one day in her life that no one else—no one else—could have contributed to this book, not even lawyers and playwrights.

— *Joni B. Cole*

Mommy Martyr

*O*nce a groovy girl lawyer intellectual . . . now an "over-educated under-achiever" who fell into the role of homemaker. "I assumed I'd be working but once I had Fletcher—What was I thinking? How could I let anyone else take care of my baby?" Five years and a second baby later, the switch in roles still throws her self-identity for a loop. "It's been hard when I thought it would be easy. We worked so hard to become professional women, to throw it away and learn how to bake bread and clean toilets and go to mommy groups. I'm trying to enjoy being a mom/homemaker because I know it's only a phase, but I don't have a lot of accomplishments to take pride in outside of motherhood." Outgoing. Outspoken. Married to a psychologist. An only child who was close to her parents, she lost them both in her late twenties. She is half Chinese, but grew up all white. "My dad was the Chinese Archie Bunker. Being Chinese was the bane of his existence." She lives in a different era—showcasing her Asian background to make herself more interesting. That's why she kept her maiden name. That's why she dyed her brown hair black. "I've tried to make it an issue because being ethnically diverse is cool now."

TRACEY SANG, 37, *Encinitas, California*

9:00 A.M. Up. I realize that I am "blessed among women" for having kids who sleep so late but it's all relative and we didn't go to bed until 10 or 11. Fletcher (recently 5YO) is recovering from his first encounter with strep throat and even though he was content to be mellow yesterday, today I anticipate he will feel better and be bouncing off the walls and back to his usual nagging for entertainment. (He only goes to pre-K MWF so Tuesday and Thursday are often a whine-fest.) But he's not the one who makes it hard: it's been the addition of number two, Rex (now ten months) who pushes me over the edge hourly. He is the sweetest, most adorable and precocious angel. And he's a fuckin' handful.

Btw, I am sick too. Just a cold, but it's enough to make things harder. Btw, I used to be (still am, I guess) a lawyer. Now I just knock myself out working for nothing. Don't get me wrong, I wouldn't have it any other way. But man, motherhood can be a hard gig.

9:30 A.M. Doing day diary. Lasts all of ten seconds because Rex is fussin'. He is screaming and clawing at me even as I type. Really, he is fine. But he is still a breast-fed baby (I nursed Fletcher 'til he was two—path of least resistance) and this one too wants a boob in his mouth 24/7. Not to say he's not a grand eater of all things and a beast of a baby. He just wants what he wants. Don't we all.

9:30–10:30 A.M. A blur of diaper and clothes changing (for them, not me—I am still in my pajamas), cereal, unloading half the dishwasher, nursing, and watching *Blues Clues*. (Fletcher declares, "I like Joe better than Steve!") I have only managed to drink half my cup of precious coffee before the baby skillfully manages to reach up to the table and grab the handle, spilling the rest of the cold but life-giving liquid onto the whitish carpet. I make only a half-assed attempt to clean it well. After all, it merely joins a myriad of predecessors.

10:30 A.M. An odd moment of calm between storms. Fletcher has gone in his room and closed the door. (A new thing for him and something I'm sure I will grow to dread in the teenager years but for now it's great.) Rex has independently wandered off and is amusing himself—always a miracle. I just made a play-date to meet at McDonald's for later this afternoon. Lining up the amusement du jour is always a chore on our off-school days so I am relieved to have accomplished this relatively early. I'm sorry to say that I don't have an abundance of other mommies with whom I'm truly compatible. I often muse that "mommy dating" has become my new social mission and I'm now on the lookout for telltale signs of compatibility in a mom—reading *Vanity Fair*? a chic twist to the outfit? maybe an irreverent comment?—like I used to be looking for compatibility in a man!

Of course, I made this play-date because my husband was planning to play tennis after work. No sooner do I hang up with the friend than he calls to tell me that he will not be playing tennis and will be home by 4:00 and isn't that nice? I can't cancel now even though one of the happiest moments in my day is the return of my husband—such a flood of relief knowing that there will be another adult to converse with and help with the kids for the whole rest of the evening. I don't know how single parents stay sane.

11:00 A.M.–12:00 P.M. Get dressed. Margot coming over. Margot is an artist who we're commissioning to do a fine art painting of our kids. It's very hip and contemporary. She takes candid photos first, then isolates them and transfers them to canvas somehow and makes a kind of Warholesque painting. It's a big undertaking, but I've decided that I need ART. No more framed prints, ART dammit! I was an art major in undergrad so you wouldn't think that's asking too much. But, since coming to this decision, my husband and I have found that a large painting of any type is surprisingly pricey. Anyway, we stumbled onto Margot and we figure that this is a neat way of killing two birds with one stone: a painting AND a picture of the kids to boot.

Clean up the house a little. Margot is one of my "cool" acquaintances and as such is deserving of my wiping off the counter.

12:00–1:00 P.M. Photo session in the backyard, the canyon behind our house. Fletcher enjoys running in the canyon and pouts when we come back to the house. I'm glad that he's enjoying participating in the "project."

Change Rex's clothes (he fell in some puddles) and diaper. Nurse him in front of the computer while looking at the Last Chance! Gap sale e-mail. "Last chance"—ha! Last chance until tomorrow's e-mail.

1:30 P.M. Rex finally sleeps! Now it's time to feed ME some lunch (a frozen Budget Gourmet pasta and a Coke) and build Fletcher a LEGO Bionicle because I PROMISED.

Mother-in-law e-mailed me that my husband and I are SITCOMs: single-income-two-kids-oppressive-mortgage.

2:00 P.M. Fletcher wants bacon for lunch. Then he agrees to taquitos instead. In the midst of unloading the other half of the dishwasher and eating my lunch standing up, I forget that I just made him two taquitos and start cooking the bacon anyway. He does NOT want to build the Bionicle any more. Now he just wants to watch TV. I am happy but feel guilty about it. I realize yet again that I am all about quantity of time rather than quality and wonder whether a "better" mother would be using this time to show how one taquito plus another taquito equals two taquitos, and did you know that "taquito" is Spanish for little taco? (It IS, isn't it?)

Rex wakes up already. Off to buy birthday presents and Halloween costume and our date at McDonald's.

5:30 P.M. Home. A long, tiring, and expensive outing:

At Target: two birthday presents for the two parties this weekend (it's a never-ending process), a Halloween decoration since I'm getting a complex from the fifty Halloween decorations the neighbor has up, a new package of dinosaur underwear (too big, but it HAD to be the ones with the raptors on them), skull socks that make a scary noise, and a shirt and bra for me that I didn't even try on. I'm sure I'll be returning them tomorrow but who can try things on with two kids?

At Party City: the Ice Wolf Ninja costume. Out of the ten available ninja costumes why does he have to pick the only one that's $25? I conclude it must be because of the cool ice spear—BUT NO! Ice spear is an additional $7! $35 (after tax) for a costume that he will not be able—nor want—to fit in next month and that his brother will despise in three years.

At McDonald's: all in all, not bad. Good toy in the Happy Meal, both kids are happy at the play place, it's unexpectedly tidy there and my friend—who has three kids—always puts things into perspective for me. Her son actually cries with sadness when we have to go. If only all my departures were so dramatically met.

Rex is still awake when we arrive home. Fucking amazing. Aren't babies supposed to need sleep?

Daddy's home! Fletcher immediately dons his new underwear, puts on his Tarzan DVD, uses the remote to skip savvily to the leopard fight and commences to reenact it on his end with his new $7 ice spear. Daddy is the audience instead of me and even such a small thing is a help. I nurse the baby in front of the computer and he is out instantly. Bad time for a nap and probably too early for him to be down for the night.

Now on to dinner decisions. Oh! First I think I'll try on my Target shirt and bra and see how good my eyeballing skills have become . . .

7:30 P.M. Made spaghetti for dinner. It's a good fallback when nothing's thawed and it's one of Fletcher's favorites. Pretty lazy tonight (didn't even make a vegetable). I know, you'd think I could at least make a stinkin' vegetable. I mean, cooking the meals IS a large part of my "job" now. You know, everyone talks about the plight of the working mom, but in some respects I think it's easier. At least you have set hours. You still get to put on pretty clothes and go out to lunch. But when you're the primary caretaker and housewife, it never ends. It's 24/7. It's like that movie *Groundhog Day*. I sometimes feel there needs to be a voice for moms like me, someone who talks about the plight of the professional woman who's become a '50s throwback and what a difficult transition that is to go from Mary Tyler Moore back to June Cleaver.

Rex woke up again after just a half hour. What's going on? At least I have high hopes for an early bed time. He screamed the whole time I was making dinner. (Craig kind of tries to distract him but does a VERY poor job.) I burned the garlic bread, as usual. I am NOT a domestic goddess. At least not at this point in my life with two little kids making two messes as I try to clean up one. Craig usually does the dishes, which is great. I still usually have to do everything else like scrubbing off all the surfaces and putting everything away, but a man who does dishes is a keeper.

Fletcher is back to his old self now and was especially needful of attention during dinner. Craig and I can barely exchange a sentence or two without being rudely interrupted with a question involving whether his costume is cooler than the boy's next door or what he plans to ask Santa for Christmas or whether Rexy should be allowed to touch the dog's water bowl. By the time dinner is over, it is a welcome break to have the excuse to come into the office and type!

How about a bath for Rex?

(Btw, the Target shirt is good but I think I can do better at Victoria's Secret on the bra. It just seems a little cheap and ill-fitting.)

8:00–10:00 P.M. I run a bath for the baby, but decide to get in it myself. I get to sit all of five minutes before the baby comes trundling in looking for me. He is pleasantly surprised to find me in his tub and plays happily for quite a while dropping things into my bath water until I reach over from the tub and get him naked, all but one blue sock. (Daddy is out in the kitchen finally making Fletcher's Bionicle with him.) The cutest sight I've seen all day is my little, naked, dimpled cherub padding out the bathroom door in one sock, dragging my *In Style* magazine behind him.

After a few minutes he comes back with Fletcher and soon all three of us are in the tub. Eventually it is just Fletcher in the tub playing with this really messy foam stuff and me wrestling the baby into his last diaper of the day and his pajamas. He nurses, I find yet another version of *Wuthering Heights* to watch on TV, Dad is on the computer, and Fletcher is back in his room dancing to the Tarzan music. Finally, the baby is NIGHT-NIGHT!

I put the finishing touches on the kitchen, clean up that goop left in the tub by the supposedly kid-friendly foam, and discuss remodeling plans with Craig (until we decide, as we always do, that we can't afford it). All the while Fletcher is interrupting, interjecting, and generally making his presence known. As I mentioned this morning, Fletcher gets up relatively late because he doesn't go to bed 'til we do. We take a lot of flak for this because we get very little non-kid time. But all this will change as of next year when he has to get up early to go to kindergarten every day. So for now let him eat cake and stay up late with us.

10:00 P.M. Craig goes to bed (he gets up at 5:30). I'm typing. Fletcher is watching *Courage the Cowardly Dog* on Cartoon Network and generally wishing I'd hurry up and finish so I can read him his requisite two to three books and he can go to bed. He would rather die than admit it, but he's tired. I, on the other hand, am a total and classic insomniac—cannot sleep even given the opportunity to do so—and must take a half a sleeping pill and/or glass of wine every night if I'm to have any hope of dozing off before midnight. Back when I "worked" (for money, that is), I was asleep the minute my head hit the pillow promptly at 10:00. Now it's like I'm in Nam and I always sleep with one eye open. Rex usually does not sleep through the night and my sleep is always interrupted. Sleep deprivation is the cruelest of punishments (and it leaves no scars, hence making it a favorite among the torture crowd).

11:00 P.M. After reading Fletcher two books, finding the proper pajamas and water bottle, and a late night pooping session during which he "needs company," we all, finally, sleep.

THE WEDDING PARTY

12:40 P.M. Two hundred direction cards for the wedding invitations are done! That wasn't so hard; now I just have to remember to bring them home. All my bridesmaids are mad and I know it's probably my fault. The maid of honor decided it would be best to have separate showers (one for my family, one for his friends and family, one for the work people). The others don't agree but are doing it because, well . . . because she's a CONTROL FREAK! She thinks I've invited too many people to the wedding and just because I invited them to the wedding doesn't mean they have to be invited to the shower. The shower should be for the people I really want there. Well, if I didn't really want them all, why would I have invited them to the wedding? God, I know way too much about this.

ZOE JOANNA PAPADAKOS, 39, *Tarpon Springs, Florida*;
nurse practitioner

TAKING NOTE

I am ten minutes late to the meeting of the Arts Council, of which I am secretary. Taking notes allows me once again to be more observer than actor. I believe our little organization is valuable. It has brought puppets, jazz bands, and potters to our schools and community. But I am struck once again by how many words people use to make fairly simple statements. Should deciding on a time to meet next month really require a paragraph from each member? I am also struck by the splendid heavy necklace our new member is wearing, and by the amount of bare chest on which it is displayed. Oh well, she's from the West Coast.

BETTY F. MOFFETT, 60, *Grinnell, Iowa*; **retired composition teacher**

PEN TO PAPER

2:15 A.M. Just finished the fun and forgiving portion of tonight's art project (forgiving because I'm using pencil at this stage). Next comes the most dreaded stage, putting pen lines over the pencil. I mentally "choke" a little just switching from my crisp-lined O.S. mechanical pencil to my fine-line ink pen. These designs are primarily symmetrical, mirror-image designs, accented with very delicate and fine scrollwork woven throughout. I feel nearly criminal to expect tattooists to repeat these designs on supple flesh when I'm feeling so apprehensive about pulling it off on paper. I pause to slowly eat a bowl of popcorn (one kernel at a time) and finish reading the newspaper, and will surely emerge bristling with extreme confidence and unflinching dexterity and total amnesia about this moment of doubt (ha!).

GAIL SOMERS, 42, *Coeur d'Alene, Idaho*;
flash artist (designs tattoo patterns)

PRIORITIES

12:45 P.M. I washed my hair Sunday and I continue twisting my locks to firm them up. I luv my hair these days! I wish that I had locked a lot sooner in my life. It was finally creating Diva Squad and understanding that dreadlocks can be styled just like any other kind of hair and having my husband joyfully play in my seriously nappy hair (after I had washed it) that convinced me it was time to lock three years ago. When I took my braids out, my hair was twisted in coils and I was just delighted! I took the extensions out of my hair and put them on the Trapunta quilt that I was working on and became officially a happy nappy dread. But it now means my hair regime takes up more time. I have to twist it with olive oil rolling it between my hands one lock at a time. Oh well, you have to make time for what is important.

CHEZIA THOMPSON CAGER, 51, *Baltimore, Maryland*;
language and literature professor

TIMES TWO

10:59 A.M. This is the thing about twins: I need, of course, to do laundry. So I pick up baby Trintje in her bouncy seat and carry her downstairs. (WARNING, MISE EN GARDE, ADVERTENCIA: To prevent serious injury: Never use as a carrier or lift while child is seated!) Then I run back upstairs and grab baby Peter and bring him down. (WARNING: Never leave child unattended!) Then I run back upstairs again and get the laundry basket, and bring that down. Then I try to remember anything else I needed or wanted to do downstairs, because for the next task I'll have to do this all again in reverse.

ANNE NYDAM, 32, *Needham, Massachusetts*; **at-home mom of seventeen-week-old twins and former middle school art teacher**

MANAGED CARE

I'll be going into work a little late today. I'm on my way to Chinatown to my bank to get a certified check, which I then must FedEx to JPMorgan Chase bank. This is in hopes of having my health insurance reinstated. I've had an individual insurance plan with Oxford since I left my last job in 1995 to free-lance. Oxford claims that I did not pay my premium for August 1997. I've been mailing, faxing, and e-mailing them proof of payment for years, but they refuse to credit my account. They've refused to put anything in writing and have refused to acknowledge receipt of my documents. They never even sent me a letter to tell me that they would cancel my insurance if I didn't pay the disputed amount by a particular date.

So, I now find myself being forced to re-pay a premium that I've already paid. The payment must be made within two business days but they won't give me an extension for yesterday, Columbus Day (even though ALL banks are closed!!!). They also won't extend my coverage during the reinstatement process, which can take up to fourteen business days. There's nothing like being held hostage by a managed care company.

ABBE G. ECKSTEIN, 36, *New York, New York*; **art director**

ASSETS

On my way up the stairs to the train. I pass two men who are cleaning the stairs with a huge hose. They stop spraying as I pass and I wonder if my ass looks good in these pants. Then I feel silly for hoping these strangers are checking out my ass.

GENEVRA GALLO, 29, *Chicago, Illinois*; **staff writer, Planned Parenthood**

Shipping and Receiving Manager, with Background in Military Intelligence

At eighteen, she joined the Army, just wanting to get away after her mom's suicide. The recruiter sold her on army intelligence: "He drew a great picture. If he'd suggested 'cook' or 'polishing boots' I would have done that." In Okinawa, she met her future husband, also in army intelligence. Love at first sight... *not.* "We annoyed each other to no end, but after a while you just sort of give up, and that's when you fall in love." Now married over twenty years—"This man needs a medal he puts up with so much." Overemotional. The Peter Pan of women. Her hang-ups? "Age, weight, thinning hair—How much time do you have, honey?" She sees the world in black and white. "I either feel very strongly about it or it's not worth thinking about." Two sons, ages twenty-two and nineteen, one grandson, and another on the way. She wants her kids close. "If I had apron strings, they'd be around their necks." Patriotic, "almost to a fault." Time spent overseas has made her appreciate American freedoms. "And, if someone threatens to take them away, you'd better be standing in their face, ready to defend them."

LAURELLEIGH CAUDILL, 44, *El Paso, Texas*

1:47 A.M. Can't sleep. Again. Insomnia is yet one more gift of menopause. It ranks somewhere between hot flashes and night sweats. I am irritated and certain on some sleep-deprived level that women really pissed off the gods at some point in history to deserve this. I catch my reflection in the window. God, I look tired. I can actually see the wrinkles without my glasses. I need something sweet so badly I could knock over a 7-Eleven for a Milk Dud.

My nights, like my days, are riddled with Jerry Springer fodder—little things I turn into neuroses. This evening it began with an innocent question on an insurance policy update:

"Age?" 43, I write absentmindedly.

A quick glance at my birth year on the form tells me something isn't right.

"Forty-three, I know how old I am," I mutter.

I'm not that sure, so I do the math. Twice. Suddenly, I am forty-four. Why do I feel cheated? How stupid is this?

Reliving the moment, I must have chocolate. I rummage through the kitchen cabinet and find a tub of chocolate frosting. Yes, here I am at 2 A.M. eating chocolate frosting with a spoon. I should be medicated.

5:00 A.M. Coffee. Hook me up to an IV, I need coffee. God bless automatic coffee makers!

7:30 A.M. I love the first thirty minutes of my day. My desk at work is organized and I am in control. The phone is silent and I accomplish more in those thirty minutes than I will in the next two hours. The warehouse door is open behind my desk and I can hear birds. Autumn is my favorite time of year. The leaves are beginning to dry on the trees and rustle softly in the cool breeze. The air carries the smoky scent of a fall burn. Chocolate for breakfast does wonders for the human soul.

My phone calls start on the East Coast, and move west with the clock. I can't believe Christmas is so close. First, I call all the component vendors with pending deliveries, then track the shipments they promise are en route. My crew begins to trickle in like sleepy kids reporting to school. The sounds of fourth quarter fill the shipping room as hundreds, then thousands, of packages are prepared to ship.

9:30 A.M. There is not enough coffee in the Western Hemisphere to get me through this manager's meeting . . . All of us are hyped about fourth quarter as we share what is going on in each department. Stahmanns Gifts is an ever-growing company. We have high hopes about the season ahead and we plot like an army cadre. Invariably, there is that time-consuming argument between two of us regarding some procedure. This time it's between me and the MIS Manager. I present my problem in three words. "This procedure sucks" (tactfully). Then, of course, I have to listen to the reason behind the offending procedure . . . yadda yadda yadda . . . blah, blah, blah . . . (Are all men born with condescending attitudes, or is there a class they attend somewhere? Yeah baby, it's all about you.) Finally, we agree on a new (not great, but at least different) procedure. Fortunately, we do all genuinely like each other. This makes it immeasurably easier to put up with each other's idiosyncrasies and idiotic behavior!

12:00 P.M. I sit on the loading dock, soaking up the fall sunshine, listening to the comfortable chitchat of my crew at lunch. They have such interesting lives. Of course, they are in their twenties, not forties. (WHY does that bother me so much???) I am intrigued by their stories—dreams, young love, plans for after work. I feel content, I have a good job, working with people I enjoy.

I call my husband to catch up on his day. Seems like we never see each other any more. He works shift work and I hate it. I really miss him. We chat briefly about having Mike (our oldest son) and Liz (his wife) over during the weekend. Their baby is due in December and it's been forever since we shopped at Toys "R" Us for Christmas presents! We work through the details and, next, I call my oldest and leave a message on his machine. It's time to get back to work.

1:00 P.M. Despite twice-a-day cleaning, packing peanuts and wrapping cover the shipping room floor like a bizarre snowfall. Music from the radio fills in the gaps as packers joke while they wrap and pack the multitude of gifts our customers send out. The smell of pecan pies baking in the kitchen mingles with the scent of dark chocolate. In the cold room next door, pickers scurry around pulling orders and shuttling them to the packing stations. Packers "*tia wrap*" (like you are sending it to your Auntie!) each gift tin with packing paper from a giant spool—*Rrrrrip*! *Crunch*! *Crunch*! *Crunch*! Then pack it in a box with Styrofoam peanuts. *Chhh*! And seal the box with Kraft tape. *Frrmp*! *Whack*! The finished box goes on the rail and rolls to the UPS machines. *Whirr*! It is weighed, addressed (*click CHING, click CHING*!), and put on a pallet to go out the door. This will continue until a few days after Christmas when the blizzard of orders becomes a snowfall, the snowfall a flurry, and fourth quarter will be over.

4:45 P.M. Wow, the whole afternoon blew right by me! This will be my seventh season. Sometimes I forget what normal Christmas seasons are about. I miss Christmas cards, carols, and church bazaars. I miss putting up decorations with my family and baking cookies with my best friend. I wonder where we put the decorations for the shipping room. I make a note to look for these tomorrow. I hear the laughter of my evening shift supervisor as he makes his rounds. Time for me to go home.

My drive home is forty-five minutes on a good day. I spend some of it singing along with the radio and much of it in mental aerobics. I will be a grandmother this Christmas. Two grandsons from my two sons. It will be fun to celebrate with little ones again. I miss the craziness of kids romping around. Adults forget how to have unbridled joy. I have always wanted to have my boys and their families close by. A big family! I need to call my oldest son and his wife. I am so happy we live close by. Thinking of them makes me smile.

6:00 P.M. I make it home in time to watch my favorite program, *Star Trek: The Next Generation*! You can keep your reality TV. I live for the future. All aliens speak English and we come in peace, baby!!! I am a believer. Beam me up. NOW!! My husband is working on "Baby" (his 4 x 4 Toyota) and after sharing a kiss and the Reader's Digest version of our day, I nuke two Hot Pockets (why don't they make chocolate hot pockets?) and nosh in front of the tube.

7:15 P.M. My youngest son is home and joins me in front of the TV. At the commercial, he casually announces he is planning on joining the military. He is joining the Army. Everything in me is raging against time. I listen to his plans, his need to stretch his wings . . .

I am avoiding him until I can talk without crying. I take my golden retrievers out for a walk in the desert. My heart is breaking. NO! You will get hurt! I can't get to you if you need me! Who will take care of you? Who will I take care of? Who will I ride the roller coaster with? Who will be my shopping buddy? Who will I hug and kiss goodnight? I already did this once with your brother! I'm not ready to do it again! I can't let go yet! How can I be so utterly pathetic on so many levels? Shouldn't I be supportive of his choices? My husband is retired military. I also served for ten years. It's what we do, what we believe in . . . except, that's my baby, and I wonder how I will learn to live with this . . . and if there is any other woman out there as lonely and frightened as I am at this minute.

My dogs keep running back to me on the dark desert road. Shasta pokes at me with her wet nose. Shiloh, her slobbering tongue hanging out, rolls adoring eyes at me. I can't help but laugh. How can people make it through life without dogs? For my husband, this is the natural progression of the boy's life. Me? I feel sad, like this season of my life is ending. I struggle with feeling old. Yes, I am a grandmother. Yes, my boys belong to other women. Yes, there are thousands, indeed millions, of women who have made this transition and lived to talk about it. Somewhere in the dark, out in the desert, *la Loba Loca* soothes me and I begin to accept my future. I desperately need to pull it together and deal with reality. It will be OK.

10:00 P.M. Time for bed, thank God. My face is all puffy and stuffy from crying. It's all good. After crying like a baby on my husband's shoulder, I cried like a bigger baby on my son's shoulder. If he thinks I'm nuts, so be it. He will never doubt that he is loved.

TECHNOLOGY

7:20 A.M. Check e-mail. I can't believe my eyes. An e-mail from Mom. This is monumental. (My mom got a computer last June and to say that she is having trouble learning to do e-mail is a drastic understatement.) She was so frustrated when I talked to her last night, she couldn't even figure out how to move the cursor. Now, after four months, success! She even had the subject line filled in. This is big. I am so happy for her.

MARILYN HOUGH, 53, *Broomfield, Colorado*;
marriage and family therapist

After I had the revelation that it was all about baby Madeleine and that anything I wanted to do had to take a back seat until she was taken care of, it made things much easier. And the realization that an e-mail doesn't have to be answered immediately certainly helped decrease my stress level, too. One thing that I still have to work on is figuring out how to deal with business calls at home. They stress me out since I worry about Mads screaming. With friends, it's one thing, but for work, it's hard. I just don't want to seem unprofessional. I'll just have to practice with the mute button before my conference call tomorrow.

ELLEN HWANG, 32, *New York, New York*;
editor-in-chief, *JADE* magazine

9:45 P.M. Howard and I chat and eat buttered popcorn while watching programs we've TiVo'd. I'm starting to get TiVo stress. All those great dramas like *Law and Order*, *West Wing*, and witty sitcoms like *Scrubs* are piling up on TiVo's hard drive. If you don't watch them quickly enough TiVo puts an exclamation point in a yellow circle next to the program to alert you it will soon delete it to make room for even more programs. It's like the e-mail of television.

GAYLE SEMINARA MANDEL, 46, *Chicago, Illinois*;
owner of Transitions Bookplace and Learning Center

10:53 A.M. I like everyone but hate telemarketers. ADT called, they want to secure my home. Jesus already does. No, I don't need to know what they offer.

SUSAN L. KOESTER, 44, *Vicksburg, Mississippi*;
mother of four

12:00 A.M. Still at work in my studio (since 8:00) going over tracks. So far these are mostly rhythm beds of drums and bass only. Figuring out direction to take. Learning too the new system and what it can do. Over six hundred pages of manual, barely touched. Technology is draining. By the time I figure it out, inspiration has passed. Sometimes I wish I could be satisfied to be a traditional artist with all the financial security widespread acceptance means. Grass is greener.

TINA WEYMOUTH, 51, *Westport, Connecticut*;
**lead guitarist for The Talking Heads,
Rock 'N Roll Hall of Fame inductee**

Like Father, Like Daughter; World-Renowned Sitar Player

Trained completely by her father, the legendary sitar player Ravi Shankar. She started playing at age nine (her mother encouraged her; her father wanted the decision to be hers). A professional debut at age thirteen. She still performs with her dad, but she's forging a solo career. Three CDs released to critical acclaim. A Grammy nomination. Seventy performances worldwide this year. She misses her freedom when she's touring. "I get really sick of knowing exactly where I'll be in two years, down to the hour." Born in London and raised in California, with frequent family trips to India. The most American thing about her? "My Southern California drawl. When it's in full force a lot of people in other countries haven't a clue what I'm saying!" Two new ventures: the recent release of the biography she wrote about her father, and her first appearance in a movie. At ease with elderly Indian musicians, high society, trance parties, and people her own age. "I'm the product of all those things so there's no point in dissecting it. It's the sum total that matters . . . I'm just Anoushka!"

Anoushka Shankar, 21, *Encinitas, California, and New Delhi, India*

10:30 A.M. Woke up, as usual, in a bed that's not mine. For once, though, it's not a generic hotel bed in a generic hotel room, so I feel quite happy to open my eyes and see the little details that made this Swetha's room before she went away to college: CDs, dance and yoga posters, the tassel from her graduation cap. It's been years since she and I really spent any time together so it's kind of strange, though nice, to try and catch up on her years through these clues she's left behind. It really is silly considering she goes to college in San Diego, just fifteen minutes from where I live, but that's a common story isn't it? She's busy enough studying and dancing professionally, and I'm always away on tour, so it's a wonder we see each other at all.

Enough daydreaming. Back to reality in Yorba Linda, California, I quickly get dressed and go downstairs to eat something before my second dance lesson. It's fun having this kind of respite from being on the road, doing something other than performing on my sitar that's also this challenging and creative.

Ramaa aunty (everyone older becomes aunty or uncle or brother or sister in India, similar to how in Japan it's impolite just to address people by name) cut up strawberries for me to put into my Special K when I came down. Moving around so much I can't help noticing the little things that make one family different from another. People actually cut up fruit to put in their cereal! I'm more of an eggs, bacon, toast, and tea person (though I did enjoy the cereal). Even better than the cereal, last night they actually lit the candles that were scattered around the house! Every room has candles with deep, telltale indents in them instead of looking spanking new as mine do. As much as I keep buying beautiful candles and holders they tend to just sit there—make a mental note to change that.

Also make note to change the amount of bath stuff that just sits in my bathroom in San Diego. Ramaa aunty suggested I take a hot bath last night so my muscles wouldn't be too sore today, and actually poured this lavender bath salt and rose oil into the water, what heaven! So swirly silky sensual . . . I need to take more baths. Somehow I never have the time for more than a shower, which is ridiculous. Nobody has time for much of anything, or so they think, it's just a question of making time for what you want. So—more candles, more baths.

Gotta go and have another dance lesson now. I'm studying *Bharatanatyam*, one of India's seven classical dance styles, known for it's intricate hand gestures and facial expressions, intricate footwork and beautiful symmetry. Technically it's mind-blowing, but as with all our classical styles, the storytelling aspect is also incredibly important and the dancers are trained to be able to express almost anything with their eyes, faces, hands, and body language. I'm acting in a movie for the first time in February, in which I play a *Bharatanatyam* dancer, and there are a few scenes where I am either practicing or performing, which is why I'm trying to get a head start on relearning and getting in shape for it now. The movie is based on an Indian play (in English thank God!) called *Dance Like a Man*, and is basically about a family of dancers. I chose this as my first film because it's quite small, closer to theatre than Bollywood, and the director Pamela Rooks is an old family friend so I feel quite comfortable that she will ease me into this new field with care. Plus I have to confess the dancing aspect really drew me, since this is sort of a double challenge—acting for the first time and also having to dance. The dancing scenes are at most a couple of minutes long, but I'm going to have to look completely polished and professional, it's quite a challenge!

It's madness how Ramaa aunty and I are trying to cram years of work into three days, but that's all I have. (Ramaa Bharadwaj is one of the best-known *Bharatanatyam* dancers in America.) I studied *Bharatanatyam* for a few years when I was a kid but it's not helping me much now. Tomorrow I drive straight to my sitar performance in Irvine and then I'm on tour in North America constantly for the next couple of months, with up to five shows a week all in different cities, so I really don't know how I'm going to do this. But I guess that's the same issue of making time when you have to. I mean, I'm the one who chooses to do all these different things, and sometimes it really does feel like too much, but I wonder if I'm just not managing my time properly. The way I see it, there are two kinds of busy. Monotonous busy, and creative busy. As much as I love music, just being on the road all year round drives me crazy. It's very easy to get stuck and not grow when you're repeating the same pattern again and again, as we do on tour in airports, hotels, and concert halls. I'm as sure as I can be that playing the sitar will always be my main profession, but that's not enough for me. I get sick of the patterns after a while and feel a need to escape.

12:40 P.M. Ouch! Ramaa aunty just worked me to the bone in her dance hall (they renovated the garage with ideal flooring, wall-to-wall mirrors, and typical South Indian red floors and white patterned borders). I'm so grateful that she's made this much time to instruct me one-on-one. We don't have the music yet but she's working more on teaching me how to look, to walk, to finish with a flourish. Basically giving me all these tips to look as professional as possible. It's true for all art forms, but it's just mind-blowing how the simplest steps require so much effort to do properly. They look so easy! I know when I leave here her voice is going to be ringing in my head, "Posture! Shoulders down! Chest out! Diaphragm open! Feet together!" To keep each hand gesture in perfect position, then to have to jump and move and land gracefully and smile and keep eyes in the right position and coordinate tricky movements with the arms, legs, and face AND look happy about it! Come to think of it that's what people say about my music too. And it's true, it took a couple of years as a kid just to get the scales right. Classical art forms require so much discipline; well, everything does, but especially classical art. Sometimes it can be overwhelming, to try and find your own voice, your patch of freedom, in the midst of so much regulation.

4:20 P.M. Had a little time to myself after lunch to take a short walk around Ramaa aunty's house, leaf through my script and even take a short nap. Woke up feeling rather irritable and displaced. I'm quite used to that feeling, and get it quite a lot on tour.

What is home? I have three, and a hundred hotels to sleep in besides. What is that attached feeling people have to one specific place? I don't even know it. Everything becomes so unstable in this lifestyle. With the shows I'm booked for this year I've been at home in San Diego less than six weeks! Then there's our new home in Delhi, which seems like it's never going to be finished so we can truly feel settled in, with all its construction and bustle. Perhaps that's why I cling so tightly to the people I love. Perhaps also why I drop so easily those I no longer feel I connect to? Time is too precious to waste on pointless relationships—and nothing is worth missing out on true connections. My career is the biggest thing in my life since it so totally dominates the way I live, but it isn't at all the most important—people are. My best friend Sharmila was studying me over a chai latte a few days ago and suddenly pronounced, "You must be very lonely, Anoushka." And this, coming from a chick who's always making fun of how sociable and enthusiastic I am, was a surprise. "Well, you have so many friends in so many cities, that no matter where you are you're always away from most of the people you're close to. It must be horrible constantly having to miss someone."

I think that's where most of my frustrations have been coming from for the past few months. As much as I love my music for its own beauty, and also on a more superficial level for the fame and fun it gives me, it's meaningless to me the longer I go on. Of course it's a great life, I don't mean to sound ungrateful for what I have. I love the music, I love being able to share it with people when I'm onstage and see the pleasure it gives them. I love that exhilarating feeling of being up there in front of people, rushing to the climax of a show all sweaty and breathless, getting thunderous applause. One of my favourite things about it is being up there with my father. That's really when we are closest to each other. It's like a culmination of our relationship. Onstage he's my guru, pushing me to do something new, we are partners making music together, we are father and daughter taking pride in each other, we have fun, we move each other, we are almost one. It's also incredible to see so much of the world, to feel at home in so many different cultures and experience so much. I love getting to meet so many people, famous and not famous, it's fun being recognized and getting fan mail, of course, it's all fun.

But I think I'm tired of always being away. Of missing old Californian school friends while on tour, of losing friends while growing apart, of missing old friends in India while at my other home, of missing the beautiful boy who eventually got tired of missing me, missing cats, missing family, missing, missing . . . and the worst part of this kind of lonely is: I'm also missing. Not too sure I can explain that, but I'm constantly away, which means I'm not essential to anybody—all the people who I'm close to are used to life without me! When I return, I need to be accommodated because everyone's lives are full enough without me there. I'm sick of it!

11:30 P.M. My body is jelly. Pure, wobbly, uncontrollable jelly. I've danced for hours today and even squeezed in almost two hours of sitar practice—good thing since I have a show tomorrow. It's really hard to find actual practice time on the road, since often with travel, shows, press, and lectures or workshops the days get completely filled up. So, surprisingly, I actually enjoyed doing some scales and different strengthening exercises for each hand. And it's also extremely important to just play, try new stuff. On stage it's hard to take total leaps, in the sense that even if I'm improvising I have a general idea of where I want to end up, because obviously I'm doing a show and don't want to screw up! So it's important to practice just being totally free in private, that helps me a lot.

The three days here has actually gone quite quickly. It has felt nice to be so productive, eat healthily, finally kick the online chatting habit (another thing about being on tour and constantly away from dozens of people—there are always friends online in SOME part of the world!) for a couple of days at least, and get out of the touring routine for a while.

ON THE JOB

JOYCE HUGHES, 51
Bullhead City, Arizona
funeral director and embalmer, Dimond & Sons Silver Bell Chapel

When a death call comes in we MUST respond immediately. This is somebody's loved one and we just can't leave them lying there. There is no one available to make the death call but the two of us. We lock the door and put a note on it saying that we will return soon. Our policy is to always send two people to a home death. This is because we never know what kind of situation we will be getting into. The deceased could be on the floor, or could be very large, and we can't ask or expect the family to help us. However, there are times the family will ask if they can help and, by all means, we let them.

I knock on the door and go inside to introduce my colleague and myself to the widow, who is sitting on the couch crying. I sit beside her, give her my condolences and she begins to talk all about her husband. Reminiscing of their fifty-three wonderful years together. I smile at her and listen intently to her stories. Then she tells me she wants him to be cremated and she wants the cremated remains returned to her. I then explain to her that we are going to bring in our equipment so that we can take her husband back to the funeral home. I ask her if she would like to be in the room with us, and she says she would. We wrap him in one of our crisp white sheets and gently place him on our gurney.

We keep his face uncovered while in the house, because I just can't cover the deceased in front of the family. We do have to completely cover the deceased once we are out of the house for legal reasons. I ask her if she would like to say goodbye to him before we leave and she says she would. She leans on him, kissing his cheek, saying, "You were my whole life. What will I do now? I love you." It is so sad. I can't help the tears in my eyes as I stand there while she is saying goodbye to her husband. Just then her daughter arrives and stands beside her mom, crying and also kissing her dad goodbye. The daughter then takes the mother back to the couch and tells us to go on.

Retired Church Secretary Who Spoils Her Grandkids and Dog

Retirement three years ago taught her how to deal with solitude and still be content. "At first, I was lonesome for the contact with people, but life just closes in around you and pretty soon you're saying, 'When did I have time to work?'" Married forty-two years to her high school sweetheart. Two sons with families of their own—one lives a thousand miles away, much to her sadness. She's lived in the same city all her life. Keeps an immaculate house. Exhibits her paintings at home and local art shows. Cackles with glee when she wins at board games. But overall a quiet, regular person. "I get overlooked much of the time. That's why, when I do make friends, I make lifetime friends." Odd things earn her attention, like the restrooms on cross-country trips. "Interesting things happen in public johns. Sometimes the seats are on springs and won't stay down by themselves. If you move at all they slap or pinch. If you try to cover them with tissue, they fling it into the air." Growing older has affected her perspective. "You learn not to take things quite so seriously, including yourself. I hope I'm gaining some wisdom because, if you don't, you're in big trouble."

DIANE NORMAN, 62, *Rockford, Illinois*

6:15 A.M. I wake, not because it is my regular time to get up, or even a good time to get up, but because of a sixty-two-year-old bladder that has its own mind. Even Abby, my dog, does not stir. It is just gray enough in the room that her "gimme food" instinct doesn't register clearly. I crawl back into bed.

7:15 A.M. The dog is beside me and staring at my face. Why would that wake someone? Do dogs possess some magic eyeball rays? If I remember right, children possess the same power: stare at Mommy or Daddy long and hard enough and they'll wake up.

I shuffle to the kitchen. I'm not good in the morning. Give me an hour with my tea, with my thoughts, in my blue bumpy robe and clunky slippers and then the day may start. While the water boils, I feed the dog and let her out. It's automatic. It takes no thought. This is the most work I want to do at this time. My husband, Bob, on the other hand, is long off to work. He deserves a medal for this. If I had to get up at 5:00 A.M. each morning, I would be so crabby no one could stand me.

I sip a little tea. I turn on the TV to catch the news. Another sniper shooting in Virginia last night. I'd be so scared if I lived there. The authorities are telling people to go about their regular lives. Huh? I think that's awful advice. I would tell people to huddle inside their homes until this is over.

I make my 8:30 call to my good friend, Judy. She just lost her dad a week ago. It brought back the sadness I felt when my parents died. Even though my dad has been gone for ten years and my mom for eight, I would still like to have them back. I still miss them. I wish I had asked them more questions about themselves and their lives. I wish I could call my mom for advice or a recipe once in a while. I wish I could cut my dad's hair again. He never complained. I wish, I wish. Sometimes, now, I feel like an orphan.

Judy and I talk for a half hour. It's a regular thing with us and has been for many years. Every weekday morning we talk at 8:30. When she's out of town, I'm lost. When I'm out of town, she's lost. We can be our very best or our very worst with each other. There's no need to pretend. We've laughed, cried, complained, rejoiced, and argued together. We're both mules in arguments. We both think we're right and must convince the other. But we both know something important: our friendship is stronger than our mulishness, so we take our disagreements and either talk them out or throw them out. Judy is a lifetime friend.

9:00 A.M. I eat a bowl of cold cereal, then take my blood pressure pill. Things change when you get older. I always had low blood pressure. Now I need pills. That sucks. I have other pills, too. Pills for arthritis, pills for sleep, pills for osteoporosis, vitamin pills, pain pills, calcium pills. The list is getting longer. That sucks, too. People say these are the "golden years." What fool made that up? I would never describe aging in terms of a precious metal. If I used any metal to describe it, it would be rusty metal.

10:00 A.M. What do I need to do today? I look at my list: make an appointment for the dog to get a haircut; go to the bank; stop by the dentist's office; clean up my sewing room; finish up some sewing projects so I can start a new one tomorrow. Not a bad list. Pretty light. I do like being "retired." It's respectable, like a station in life one gets to. It's kind of a misnomer, though. People ask me, "Do you work?" I want to say, "Of course I work, you ninny. I cook and do laundry and grocery shop and scrub toilets and bathe the dog and clean up the house and rearrange closets, etc. Oh, did you mean do I do something someone pays me for? No. I'm retired."

I'm starting to think that the whole work scene has been glorified. For most of my adult life I was a homemaker and mother. I stayed home, raised two children, and did all the work that was required. As they grew up, I took part-time jobs. They filled time, were fun to a point, and earned me some money. Do I miss them? No. Do I yearn to be remembered for being the best secretary in the universe? No. I'd rather be remembered for being a loving wife and mother; a faithful, listening friend; and a grandmother who can't contain her joy over her grandchildren. I know many people in their eighties who I like and respect very much. They are productive, they are interesting, they work hard at home and in volunteer jobs. What they did for a living during their official working years is not at all important. I know them free of those roles, and love them for the people they really are. Jobs and titles can be great seducers, but relationships are what bring lasting joy.

OK, enough pondering. The day has begun. Do the regular things first. Get dressed. Make the bed. Clean up the bathrooms. Tidy up. I like to blame my husband for making messes. The truth is, I make as many as he does or more. (Do not tell him this.) Anyway, I tidy up and let the dog in and out. The sun has come out and it's a beautiful fall day. She thinks she needs to go out every seven seconds. There are three reasons for this: her dog friend next door might be out; chipmunks may need to be chased; she gets a treat every time she comes in. The more in-and-out trips, the more dog treats. I'm not a dumb dog-mother.

11:00 A.M. I run to the dentist's office to pick up a magic potion for fever blisters. To get there, I have to maneuver my car though a maze created by road construction people who think they're building a pathway to the moon. I didn't know there were that many orange fluorescent barrels on the planet, yet there they are channeling the flow of traffic. If you don't get your car in the correct position, you may end up headed in the wrong direction, or enclosed in an oblong ring of barrels with no way out, while people snicker as they whiz by.

11:30 A.M. Back home. It's amazing how relaxed I feel walking into the dentist's office when I don't have to have anything done. I was actually cheerful with the receptionist. Normally, I'm a nervous wreck. I always thought that once I was an adult I'd get over being scared to go to the dentist, but it hasn't happened. I once told him that maybe I should have all my teeth pulled, get dentures, and mail them in when they needed work. He just laughed at me.

Well, there's time for a little sewing before lunch. The cubicle I call my sewing room is a mess, as usual. There's no way to keep a sewing room neat unless you don't sew in it. I have a love/hate relationship with sewing, and am what you might call a grateful sewer. I'm grateful when things turn out. Sewing fulfills something in me that says, "Go . . . take a blob of nothing and create." Maybe it's a long-dormant pioneer gene I got from my grandmother who crossed the plains in a covered wagon. Today I sew a wee little tag with my granddaughter's name on it and attach it to the inside back of a pair of slacklets I made for her. I call them slacklets because she's only one year old. That's too young for slacks, way too young for trousers, and the word pants could be inner or outer garments. What is the proper name for the little things babies wear to cover their legs? My granddaughter lives a long way from me, so I have to mail the things I make her. She'll be here at Christmas with her mommy and daddy, but nothing fits a toddler for two months. I get a kick out of sewing for my seven-year-old granddaughter, too. She likes straight-up-and-down dresses (no frills, no poufs, no gathers, and no ruffles). Straight. That makes it easier, as does the fact that she lives in town and measurements are easier to get.

12:30 P.M. Now it is officially lunchtime. I know that because the dog is eyeballing me again. Yes, she eats three times a day, just like us. And she doesn't eat just any old dog food. No. She eats food that costs one dollar a can, a special prescription concoction because she has irritable bowel syndrome. So, doesn't everyone? No, wait, that's just me. Anyway I feed her and I feed me. I have her on a little diet because she's a tad overweight. I finish up a pork chop from dinner the night before and then decide to make chocolate pudding for dessert. The absurdity of this hits me while I am spooning Cool Whip onto my pudding. I have the dog on a diet because she's maybe two or three pounds overweight. I, on the other hand, am probably twenty pounds overweight and am eating pork and chocolate pudding. What is the lesson here?

Afternoon. Laundry switches: into the washer, into the dryer, onto the hangers, into the closets. Repeat 'til you can see the floor. In between, I listen to a little news, none of which is good. I talk with another friend on the phone. Aren't friends great? She will try and come over tomorrow. I have her Harry Potter movie and she has some doilies for me. Marcia and I have known each other for over thirty years, starting out as neighbors when we both had teeny little houses and teeny little children. We've sort of grown up together. Marcia has a big and loving heart. I know that when I'm hurting she'll open her arms and I can just walk in and be comforted. I know I can trust her with stuff I don't want anybody else to know. I know I can be wise or stupid with her and she'll still like me. She is a forever friend. Marcia has a wonderful mind and she can think on her feet. I admire that about her. She can call in to a talk radio program, express her views, and when challenged on those views she can reply with facts that not only support her position but are convincing! In contrast, I can barely think when I'm on my feet, such as at an important occasion. I need time and paper and pencil to get my head on straight. I'm smart the next day. It's all crystal clear then, and if I could repeat the scenario, I'm sure I'd be elected to some important office.

Today we talk about our husbands retiring and wonder if any of us will have enough money to be comfortable. Isn't the economy pukey right now? Companies sending their business offshore have hurt her husband's plastic molding business and for a couple of years my husband's hours have been miserably down. His shop makes tools for the fastener industry, and he has worked fifty to fifty-five hours a week for years. All of a sudden, he is down to forty hours. That's scary when you're just a few years from retirement.

Well, so far this day sounds plain and boring. But I've learned something as I've gotten older: Boring is good! It means there are no crises, no places I have to go that require pantyhose, no getting somewhere at a prescribed time, nobody I have to look or sound good for, no life-changing decisions to be made. You know . . . boring. However, I've also learned, the day isn't over yet and anything can happen.

3:00 P.M. I bought an emerald green nubby chenille shirt the other day, and wonder of wonders, I have double knit fabric on my fabric shelf that is guess what . . . emerald green! So I will get out my trusty slack pattern and cut out some slacks. The pattern is a miracle. Anyone who sews—well, any regular person who sews—knows how hard it is to fit slacks. Most regular sewers have oodles of slacks they've made that are either gardening slacks, around-the-house slacks, slacks in a bag, or pieces of junk fabric that were once slacks. That's because homemade slacks seldom fit well enough to be seen in public. My slack pattern is the result of a quest—a ten-year quest to get the crotch depth right, the hip curve right, the leg width somewhere decent between an elephant-leg look and a squeezed-into-cellophane look. It didn't help that my body kept changing every fifteen minutes. Ten years ago I was much smaller and an inch taller. Ten years ago things didn't droop so much. Ten years ago I didn't look like I was four months pregnant. All that makes a huge difference when fitting a pattern. But I hung in there. Quests are important. My husband helped me, pinning and unpinning, drawing white chalk lines where I told him to. I tried so many patterns I lost count. I don't know who they were designed for but it wasn't me . . . until I found THE PATTERN! The one whose only fault was a thigh measurement slightly elephanty but easily fixable. So, today I will sew a pair of slacks, cinchy when you have THE PATTERN.

4:25 P.M. The dog is running back and forth from the window to the door, yipping, wailing with excited abandon. Our favorite man is home, my hubby of almost forty-two years, her dad. Life is good!

5:00 P.M. We sit at the kitchen table and share our day. He's in charge of many people at work, so he gets lots of talk, lots of complaints, and lots of problems. Sometimes he needs to unload. Other times we share briefly and then I disappear on purpose to give him some quiet moments with the newspaper. He likes to go down to the basement to exercise. We recently bought a motorized treadmill. I had to have one you could simply walk on, no jogging or running for me. For heaven's sake, I can barely walk on flat, straight roads, let alone run on a moving strip of rubber. No, slow is the word, just enough to feel like I'm doing something and perhaps inch by inch do a little good healthwise. Bob does thirty minutes. He has a program. A PROGRAM! It goes slower, and then faster, then inclines up and back down again. Does that not sound professional? He even has a water bottle. Well, there you are. He'll probably outlive me by thirty years and his new wife will get all my stuff. Poo.

I am starting supper. We'll have chicken breasts on the grill, baked potatoes, and a veggie. Pretty standard and not too much fuss. Man, am I sick of chicken. I'd love to cook roast beef and have gravy on mashed potatoes, and vegetables in a casserole so creamy, crusty, and thick that you wouldn't even know they're vegetables. With dessert afterwards, for sure. Lowfat eating is boring, boring, boring, but cholesterol seems to be the name of the game. Mine was too high, due to the fact I had fallen in love with a certain little chocolate nugget (which shall go unnamed) and ate not one, not two, but handfuls every day. So, instead of taking yet another pill, I went on a diet, and for five minutes about two years ago, my cholesterol, triglycerides, and other stuff were in perfect condition. That was the result of twelve months of eating things that had absolutely no taste or texture. Twelve months! How disgusting is that, especially since all the numbers went south the minute I went off the ugly diet and dared to put a fat gram in my mouth again. I blame having to cook Thanksgiving dinner for my falling off the food wagon. The aroma of turkey and dressing cooking was way too tempting! But, in reality, no one held me down and forced me to eat. Since then I've tried to contain my appetite for real food, have succeeded at times and failed miserably other times. I wonder how many pills I'd have to take to be able to eat anything I want?

5:40 P.M. Time for my extensive, hard-driving ten-minute workout. My polyester slacks and navy blue moccasins with the white ties are not workout garb. Do I care? Heck no. You can sweat in polyester just as well as spandex, but I don't plan to sweat anyway. It will be a new century before I personally rev that treadmill up to sweating speed. I hate to sweat. Sweating is a wet and sticky business.

6:00 P.M. We eat. The dog eats. While I eat, I let her out twice. We can't seem to get the supper routine right. If we eat first, she annoys us the best she can. You know the doggy look—panting, whining, barking at us, etc. If she eats first, she still wants to go out twice while I'm eating. Go figure out a dog. Bob gets a little annoyed at this in/out routine. He says, "Make her wait." I say to him, "How would you like it if the next time you have to go to the bathroom I make you wait?" He's a dog owner—good to the dog and takes care of basics, and I'm a dog-mother—treat the dog like my child. It's a shortcoming I have, and is accompanied by babying, coddling, worrying about, and generally behaving in weird caretaking ways only another human dog-mother would understand.

6:30 P.M. Last dishes of the day. Spiffy up the kitchen. That's like making your bed before you leave the house. You know, in case you die nobody will think you're a slob. Same goes for a spiffed-up kitchen. Besides, who likes to look at dirty dishes in the morning?

7:00 P.M. Television time is coming. It's pretty much our routine. But first we must go out and cover the flowers. Tonight there's frost in the forecast. I hate to see the flowers go. I'm never ready for that.

8:00 P.M. *Frasier* and *Amy* time. I read a book on sewing tips during the commercials. Bob is awake again after his in-the-chair nap for the night. It's our easy time, the kind of time that is born from being married a long, long time. We can talk or not talk. We can watch TV or not watch TV. We can read or not read. There's no right or wrong way to do evenings. We're just together, relaxing, doing what we want to do.

10:00 P.M. The bedtime routine: put eyedrops in the dog's eyes; give dog a treat for being a good girl; let dog out, let dog in; give dog a treat for going poddy. Button up the house, light's off, alarm on. Floss and brush. Wash face, eyedrops for me, kiss hubby goodnight. A little TV, then to sleep.

Thank you, God, for the blessings of a regular day.

COLLECTIVE GLIMPSES

32% of day diarists talked to their mothers . . . 84% of those enjoyed the conversation

4% fought with their partners . . . 85% of those made up

10% had sex

84% said, "I love you"

3:10 P.M. As usual when I try to take a nap, my loving husband is talking to me! Yes honey, no honey, what the hell is he talking about?

BELINDA GIANOLA, 37, *Lake City, Colorado;* receptionist

Life in the Blackboard Jungle

An English teacher who went into the field because it was an obvious—if not inspired—choice. "It was something until I figured out what I wanted to do." And has she? "No!" She married her husband six months after they met. "The only time in my life I've ever been certain of anything." He died six years ago. Two years ago, following the deaths of three of her students, she took a one-year assignment running a high school program for troubled kids. The job was an opportunity to build her own curriculum. Over time, she's seen more anger, unhappiness, and lack of commitment in students ("Why read the whole book when things may blow up?"), but she still likes teaching. "It's real—not on paper, not theoretical, not virtual, not deferred." She's glad she grew up in the fifties, then participated in the sixties peace movement. Regrets she can't give her two children, or her students, that kind of security . . . or belief. "Today the truth is no longer absolute." Regrets she's lost her zeal. "I think I should be doing something but I don't know what." Last Christmas, she got a Barbie from one of her oldest friends, who asked, "Wasn't it fun when we controlled the world?" "It was."

SUSAN HESLEP, 51, *Richmond, Virginia*

12:30 A.M. Great start; woke up to realize I'd fallen asleep under a mound of ungraded test papers, turned off light. Will get up early.

1:00 A.M. Toilet running. How can something with three moving parts not work and totally defy my efforts to understand, much less repair??? Must get up and jiggle the handle.

1:15 A.M. Wide awake, plumbing calm for now, but mind racing. Worries about what to do with son who is just not achieving in school. He is bright, but failing most classes, a sweet, friendly kid, who seems disappointingly influenced by the older guys who have sort of adopted him. He is pushing every limit in his bid for independence, but shows no sense of responsibility and I have trouble being both "the cheerleader" and "the hammer." I keep debating boarding school, etc., because he needs male influences, I think. He's sixteen, and his dad died when he was ten. However, tuition is a real concern. Do I blow his college money on high school? At the rate he's going, a college fund may be pointless.

He makes me crazy and I would miss him dreadfully. I just don't feel strong enough for all of the issues and problems that keep popping up.

1:20 A.M. Damn toilet running again; I'm neither a good plumber nor a good mother!!! Such a range of failure. Sigh . . .

5:15 A.M. Hit snooze button for the third time. In an effort to be insightful, I have had the brilliant notion that hitting the snooze is the last vestige of independence I'll experience today. From here on, what I do is determined by what others need or want. Not much to look forward to today . . .

5:40 A.M. Fed dog and cat, iron on, coffee on.

6:00 A.M. At fifty-one, I suddenly cannot drink espresso or even freshly ground French roast any more. I drink nasty generic stuff out of a big red can and seem to like it. Can standards be dropping??? And coffee was such simple pleasure.

6:30 A.M. First attempt to get son up—no luck—so worried! Decision about boarding school looming, money issues vs. what's best for him vs. my not wanting to have him far away. How can a teacher not help her own kid?? Plumbing OK.

6:40 A.M. Check e-mail. College roommate and continuous chum sent address I keep losing to send care package to Jane's sons. Jane was another college roommate, who died of cancer two years ago. Hannah does a lot with Jane's sons, like taking them Father's Day and Christmas shopping; all I seem to do is to send chocolate chip cookies. Thank goodness for friends! Hannah never questions my forgetfulness, and we are sharing the same questions about what the next twenty or so years of our lives hold. Her nest will be empty in the fall, a bit earlier than mine, but we both feel an antsiness, a restlessness for some change, some new sense of purpose. I used to joke about chucking everything and going to Tahiti, like that painter. Not now!

Cleared out spam. My mother responds to every phone solicitation from anyone identifying himself with the police and sends off little checks (despite my warnings about scams) and I am paranoid about any odd e-mail about my credit (which is fine I think). Why can I not recognize that the credit e-mails are as bogus (or at least as unneeded) as the penis enlargement offers??? A trouble with widowhood is that there's no one to tell you when you're being a fool. (The sixteen-year-old doesn't count.) Mom should just drive more slowly, so she won't think contributing to every police fund will spare her a ticket, and I should just delete e-mails before reading what I know is phony.

Hit "hunger site" and others; pitiful that my most useful action of the day may be being counted as a "hit" on a Web site. Quick read of headlines in newspaper. I worry about news of ships gathering in the Gulf; Congress gave in to Bush too readily. Where is the protester in me? Thirty years later I am tired and afraid—not indignant and filled with the possibility of change. Guess I have a daughter for that, now. I am proud that she knows how to protest fearlessly. Son too wanted to go with me to protest neo-Nazi's appearance near here. That's a good thing.

7:15 A.M. Son up—four wake-up calls filled with increasing volume and annoyance. I wish the term "oppositional child" had never been introduced into my vocabulary. I don't know if he is, but A.M. does nothing to dispel the notion.

8:45 A.M. At school, an oddly varied demographic, ethnic, and economic mix, with sixteen hundred kids. Have been here for eighteen years. News and talk of another sniper shooting . . . too big to comprehend. A kid told me he wasn't worried because "everybody dies sometime." I mentioned that perhaps no one was depending on him yet in life and that his view might change. Is he the more practical or just nihilistic or naive?

9:45 A.M. Giving practice PSATs for several hours to homeroom kids I only see for things like this, so I barely know them. One girl is nodding off. Her hair is spiked so stiffly I'm surprised sleep is possible. Poor little thing—eyes like a raccoon, plumbing supplies for jewelry, and such an assumed air of ennui. She's repeating ninth grade for the third time, but is bright. Must see counselor about the GED program for sharp kids. She seems the perfect candidate. Her dad came with very liquory breath on fee night and paid no fees but talked about how brilliant she and her jobless brother are. What good is genius if it has no outlet?

9:55 A.M. Surprise e-mail from son's unofficial godmother who teaches at his school. She too is worried. Says he's "loved there, but having problems." E-mail during the day is a luxury, the payoff for boring standardized testing! People in "real jobs" probably get to do this often, just like they can go to the restroom when they have to, or go out for lunch once in a while. Just don't know what to do for son—have gone through psychiatrist, psychologist, medications, another two counselors, educational consultant, testing, etc., etc. Everyone finds him charming, bright, and unmotivated???

10:15 A.M. Another kid sleeping now; he too is repeating the grade. What will happen to these kids (and mine)? I am really afraid that as a mother and a teacher I have lost the capacity to reach them. I am not sure that I understand what they think is important, if anything, or that I share their vision of a future. I used to be one of the slightly more attuned teachers, I thought. I'm not sure which is the chicken and which is the egg here. I think my failure as a parent has kicked my confidence as a teacher straight in the teeth. "Physician heal thyself." Hah! (This diary thing is painful; I had expected to be cheery and clever, and now I'm defensive and depressed.)

10:30 A.M. Great . . . more sleepers now. The test does not count at all for these kids. With no pressure, they're choosing not to try. Maybe they're very bright and finished early??? I would know if they were kids I taught, and I could cajole them into keeping going at least. How to motivate strangers? I think fear has motivated me my whole life; while I'm glad that kids don't seem fearful, nothing seems to have replaced it as incentive.

12:30 P.M. Study hall—yet another group of people I don't teach or know well. My major task here is to ask them not to play games or music on their laptops (provided by the school system). I wonder if somewhere someone's study hall is skipping through educational sites, learning other languages or chatting with newsmakers, keeping current with events in foreign countries. I believe these were among the projected uses when the laptops were introduced, to the tune of eighteen million dollars. To whom are all these kids illicitly e-mailing and what can they possibly be talking about??? And does anyone else see this as the demise of all punctuation and grammar??? Threatened to refer two guys to their administrators for "talkin' 'bout mamas." That's an oddly reassuring constant in a twenty-eight-year career.

1:15 P.M. Nice walk during lunch with two friends my age. We are the dinosaurs of our department. The lounge has become "bitch central" and it makes me sad. The new teachers are too young to be so angry. So frequently they blame the kids, when much of the problems stem from their own defensive posturing or need to assert CONTROL. I think teaching is no longer a profession for life (life sentence?). It seems more like a job until these twenty-somethings figure out what to do next. That's fine (after all, that's how I started out), but something about really understanding kids takes a lot of time, and putting aside much of one's own biases and prejudices takes some effort. (OK, *King Lear* requires the bathos of midlife to appreciate perhaps . . . and when some kids think Emerson is "stupid"—horrors! I do jump!) Just missed catching two smokers. They heard us coming and ditched smokes before we rounded the corner. Good—no "smoking butt" to deal with—lingering odor not enough for a bust.

2:00 P.M. Two nice students came to finish a test during study hall. That's somewhat fulfilling; first teacherly thing I've done today. They care—yippee! Book reports (yes, this fossil still assigns the reading of books, much to students' amazement; most did not have school library cards and they're juniors). They're due tomorrow.

2:30 P.M. Finally a real class; usually a difficult one because it's the end of the day, and they're tired; three repeaters and everyone must pass the class and the state-mandated standardized tests to graduate. Those tests have taken some of the joy out of teaching—pacing guides, uniformity, not being able to seize a moment are disappointments. However . . . they are the new reality. Dumped plan to read Act 3 of *The Crucible* and retaught when to use apostrophes and commas. Oddly, it was fun and very calming. Kids actually said they'd never understood apostrophes, so they just didn't use them. (Duh . . . I had noticed this.) Silly sentences and examples helped, and they left actually knowing something. The PSATs were real for them and I think they were humbled by the test's difficulty. I wanted them to end the day feeling better. Who knew apostrophes could cheer up anyone? I was actually pretty perky myself.

4:00 P.M. Alumnus visit—always a treat and I thrive on these visits. I am always delighted to hear that college is "fun" or that kids continue to read, or that the young mothers are reading to their children, or that Emerson's "Trust thyself" has become a personal mantra (or tattoo in one guy's case). I have been blessed this year—every few days a random former student appears. I was in another school last year—sort of a sabbatical—and totally out of the loop. It is very nice to see "my" kids and hear what they're doing. I always think these may be the last of the returnees though. I cannot imagine the girl with the spikes and chains and sad, sad eyes coming by.

4:45 P.M. Late picking up son from a detention for tardies. I didn't know the guy across the street with whom he rides had overslept three times. "No, you didn't mention it" . . . and as I was frantically driving up to his school, friends were arriving to give him a ride home. Ah, the convenience of one cell phone. I mentioned that I was sorry he'd waited, but wouldn't I have waited for a long time had he gone off with them? "Hmm . . . maybe." Aaarrrggghhhhhhh!!!

5:15 P.M. Home; have run out of gas (metaphorically). An unproductive day, worries . . . read newspaper and fell asleep.

7:00 P.M. Avoiding grading papers again. The grading just takes all the hopefulness out of the enterprise. I haven't spotted magic yet this year; actually I really like the writing of one very science-oriented guy, and one girl thinks totally differently, but wisely. They are the treasures so far, with assorted bright spots provided by hard workers. I just am not reaching enough. They should adore The Crucible; they liked the sex part and don't quite see what all the fuss is about, and oddly, this year, there is some respect for Abigail's wily ways. There used to be righteous indignation that she could cold-heartedly set up Elizabeth Proctor. It seems that Truth is now relative, rather than absolute, thanks to politicians, corporate executives, and other adults who have failed this generation. Now, Abigail is considered clever. Uh oh . . . this does not bode well for the lessons of *The Scarlet Letter* . . .

7:30 P.M. Ate oatmeal for dinner—blech—oatmeal! Son ate pizza with neighbor, so I boiled water, didn't cook. Did not feel it lowering my cholesterol as I swallowed it with great gulps of martyrdom.

8:30 P.M. Nightly call from Mom, who lives four hours away. Daddy died six weeks after my husband did, so we are bound in even more ways than typical mothers and daughters, I think. She's been out to dinner, as usual for Wednesday, had usual dinner with usual companion . . . but she's pretty happy and busy. Sometimes I feel older than she. Oddly, I got breast cancer first, became a widow first . . . feel some pressure to be responsible for both of us. Have thought of moving "back home" if she needs me, but I don't think I can do that. I would revert to being the daughter of my parents in a tiny town and whoever I am (and that is a puzzle these days) wouldn't be any more. I'm almost superstitious about it, and terrified that I'll wind up there as a missing person. Luckily Mom is still independent and has a good network of friends and people who care about her. But some day I'll get a call that she's fallen or that she's in the hospital or something, and I'll need to react. Hopefully my kids will be OK by then. How does one choose between the needs of one's children and one's parent??? And I am obsessed that kids won't be worried about me, ever. Having trouble getting long-term-care insurance because of the cancer and its reoccurrence. Is there a way to reserve a spot on an ice floe??? I like that idea.

9:00 P.M. Fading again, tried to read *Newsweek* and the *Southern Poverty Law Center* magazine about hate groups. Very saddening. Where do these wackos come from?? And the neo-Nazi who was in the area in September is returning soon. Guess I'll get to sing "Kumbaya" twice in one year after a thirty-year hiatus . . . I DON'T sing.

9:15 P.M. Have come full circle—fading amidst a stack of ungraded papers with the damn, damn toilet running on its own again . . .

SINGULAR PERSPECTIVES

I'm out the door about 8:30 to stop by Sav-On to pick up birth control pills. I haven't taken them for years, but I freaked myself out and decided to just go back on them. Don't really like the idea of taking hormones, but really don't need to panic about a child with a guy that is too "not where he wants to be" to even give our relationship a label. He says we're hanging out. I'm too old for this shit but I like him. He's cute and sexy and funny and we have a good time. He's clean and articulate, nice and thoughtful. I live in L.A. and this is hard to find.

SUSAN DAWSON, 39, *Hermosa Beach, California*;
executive producer at a post-production company

Andrea, my super, the only man who is a constant. When I lived in Florida, it was my dentist. I would tell him, "Dr. G, You know? You're the only man I see on a regular basis. I love the way you send me cute cards and have your receptionist call me to make sure I'm coming to see you." And it was always the same laugh between us when he would reply, "Oh Madeleine. You sure know how to make a black man blush."

So now it's Andrea, my sixty-four-year-old Italian widower with two lovely daughters and an elderly mother, who cares for this building as I imagine he would a wife. And then there's me, a little shy about taking his time for things I cannot do myself and that I have no one else to help me do. The air conditioner has got to come out of the window. Is there time today? I'll make it, if now is when he wants to do it. My time is never my own. Who's responsible for that? People think when you're single you have all the time in the world. But if I don't get the groceries, there are none. If I don't do the laundry, there's no clean underwear. When you live alone, you don't get touched and you hardly get any presents. Still, I don't discount my riches, the greatest of which is my independence.

MADELEINE L. DALE, 53, *New York, New York*;
lecturer and faculty advisor, School of Social Work, Yeshiva University

10:34 P.M. I think I will play some more computer Scrabble. It soothes me and takes my mind off the troubles of the world. It's fun, sitting around playing four rounds. I usually name three of my opponents after past boyfriends so I can WHUP them.

CHERYL L. SMITH, 44, *Dallas, Texas*;
Dallas *Weekly* columnist and radio host of *Reporters Roundtable*

6:55 A.M. I think I will do my hair curly today. He likes it better that way. I always feel like I am letting him down when I do it straight. I need to buy more mousse and go grocery shopping, the refrigerator is looking pretty pathetic, but when am I going to find time to do that? Maybe I can hit the twenty-four-hour grocery store in the middle of the night. That seems to be my only free time. My boyfriend seems to be getting ready fast this morning. Wonder what the hurry is? I wonder if he ever took those pictures of his old girlfriends out of his drawer? Why the heck does he keep them, especially where I have to look at them all the time?

LINDSEY NORMAN, 28, *Cheyenne, Wyoming*;
safety supervisor at a correctional facility

10:30 P.M. I know we're both trying to pretend we can just stay this way forever, even though it gets harder and harder to forget that we probably have to let go soon. In a way it's a mercy that the baby question seems to have cast the deciding vote. My greatest fear is the thought of being together for a few years, and then having him lose his attraction to me and leave me for someone younger and more beautiful. And then on my end, he really hasn't had much experience. It's fine now, but if we tried to make it work long-term, would I start to mind? Last weekend I had to explain to him who the Beat writers were. Will it eventually matter that he doesn't like to read? With everything as good as it's been so far, it seems insane to consider saying goodbye to the best relationship I've ever had. But at times, all points but one become moot: Doug's not ready, and I can't wait anymore. In the spring, once I'm in my own house, I'm going it alone. I can't risk missing the chance of being a mother.

JENEFER ANGELL, 37, *Portland, Oregon*
(DATING A MAN TWELVE YEARS HER JUNIOR); **editor**

11:45 P.M. Oprah's rerun on the dating challenges of women over thirty-five makes me chuckle. I remember several losers I dated after Frank's death. I wonder why I even tried. It is so much more satisfying to be responsible for only one's own happiness.

SEL ERDER YACKLEY, 62, *Chicago, Illinois*; **retired travel agency manager**

Miss America 2003

*H*er platform: empowering youth against violence, a cause embedded in her own terrifying experiences as the target of high school bullies. Resilient. Tenacious. (It took three tries to become Miss Illinois). Focused. "The night of the pageant I felt completely calm. I was in competition mode. When I was on stage, I wasn't thinking about the camera and the millions of viewers. I was thinking about points." Winning the crown was surreal. "You go to the competition as an ordinary person then your name is called and you can't comprehend it." Life as an American icon? "You don't change intrinsically; it's the way others treat you that changes. It's particularly weird when family and friends ask you for your autograph—What?" Personal perks of the job? "Meeting John Ashcroft. I have a deep amount of admiration for him. His confirmation hearings were contentious and he never lost his composure. And—on the Miss America-y side—meeting Bruce Willis and Bill O'Reilly." The oldest of four children born to a white father and a black and Native American mother. A nerd. A beauty queen. A Christian. A Hollywood Square. After her reign, Harvard Law School, then a career in public interest law and public policy. Ultimate career aspiration—to become President of the United States. Here she comes . . .

ERIKA HAROLD, 22, *Urbana, Illinois*

5:30 A.M. I awaken to realize that I have left the television on all evening. The reporter on CNN is talking about law enforcement officials' progress in apprehending the Washington sniper. I want to pay attention to the reporter, but my cold has left me groggy and with a headache. I fall back asleep.

10:00 A.M. I reawaken to find the reporter still talking about the sniper. I wonder whether or not this constant media coverage may serve as the catalyst for attention-starved individuals to engage in criminal activities. I get out of bed, put Celine Dion's "I'm Alive" in the CD player, and begin dancing around the hotel room to stimulate my muscles and blood flow. This hotel is one of my favorites in that it comes equipped with a CD player. Adjusting to new hotel rooms, usually every other night, can be slightly unsettling. I sleep on a wide variety of pillows and beds, some more comfortable than others, and try to settle in to each room without unpacking any more than is absolutely necessary.

Since the quality of room service varies from hotel to hotel, I usually order grilled chicken Caesar salads and raspberry sorbet, as there tends to be very little that can go awry during the preparation process. I have often thought that perhaps someone should pay me to write a comparison piece on salads and sorbets from around the country.

11:00 A.M. I do a telephone interview for a morning radio show. We discuss a plethora of topics, including bullying, youth violence prevention, abstinence education, my future attendance at Harvard Law School, and the monetary value of the Miss America crown. People always seem to be curious about the stones used in the creation of the crown and how much money I would receive if I pawned it. I was told that the crown comprises 733 Austrian crystals and that, should I ever have free time, I was welcome to count them. I've decided that I will never have the inclination to do so. However, I always tell people that I would never desire to pawn the crown because it is not only a symbol of a personal achievement, but it also represents a time-honored American tradition and has gained iconic status. To step into the role of American icon for a year is a bit daunting, as people have so many different expectations and cherished memories. However, I attempt to keep perspective by reminding myself that my role is not to embody every aspect of the legacy, but rather to add to it.

11:15 A.M. I do a telephone interview with a reporter for the *National Jurist* magazine, a magazine for law school students. I talk about the ways in which my experiences as Miss America will help to prepare me for law school. While in law school, I hope to study public interest law, which entails utilizing your legal education to, in some way, improve the lives of others. By traveling around the country, directly listening to the needs of a variety of Americans, I hope to be in a position to better understand how I can use my legal education to make a difference in their lives.

12:00 P.M. I talk to a photo editor at *People* magazine regarding the article they are writing about the harassment I experienced in high school. She tells me that she needs some photographs of me from ninth grade. I have my parents send them some, silently hoping that they choose photographs that won't embarrass me. However, as I am photographed so often, I have made peace with the fact that there will inevitably be unflattering pictures taken. Therefore, I have decided that if approximately 70 percent of the pictures taken are flattering, I won't worry about the other 30 percent (at least not too much).

1:00 P.M. My traveling companion and I arrive at a fancy New York hotel to meet with the directors of Words Can Heal, a nonprofit organization dedicated to the diminishment of negativity in discourse and the promotion of positive language. They seek to show the detrimental impact gossip, rumors, and cruel language can have upon someone's relationships, sense of self, and dignity. Tonight, they are having a gala event to honor three Ambassadors of Healing, including Goldie Hawn and Susan Sarandon. Even though I don't follow their careers very closely, I am still excited about the prospect of meeting movie stars. These types of encounters certainly enhance the level of glamour in the stories I tell family and friends about my time on the road. I was invited to attend the function because my goal as Miss America is to prevent bullying and violence among young people and empower all segments of society to proactively work towards the elimination of this behavior. I will make a brief speech at the beginning of the event, describing the way in which I was mercilessly harassed in the ninth grade and congratulating Words Can Heal for their efforts to eradicate harassment. It's gratifying to find power in negative experiences by using them to empower others. I've found that speaking out about victimization and telling my own story makes me feel like less of a victim.

4:30 P.M. I practice my speech for the gala event a few times. Many people tell me that I overprepare for most things, but I find that preparation calms my nerves and helps me to focus my energy and concentration. I alter a few of the words to make the delivery more conversational and decide that the speech is in a presentable form.

5:30–7:00 P.M. I pose for photographs with Goldie Hawn, Susan Sarandon, Sen. Harry Reid, and members of the Words Can Heal organization. Sen. Reid asks me about the process of being plucked from anonymity and placed in the public spotlight as Miss America. I tell him that nothing really prepares one for that process, and that it is slightly disconcerting. I didn't fully expect the high level of visibility that accompanies the position or the fact that any comment I make, whether intended to be taken seriously or not, could be widely disseminated. In my very first press conference in Atlantic City, the issue of my race came up, and I joked that as a result of my multiracial background, I fill out "Other" on the Census form. The next day on CNN, the words "Miss America identifies herself as other" scrolled across the bottom of the TV screen. However, they failed to mention, or perhaps even realize, that it was a comment made in jest. But, with a higher level of visibility comes the opportunity to serve as an agent of change, so I'm grateful for it.

7:10 P.M. I give my speech and all goes well. I then do mock crownings for some of the guests in attendance, placing the crown upon their heads while their friends and family members take photographs of them experiencing their own Miss America moment. I always enjoy the mock crownings because it is a way to give people a taste of the shock and exhilaration I felt the night the fabled crown was placed upon my head. Some people put their hands over their faces, others jump up and down, and still others pretend to cry. Since that moment is one that the country collectively experiences every year, it seems that everyone has given some thought as to how they would react if they were the recipient of the crown.

7:30–9:45 P.M. I enjoy the rest of the gala, complete with speeches from the honorees and a performance by a group of teenagers who use music and dance to illustrate the impact of social cruelty. Although it reminds me of some of my more painful experiences, I am pleased that these teenagers have so accurately and poignantly captured the horror of this degradation. I feel hopeful that as they perform for students throughout the nation they will serve as a catalyst for others to take action.

10:15 P.M. I attempt to check my e-mail but am overwhelmed by the number of messages in my inbox (110 unchecked messages).

11:00 P.M. I watch the news and read the paper to keep abreast of current events. The sniper's activities are still dominating all of the coverage.

11:45 P.M. I reread some of the materials distributed by Words Can Heal, looking for ways in which I can develop partnerships with them during my year of service as Miss America. It is exciting to realize that during this year, as a result of my title, I will have the opportunity to collaborate with some of the most prominent leaders in the field of youth violence prevention. This prospect, combined with the knowledge that I have but one short year to accomplish many of my platform-related goals, makes me recognize that I have an obligation not to squander any of the time or resources that have been afforded to me. It can be a daunting prospect, hoping to make the most of a year. But it is a challenge I am honored to take on.

1:00 A.M. I go to bed, making sure to turn off the television.

THE ASK

10:10 A.M. I've been up for about a half hour. Long enough to face ugly reality. I must call my younger sister, Kim, and ask for an emergency cash infusion. I have enough food to get by but some bills are due and with a whopping $15 in my account, I need help. It's gay newspapers from around the country that owe me money. These papers that run my humor column "General Gayety" are my blessing and my bane. I'm able to comment on all things sensible and silly impacting us gay people, and be funny too. But due to lack of staff and budget constraints, and sometimes ineptness, payments can be as erratic as a bumblebee on speed. So I wait. And harass them. And beg from my sister.

She calls back and gets to play the modern game of driving, talking on the phone, and digging around in her purse for a pen to write down my account number. If I know Kim, coffee is involved too. When I ask her for $100, she responds, "That's all?"

My family expects dire results from my having quit a survival job two months ago to write full time. I've had part-time survival jobs through most of the many inglorious years that I've been a freelance writer. My résumé includes librarian, market researcher, temp, you name it. In my most recent star turn I stocked shoes at Sears for a year and three-quarters. My family might be right about the results of giving up that dreadful job but they're gamely hoping for the best. Before her phone dies, Kim tells me she'll call her husband to transfer the money into my account. Great. My embarrassment spreads.

LESLIE ROBINSON, 39, *Seattle, Washington*; **writer**

Caregiver to Husband with Lou Gehrig's Disease

*M*other to two daughters, ages nine and four. Her husband was thirty-four when he was diagnosed with ALS (amyotrophic lateral sclerosis) four years ago. Life expectancy of patients with Lou Gehrig's disease: two to five years. "When Ian first got sick, I was naive about what it meant to be a caregiver. I wanted to take care of him." Now she is burnt out, struggling to balance what he needs for quality of life with what she needs to have a life. "It's becoming clear that it's not a good idea for me to be doing his personal care. It tears me apart, but I need to say I can't do it. I feel like I continually put my life on hold. And it's horrible on the relationship." She has worked part-time, but she likes being at home, taking care of the kids. Her head swims with projects—knitting, beading, training horses, travel. She wants to make plans, rather than just react to the disease. "The girls have a life to live and I want to make it as normal and fulfilling as possible." Life, she believes, happens in phases. "I can look to the girls and see a future there. Knowing I'll have two girls on my own, that doesn't bother me. We're a pretty tight group."

KATE N. PEARSON, 38, *Parker, Colorado*

6:30 A.M. Out of my bath. My indulgence of the day, the one time I have to relax and be by myself. Didn't relax as much as I should. I was running through commitments at the end of the day and what I need to do to get there.

6:50 A.M. Check on my husband Ian. Move his arm to a more comfortable position and pull covers up. He hit his head on Sunday so he is not using the BiPAP to assist his breathing at night. Go out and feed our four horses and move Percy the rooster. Check phone messages.

7:00 A.M. Wake up nine-year-old Clare. Help her choose what to wear to school. Start on a mound of dishes left in sink from last night. Dishes did not get done yesterday because I was sick with the flu. Dinner wasn't much, ravioli for the girls and soup from a can for Ian, but it still generated dishes.

7:40 A.M. Still cooking breakfast. Help Clare make lunch for school. Trying to clean kitchen from yesterday. Send Clare out to feed her fowl (six chickens and one rooster). Summons from bedroom. Ian wants to get up.

7:50 A.M. Alice, four, has woken up. I am in the bathroom helping Ian use the toilet. Take him to the computer. Carpool comes to pick up Clare. Check in with Kathe, woman I carpool with. She is worried because I was sick yesterday. Alice turns on TV to watch *Arthur*, while I make spice donuts in electric donut-maker for her breakfast. Get Ian water and ibuprofen for his headache. After he fell on Sunday, I took him to the ER for CAT scan. They said it was normal but he has been sleepy with a headache. Need to keep an eye on him.

Donuts are done, take them out. Then go to help Ian put pants on. He is mad at me because he had to wait. Explain that I had to take donuts out of electric maker so that they would not burn and that he is one of four people I have to take care of. He implies that he should come first, the other stuff can wait.

8:00 A.M. Our caregiver, Terrence, arrives. In a sarcastic voice Ian says, "Oh good, you won't have to do any more." When Terrence walks into computer room, Ian looks at me and says, "You may go now." It is very dismissive.

8:15 A.M. Start coffee for Terrence and hot cereal for Ian's breakfast.

8:30 A.M. Give Ian telephone messages. Terrence says he needs to leave early today (3:00 or 3:30 P.M.) to take his daughter to an appointment. Verify with Ian that he wants to attend his ALS support-group meeting this evening. I need to call Tom, Ian's ride, and make sure he is still able to take him. Have one spice donut and cup of tea for breakfast. Just eat standing at the counter. Serve Ian's breakfast and coffee to Terrence. Will finish cleaning the kitchen when they are done.

8:45 A.M. Take my tea upstairs to make phone calls and fold laundry. Still trying to reach Tom about Ian's ride tonight and calling about getting a problem with the handicapped van fixed. Leave messages at both places.

9:15 A.M. Check phone messages again and return calls. Call Kathe and set up carpool schedule through Christmas vacation. Call my neighbor Bette. Her husband Jim helped me pick Ian up Sunday when he fell. She is glad they were home to help out but is upset at the situation. (Ian falling, me unable to get him up without help.) Betty wants to know if I am going to change things and what, if anything, is preventing me—money, lack of help? Personally, I need to figure out finances and get Ian to cooperate. He thinks I am obligated to be his primary physical caregiver. He gets angry when I say I don't want to do his personal physical care. Alice is upstairs playing in her pajamas. She doesn't want to go anywhere. She feels tired.

9:45 A.M. My neighbor Nancy calls. I've become her project. She is helping me keep from falling behind in housework. It is wonderful and generous of her. She called up this fall and offered to come over once a week and clean toilets for me. I couldn't ask her to do that so we are working on other projects, like cleaning up all the backlog of our move within the house when we remodeled for Ian two years ago. It has been hard to find time to tackle any big projects—doing day-to-day chores, caring for Ian on weekends and evenings, and the girls, together take all of my time. Hence surface scratched on housework. Just got Alice out of bath and dressed. She doesn't want to go to school today. She likes it when she is there, but protests about going.

10:50 A.M. Have hung the laundry on the line. Taken care of feeding the chickens. Clare didn't have time to do it before school. While I was hanging laundry my mother called to see how we are doing after the trauma of our weekend. Also, got cooking tips for this evening's dinner, pot roast. I need supper to be ready after school, before dance at 5:30, and before Ian's support group meeting.

Alice is unhappy this morning. Keeps telling me she loves me and then laying down. Not her usual self. She likes to be independent and do things on her own. Just took her temperature, 101. I will be keeping her home from preschool. Call school and let them know about Alice's absence and to say I won't be able to tutor the two students I usually work with. Also I have been on the phone with a friend who has just asked her husband to move out. I have two other close friends going through separation/divorce. Hard to listen to sometimes. I don't want to see people I care about have such trauma in their lives.

1:00 P.M. Have made lunch for Ian and Terrence and making the roast for dinner. Helped Ian get set up at the computer (minimal amount of time required on my part). He has no use of his arms but he can move his fingers to work the computer mouse. Also unpacked three boxes sent by my mother-in-law. She moved to a smaller house and is sorting out her possessions. She sent a tea set from her great aunt to Clare and clay masks Ian made when he was eleven. Alice is crying and not feeling well. I am going to read books to her. I know when she is sick she just wants me close by so she can hold onto me. I am trying to get her to fall asleep without falling asleep myself in the process. We keep reading. I sit with her but wish she would fall asleep so I could get more chores done. The kitchen is cleaned, the living room semi-cleaned up, dinner started and cinnamon rolls started in bread machine. Still have more laundry to do and horses to feed midday. But it is also good for me to take some time to sit down. I want to get more done now because I know we are going to face a time crunch later this afternoon. Tell Ian we will be eating early tonight because Clare has dance class and he has his meeting. At 1:30 he is just eating lunch. Meals take at least an hour for him to eat. I have to start feeding him at 4:00 to get us out of the house at 5:30 for dance. Terrence is helping him eat lunch, which frees me up. Alice is falling asleep next to me.

2:00 P.M. Put on another video for Alice. Fold and put away another load of laundry. Try making phone calls to deal with the van problem. No luck getting through. Nice to have a quiet day at home to get caught up with problems. Check in with Ian while Terrence is giving him lunch. He can't remember what we are having for supper. I had told him earlier in the day. His head still hurts. I ask if he thinks his memory problems/pain are due to a change in his medication or solely due to his fall. He has been very subdued, both yesterday and today. He also asks why Alice is not in school. I remind him that she has a temperature of 101. Am going to feed horses now.

2:35 P.M. Just brought in laundry. One of my favorite chores, and my mother's as well. On days like this, when I don't have time to exercise, it is a good excuse to be outside. It is also a good place to daydream or meditate. Plus, I love the smell of sheets and clothes dried in the sun. I am enjoying writing this day diary. It is making me think about the internal dialogue I have with myself each day. In the recommendations for caregivers, one piece of advice is to keep a journal. Like everything else I am supposed to do for myself, it is hard to find/make the time to do it. Ian has just finished lunch. It is my turn to drive carpool and pick the girls up from school.

3:00 P.M. Sitting in carpool line, listening to Public Radio International. Thinking about my day. It has not been a typical day for me but compared to one of my "normal" days it has been an easy one. Two reasons: I didn't have to drive anywhere until school pickup; and I didn't have a lot of demands on me. Ian had Terrence to take care of feeding and dressing him and helping him with the computer. Furthermore, he was preoccupied with his new computer and not feeling well so he did not worry about what I was (or wasn't) doing. I was left to do my own thing at home without commentary—a rarity for me.

3:30 P.M. Back at home. Alice started crying on the way home because she is tired and sick. Had to sit and hold her when we returned. Terrence is out the door. He has me call his daughter so she will be ready when he shows up at home.

4:10 P.M. Thought: We can all be better people but the question we need to ask ourselves is—are we actively working on ourselves to be better or are we fighting ourselves because we are afraid to change? Don't know where that thought came from . . . Made cinnamon rolls, they are rising. Fed and watered the horses. Will feed again after we get back from dance. With drought there is very little pasture so I am trying to spread their meals out. Help Ian put a tape in his talking book. He is at his Page Turner. Alice is asleep on the sofa and Clare is at loose ends. She is hungry.

Clare notices her beads are knocked over and mixed up. She blames Terrence for it. I tell her Alice and I had knocked them over and cleaned them up. The girls want to pin blame on Terrence. I think it is because they are frustrated with the situation—having a terminally ill father who takes up a lot of time and attention. It is not "safe" to get mad at Ian so they shift the blame sideways to Terrence. He takes care of Ian and thus is associated with him, but he is much easier going so it is safer to act out and blame him. I tell the girls that Terrence is good for all of us, he gives both Ian and I freedom. But he's a big, unrelated male in the house so he is a little scary no matter how wonderful he is. There are so many ways that living with a totally dependent, ill person affects the family.

5:30 P.M. Served dinner an hour ago. Finished feeding Ian about five minutes ago. Help him use the bathroom. I left the dishes dirty. Wake Alice up and get both girls in the car to go to dance class. At supper, Clare asked Ian if there is a color darker than black. I am suddenly feeling tired and I can feel the tension between my shoulders. I have been on my feet all day and catching up from having the flu yesterday.

7:20 P.M. Home from dance. Alice is now hungry so I am getting her supper. My cousin Anne showed up at dance class. She lives in Iowa but is in Denver for a financial class. Anne made two quilts: a horse one for Alice and a rooster one for Clare. She could have mailed them but she wanted to see the girls' reactions. Anne stayed to watch the end of class and visit. At home, Clare is having a second dinner of pot roast. I need to give horses last meal, do dishes, and get girls in bed.

7:40 P.M. Clare is reading to Alice. They have a special contest at school this month. For every thirty minutes Clare reads out loud, or is read to, she gets a "coyote coupon." Each class is trying to accumulate the most coupons to win an ice cream party. Kitchen is a mess again. Cinnamon rolls done, making iced tea for tomorrow and need to do dishes. I hate coming down to dirty dishes in the morning.

8:05 P.M. Finished dishes and girls finished reading. Cinnamon rolls for dessert. Our twelve-year-old dog urinated on the floor while we were at dance class. She gets stressed out when she is left alone. As I clean up the mess I quiz Clare on her spelling words. One more pan and dessert dishes to wash.

8:20 P.M. Girls upstairs brushing teeth. I am bagging up garbage and recyclables for pickup tomorrow morning. One consequence of having a disabled husband is that he cannot do the household chores, so we don't argue about whose turn it is. (We do argue about whether or not I did the chore "correctly," but that is another issue.) Girls are arguing in the bathroom; I need to go check on them. Alice cannot brush her teeth without me. Brush her teeth and get both girls into bed at 8:30.

8:30 P.M. Just put Ian's daily vitamins in his pillbox. I need to sort them each week. He takes seven a day plus medication at night. I put his three evening meds on the table. I've been getting them for him for the last few years, ever since he lost the use of his arms, and he still has to examine the pills nightly to make sure I have done it correctly. It drives me crazy because I feel like he does not trust me. Maybe he is just being judicious.

I now have some time to sit down and think about my day. On the way home from dance, I told Clare she looked good in class. I thought she was learning the new steps and routine. She replied, "I don't like compliments about myself." I realized in the last couple of years that I had not learned to take compliments graciously. I always wanted to brush them off or not accept them in the way in which they were given. ("Thanks, but I was just lucky," or "I had help," etc. . . .) I realized that I should accept sincere comments as they are given, freely. A person says them because they value you and appreciate what you have done. I want to teach Clare and myself to acknowledge and feel good about who we are and what we do.

Usually, I look forward to the support-group meeting evening out for Ian. Our friend Tom who takes him will feed him supper and then help him into bed when he brings him home. They usually get home late so I appreciate not having to stay up 'til 11 P.M. It is a treat to go to bed when I want once a month. I'll have to skip it tonight though. Tom is stressed out so he has asked me to put Ian to bed when they return. Need to make juice and soak Ian's drinking straws in denture tablets. I bring the cat in so she won't fall victim to the coyotes.

When I sit down, fatigue starts to come over me. I can stay up as long as I keep busy. I need to feed the fish, turn on the baby monitor in Ian's room, and turn down his bed. Wrap up one pan of cinnamon rolls for Tom to take home when he drops Ian off. Comfort food.

9:00 P.M. Friend calls to talk about separation from husband. Listen.

9:20 P.M. Going to take a bubble bath and read. Indulge myself. I am a little peeved I have to stay up for Ian. I want Ian to make the connection that it is a lot of work to take care of him. He keeps telling me that he isn't that hard to take care of. I think he is in denial about how much I do for him because it is a way to deny that his disease has progressed as much as it has. It is very difficult to find common ground sometimes because we see things so differently and face such a big challenge—ALS. Sometimes I feel like we are living in different realities. Into the bath and bubbles.

9:55 P.M. Out of the bath. Started a new book, *Away*, by Jane Urquhart. Have been reading lots of stories about Ireland in the last year. I need a little magic and a little luck in my life. I am a realist (as a therapist once described me) but look for the magic in life. I like reading fairy tales with the girls. They too look for the magic in life. I am going to lay down for a nap until Tom brings Ian home. I've been craving sleep and will take it when I can.

10:30 P.M. The garage door opening wakes me up. Ian is home. I need to get him into bed.

11:05 P.M. Just finished putting Ian to bed. Tom and Ian wanted to chat about support-group meeting, which puts me on the defensive. I stopped going because it upset me so much. Caregivers and PALS (People with ALS) all stayed in one group; they didn't split us up. I am a private person; Ian, public. He will discuss anything in public. I did not feel comfortable. He was a leader of the support group and people looked up to him. I had mixed and negative feelings about the admiration others expressed for him because his behavior towards the girls and me at home was so awful. I felt like I was at a pep rally for a lie. I wasn't getting the help or support I needed from the support group. At home, I feel like he treats the girls and me like dirt. I don't know if he ever looks at me and sees me as who I am. He has great affection from his "public" but fear and mistrust from his immediate family. He blames our mistrust and dislike on us, not his behavior. Often when I take care of him I am angry and saddened because he says I am not helping and I am incapable of helping him. I view him with a tangle of negative emotions.

I help him urinate, brush his teeth, get out of his clothes and into his pajamas.

11:21 P.M. Up to bed, lights out.

11:30 P.M. Back downstairs. I forgot to turn off the outside lights and shut the garage door. I need to read for a few minutes to decompress.

11:50 P.M. Lights out.

How to make a buck

7:30 P.M. Left the office and headed to the Port Authority to take my bus home to New Jersey. I walk through Times Square twice a day—once in the morning and once at night on my way home. At least once a week I see something really bizarre. Tonight was the night. I am walking along 42nd street and encounter a homeless guy. He is holding a sign that says, "Tell me off for $1." It was the first thing all day that put a smile on my face. I thought, Wow, now that is original and what a clever way to try to earn money! While I didn't tell him off, I did stop and give him a dollar for putting a smile on my face—it was the best money I spent all day.

NICOLE ST. PIERRE, 30, *Little Falls, New Jersey*;
vice president, JPMorgan Fleming

Family

8:30 A.M. Michael and I arrive at the adoption agency. I recall our first appointment there, dreaming of a family. Now we have Ben and hope for another. After a year of waiting, we corner the social worker to ask how we can put a rush on it! We're so ready for our family to grow, for a sibling for Ben, for some balance to our disability-focused life.

8:55 A.M. We learn that a birth mother selected our family to parent her child, but changed her mind after giving birth and decided to give parenting a try. We're amazed by the drama that went on without us knowing. Who is that child? We wish him/her love and happiness in his/her birth family. We discuss broadening our application to include an African American baby. Now that our family includes a significant difference in the form of Ben's physical disability, we are less concerned about "passing" for a birth family or blending in.

VALERIE L. WOOD-LEWIS, 37, *Burlington, Vermont*;
teacher on leave

Cambridge

4:15 P.M. We are at "tea." Every day my whole laboratory gets together for tea upstairs in the cafeteria. It's not just us—most of the labs go. We take twenty minutes and chat about the weather, eating biscuits and drinking tea. Strangely, I drink tea and my coworkers from the U.K. are drinking coffee. It's amazing to me, this calm ritual, this moment of social sanity, fingers wrapped around hot steaming mugs, no rushing about it—no nervous frenetic gulping. It's something these people have always done—stopped for tea—but to me it's a rare delicacy, a moment of slowing down that I wish I had done more of in graduate school in the U.S. During the tea, a lab-mate invites me horseback riding this weekend. Horseback riding!

GIULIETTA SPUDICH, 28, *Cambridge, England*;
molecular biologist

COPY SHOP

6:35 P.M. Putting pages in sheet protectors is very time consuming. This job will take 1,450 sheet protectors and we will make 2,225 copies. Can you imagine putting that many pages in sheet protectors? We have to make eight copies of two larger binders. Then we have to put the copies in the sheet protectors. So, after the small binders, I have the bigger binders to do. I love this work. I enjoy taking stacks of papers and ideas and combining them to make a book. It's fascinating to see some of the ideas that people come up with. My favorite idea was a Christmas card that a lady had made. She painted a small scene of a cabin in the N.C. mountains and wrote her own Christmas greeting. We had to put it together and make a card. It was very beautiful.

KIMBERLY G. GARRETT, 33, *Washington, North Carolina*;
part-time copy center employee and online college student

NOTHING PERSONAL

12:40 P.M. Drive back to office talking to my girlfriend Stace on cell phone. Break down the whole meeting with Sue and the rest of my students, though I'm focused on Sue. Stace says I take it too personally, but when Sue said my class was, "hippy dippy bullshit, no offense," I guess I didn't see my way out of taking it personally. All the work I do for that class and everything I put into it, God, it's my heart. Then Sue's final question to me before leaving the conference, "Are you queer?" Geesh. "Yes." Though I don't typically call myself queer. Aw, who cares? It's all just rhetoric anyway. All of it. Hippy Dippy Bullshit. TIME FOR SOME PERSPECTIVE!!! Wish I could say I won't even remember this in a year, but the truth is I probably won't forget that.

CINDI HARRISON, 32, *San Francisco, California*;
college instructor

THE *KIPPAH*

7:50 A.M. We are finally in the car, ten minutes later than usual. Anna is in the backseat doing fancy cat's cradle tricks with orange string. Adam is on a bench in the rear of my Volvo wagon eating a breakfast bar, washing it down with milk in a sippy cup. We are quiet this morning. Adam is waving to the cars behind us. He wears a bright red *kippah* head-covering held in place with two silver clips.

I always feel a bit fraudulent when he ventures out with the *kippah*. I want to say that it gives people the wrong impression about our family's level of observance, but that's not exactly what I mean. The *kippah* is a strong statement. It tells the world that I am a committed enough Jew that my five-year-old son wears a *kippah*. But the truth of the matter is that we hardly approach the benchmark of observance for wearing a *kippah*. But there it sits on his head and it looks as if he is wearing some sort of costume. He's jaunty about the whole thing because it's red, his favorite color, and on his head at just the angle he likes it. With him so conspicuously sitting in the rear, he's a human ideological bumper sticker, a *kippah*-wearing poster boy for Jewish education.

JUDITH BOLTON-FASMAN, 41, *Newton Centre, Massachusetts*; **writer**

HELLO KITTY

6:50 A.M. Snacked on the roasted chicken carcass and made a salad for lunch. Atkins diet better kick in. Feels like I'm carrying a sack of cats in my butt when I wear jeans.

LINDA TAYLOR, 53, *Redwood Shores, California*;
artist and promotional marketing expert

President of the National Organization for Women

Brings to the job twenty-nine years of activism, a law degree, and a soft spot for the underdog. "Even as a kid in Louisiana, I'd poke my finger in the face of the bully." Trial by fire. Five weeks after taking office—September 11. "Women's voices were completely eclipsed in the news. It has been hard to get our message heard amidst all the talk of terrorism." Other challenges? Calculated media campaigns that depict feminists as ugly, harried, man-hating shrews. Periodically, she encounters people who know her first as Kim, a married mother of two young girls. Their response when they discover she's the President of NOW— "Gee, you look so normal." A "Type A" personality. A Southerner. A guarded optimist. "I find that even women who avoid the label 'feminist' still support feminist issues." Passionate about progress. In 1977, working women earned 59 cents for every dollar brought home by men. Today, that figure has risen to 76 cents. "I want to continue changing the way U.S. society views and values women. I want the world to be a different place for our daughters, one that respects their entire humanity. I want that other 24 cents."

KIM GANDY, 48, *Washington, D.C.*

12:44 A.M. I'm finally in bed, the earliest time in several days. Last things before sleep: putting away the laundry that my husband Kip has sorted all over the bed, adding the Dollar Store clothesline and spare flashlight to the pile that is accumulating for Cady's Junior Girl Scout camping trip this weekend. Some final conversation about the day past and the one to come, a check on our respective schedules for tomorrow, and a snuggle. My last thought is of our political action committee organizer, Suzannah Porter, who is leaving at 5 A.M. in a rental car, driving from Baltimore to Missouri to help reelect Sen. Jean Carnahan. She's probably having her last full night of sleep until election day . . .

7:17 A.M. Wake to NPR and jump in the shower. Yet another night of not-catching-up-on-sleep and feeling-like-it-in-the-morning. It's the first cold morning and I consider going to the basement for a turtleneck to put under my suit, but decide to wear a coat instead—because it's not in the basement. Saving steps and seconds is getting to be an art form. I sit down at the computer to write these notes and ten minutes pass as I relive the first forty-five. I can tell this diary thing is going to be interesting—already it's making me pay attention to what I'm thinking about. Which is mostly that there is Not Enough Time.

8:00 A.M. A mom and dad chorus of "Good Morning to You" wakes our daughters Cady (age nine) and Max (age seven) for a change. Usually Cady and Max are the ones who wake me. A bounce on the bed, two snuggles, and two kisses are a really lovely way to wake up. Fortunately I retrieved the bin of their cold-weather clothes from the basement last weekend. I pull out matching outfits—possibly for the last time until spring.

8:15 A.M. Pouring bowls of sweet cereal reminds me that I wish they'd eat unfrosted flakes, which they don't. But that's a battle I've given up in favor of their eating broccoli, which they do. I push back from the table a bit so I can use the curling iron (yes, I know I shouldn't do it at the table—my mama did raise me right, but that bit of decorum has yielded to the need for morning multitasking). This way I can get my hair done, skim the day's news, and talk with the girls (this morning about why there is a sniper killing people in the D.C. area). Number 11 was shot yesterday at the Home Depot, in a covered parking lot no less. Kip is making lunches and emptying the dishwasher.

8:35 A.M. We're all headed out the door. Max gives me her signature kiss on each cheek, followed by a nose rub. Cady awards me a hug and an "I love you, Mom." Kip will drop them off at school before heading to George Washington University, where he teaches two classes this afternoon.

8:50 A.M. The traffic is unusually light and I get to the parking garage in time to walk the four blocks to a breakfast meeting. It's a pre-meeting with Eve Ensler (of *Vagina Monologues* fame), V-Day executive director Jerri Lynn Fields, and NOW Foundation's policy consultant Pat Reuss, to plan for a 10 A.M. group meeting about a proposed "1 percent project." My assistant, Athena Jackson, successfully lobbies to come along and take notes. We get the buffet because it's easy, and I do what everyone does at buffets—eat too much.

10:05 A.M. The meeting starts mostly on time, but the discussion is heated. The idea of a campaign to allocate 1 percent of the defense budget to ending violence against women seems like an instant winner—using the defense budget to defend women, making women's security part of Homeland Security. But the idea is a controversial one. There is a broad range among activists, and many love the idea (pointing out that the most substantial funding for breast cancer research has come from the Department of Defense), but others are concerned that it will compete with (rather than complement) the Violence Against Women Act, which we all worked to pass and get funded. NOW, V-Day, and Lifetime TV are on board, and many other groups offer to spread the word. We agree that we need to start garnering support from women across the country, and we schedule the next discussion in a different city. Time will tell . . .

12:15 P.M. The meeting is breaking up. My assistant hands me her cell phone just outside the door—it's Rebecca Farmer, our press secretary, frantic that we can't have our 2 P.M. press conference tomorrow to oppose the FDA's reckless nomination of a right-wing physician (who wrote a book prescribing scripture for eating disorders and PMS) to an important advisory panel on women's health. A House vote has just been scheduled at the same time, immediately after the 12–2 P.M. House tribute to one of my personal heroes, the late Rep. Patsy Takemoto Mink (D-Hawaii). Moving it to 3 P.M. would be too late for the news cycle and I have to leave for NYC early the next morning for an endorsement appearance, so we agree to move the press conference earlier—to 11 A.M.— knowing that the loss of three hours will make our preparation more difficult.

1:00 P.M. Returned from the 1 percent meeting to find a note on my office chair—the Supreme Court has scheduled oral arguments December 4 on our racketeering case against anti-abortion violence (NOW v. Scheidler). We're defending our nationwide injunction, which prohibits the defendants from continuing to use unlawful fear, force, and violence to close clinics. This nationwide injunction, which we obtained in 1999 after thirteen years of litigation, has dramatically reduced the violence.

I'm really tired of our opponents comparing themselves with Martin Luther King, Jr., and Mohandas Gandhi, who were the epitome of nonviolence. These guys and their violent tactics are more like those of the Klan, or like Alabama Governor George Wallace blocking the doors of the university, preventing others from exercising their rights. It's our second trip to the Supreme Court on this case. If they uphold the injunction, it will have been worth all these years of effort.

1:25 P.M. Our debriefing from the 1 percent meeting keeps being interrupted— first by Lisa Bennett, our communications director, bringing in a draft of a media advisory for tomorrow, then by Bonnie Erbe, host of *To the Contrary*, who calls with updated information about the PBS stations in Boston and

Washington, D.C. moving her show to 6 A.M. Sunday morning. It's the only news talk show featuring women's opinions at all, and it includes women across the political spectrum. We are urging PBS to restore their noon Saturday time slot, and to provide more women's voices among the "newsmakers." The 1 percent debriefers have given up and left my office by now, and I'll have to pull them back together. Then my phone rings and it's a woman from Texas who wants NOW to take up her lawsuit against the state Attorney General.

2:40 P.M. I need to get some lunch, but decide to check voice mail first, in case there's anything urgent. I still haven't checked e-mail today, and know there are dozens of new messages waiting. I can't decide whether the inventor of e-mail has made my life easier or harder, but it has completely wiped out my home life between 10 P.M. and midnight every night, which seems to be the only time I can find to answer it!

Call from Eve, she's happy with the outcome of this morning's meeting. We'll continue to work with the groups that are supportive and will worry later about what happens inside the "beltway."

Good news—tomorrow's press conference is back to 2 P.M. We've got Sen. Barbara Boxer, Rep. Carolyn Maloney, and a host of women's health groups—and the use of the Cannon House Office Building terrace, just steps from the Mink tribute. The logistics are getting better all the time.

2:55 P.M. Breakfast finally wears off and I make a mad dash for soup-to-go at the corner Quizno's and return only three minutes late for a meeting to discuss our Action Alert e-mail system. All of the action and Web staff are there, and agree on ways to make the system—which is generating hundreds of thousands of messages, to everyone from Congress to media outlets—even more effective. We also decide to start an e-mail digest of Web stories and alerts, plus updates and info from TheTruthAboutGeorge.com for people who don't visit the NOW and NOW Foundation Web sites every day. Wish we had better blast-e-mail software, but the really good stuff costs a small fortune.

4:45 P.M. Interview with Debbie Zabarenko from Reuters news service about Dr. Hager and his "prayers for PMS." We start out talking about the sniper (she has been covering the story) and our kids' reactions—we both have seven-year-olds whose elementary schools are essentially locked down. Terry O'Neill, also a lawyer (and a NOW vice president), fills me in on a lawsuit seeking to suspend our internal grievance procedures and I discuss organizing plans with Barbara Hays, our chapter development director.

7:45 P.M. I've missed dinner (franks and beans—and broccoli) but the math homework has been saved for me. I was a math major in college, and both girls love math, though the endless pages of addition and subtraction homework are boring for all three of us—I try to think of more interesting and challenging problems for them. I try to lure them away from the television, which is increasingly violent. So far Nickelodeon and Disney are the best options, and even they often portray girls as airheads. Cady picks out three days of outfits for camping this weekend. We start packing tonight because I have a conference in Cincinnati all weekend and tomorrow evening is booked with *Disney on Ice.*

9:45 P.M. "Lights Out." I'm curled up with Cady for our before-bed snuggle time. She's excited about the camping trip. I tell her that I may be one of the parents on the next trip, which pleases her enormously. We trade places—Kip comes to tell Cady a story, and I cross the room to snuggle with Max.

Max is upset because her friend Rachel said she was fat and the other girls laughed. I said they probably laughed because they thought Rachel was being silly. Max said "I know I'm not fat—am I?" She isn't, but the ease with which even a seven-year-old questions the shape of her body—something that simply didn't happen when I was growing up—made me both sad and angry.

Her comments remind me for the first time today that tomorrow, October 16, is Love Your Body Day, an annual campaign by NOW Foundation to target the media's unhealthy images of women and girls—the kind that lead to unhealthy diets, smoking, and dangerous weight-loss fads. A campus in Nebraska is having a "mirrorless" day, where they are covering up all the mirrors on campus. Another is having a "Feed the Models" action. It's hard for a woman to live in this society and truly love her body, because everything you see and hear says you need to be "fixed" in some way. I realize that we haven't done a news release for LYBD because we were so focused on Hager and on preparing our tribute to Patsy Mink. I'll have to think of what I could wear tomorrow that I would actually love my body in . . .

10:05 P.M. Hugs and kisses all around. *Judging Amy* has just started (I adore this show—especially Tyne Daly), which is my cue to open up my e-mail. I've managed to situate the computer so that I can both watch TV and work at the computer. Now if I could figure out how to return a few phone calls at the same time . . . Sent eighteen e-mails between 10:10 P.M. and 12:20 A.M., including approving an update of NOW's online merchandise catalog and confirming a speech at U. Michigan on affirmative action. Finally, off to bed at a reasonable hour—a good thing, because tomorrow will be a busy day!

NINE TO FIVE

6:38 A.M. I'm at my desk at work, not as early as I'd like to be but still early enough to be considered "extra time put in" or the so-called "casual overtime." My boss won't get here until 7:30, but hopefully he'll hear that I'm working extra. I think about how I'll probably end up staying a little late at the end of the day too. Should I go home immediately to be with my husband? It would be nice, after all, we just got back from our honeymoon and are already back into the routine of things, back to the grind. I think about how work would look upon that. Is it a legitimate excuse . . . I need to go home right away because I'm a newlywed. Nope, probably doesn't cut it. When is a legit time? When kids are waiting? When someone is sick and needs to be taken care of? When I just feel like devoting more time to being at home? I'll probably never have the answer.

MEREDITH OAKES, 24, *Niskayuna, New York*;
financial analyst, Lockheed Martin

8:20 A.M. I stop by Au Bon Pain for my morning caffeine fix. There must be a conference in town as the line is twenty-five people long. It is annoying. I see my vice president in line ahead of me and try to be inconspicuous knowing that he has already been at work for two hours and feeling guilty that I have not even turned on my computer yet. Not only do I need to work out in the morning, I also need to start getting to work earlier.

KELLY STUART, 35, *Cambridge, Massachusetts*;
marketer, The Gillette Company

9:30 A.M. Well the same old thing on the job. It's a man's world. The school has called. My daughter is sick. I can't leave work. I called my husband at his job, he's closer to school. He will go get her. But he acts like I have pulled his teeth out. I want to know who wrote that women are to leave work and take care of the kids, home, money, etc.

VALLARY JEFFERSON, 37, *Hampstead, North Carolina*;
office manager, Royster-Clark, Inc., fertilizer plant

10:00 A.M. At work now. I'm nervous and frightened. My boss is in a foul mood and I'm worried it's something I've done. I have to practically holler "good morning" at him as he blasts by me to get the mail. He seems unaware what effects his moods have on other people here.

MEG HOUSTON MAKER, 36, *Hanover, New Hampshire*;
product management director, NextMark Inc.

12:26 P.M. "Never be perturbed by people who take themselves too seriously," says Lisa, sage coworker, in regard to the copywriting shakedown. So clear, so true, but such a challenge to recall when being barraged by e-mails requesting copy, revoking my "privileges," not so subtly telling me the job I'm doing isn't up to snuff. There are people—alright, just that one person here, who is bent on sabotaging the egos of fledgling professionals. Old Ph.D.-guard versus the bright B.A.-toting young'uns. She actually shushed me once when I was laughing at something in the privacy of my own office. Shushed! A grown woman shushing a coworker!

ROCHELLE A. BOURGAULT, 23, *Enfield, New Hampshire*;
direct mail and advertising assistant, University Press of New England

One boss out of town . . . one in meetings . . . time to do Web work. Donate food, Save the Rainforest, etc. I also go to activists' sites and send letters, e-mails, and faxes to my representatives. Since our War on Terrorism started, I try to let my voice be heard. I guess most people would call me a liberal because I believe in civil liberties, the environment, and such. I just think that too many people do not care about what the government is doing. I have a wall of letters (mostly form letters) from senators, congressmen, and the White House. I keep them to remind me to keep on top of things. Hopefully, I am doing some good. Saving the world for my daughter and her children.

PAULA RAVEN, 34, *Richmond, Virginia*; **administrative assistant, CapitolOne**

5:01 P.M. I'm so damn tired. I have so much work to do. I come back from my interviews and suddenly I'm popular. Messages from some bureau chief and a bureau reporter. Gee, wonder why? Someone needs something translated!!! Hispanic Helen to the freakin' rescue. They want me to call Costa Rica. I don't have time to call Costa Rica!!! I have two columns to write before I leave in two days!!! How can they not get why I get upset about stuff like this!? I guess they have some paperwork from lawyers in Costa Rica about this priest who molested a kid there and then came to Connecticut. He's missing now, the priest. Weird, there's a passage in *Browngirl*, the book I am reading, that reminds me of all this, about being used for your color. Or maybe I'm reading too much into it because stuff like this drives me so nuts. It's just that I become such a valuable reporter when someone needs something like this, and when they don't, well, not so valuable. But it's McIntire asking, and I can't say no to him. He's always been great to me. Still, part of me wants to say, No, I'm not a translator, people . . .

HELEN UBIÑAS, 32, *Coventry, Connecticut*;
reporter and columnist, *The Hartford Courant*

A Mennonite Way of Life

She believes in a literal interpretation of the Bible; in maintaining modesty and simplicity in the midst of a decidedly secular world. A minister's daughter, she grew up to become a minister's wife. She and her husband met as missionaries in Guatemala. The mother of five children and one foster child, ranging in age from nine to nineteen. Like mother, like daughter, her oldest girl left school after tenth grade to teach in the younger classes. Her husband leads the household; she takes care of the house. Sews. Gardens. Maintains two chicken houses (home to thirty-three thousand chickens). She gets frustrated when she doesn't get more things done in a day. During trips to town, her plain dress and headship veiling often draw stares from "the worldly." Usually it doesn't bother her. "The things we practice, we can find a reason for them in the Bible so I can look different from our neighbors and it doesn't make me feel strange." It pleases her when people ask about her life and her faith. "I don't want anything to my credit, but if they can see God working in someone who is a human person that has feelings and struggles like anyone else . . . if they can see Christ in a busy housewife, that's the main thing."

SHARON L. MILLER, 49, *Margarettsville, North Carolina*

12:30 A.M. Just ready to call it a day. I was listening to a tape recording where my husband, Dale, had expressed some concerns about church-related issues and wanted my opinions. Did I think that he had really expressed things that way?

6:25 A.M. It was hard to get up this morning. Seems like I kept waking up. Usually I don't hear the alarm but this morning I did. Often I have a little prayer time before I get up. It's going to be a busy morning as my niece Sharon and I are taking hot lunch to school today. (We have nineteen students in our church school plus three teachers with grades 1 through 10.)

6:45 A.M. Dale and I spent time in prayer together, as we do most every morning. We have a different prayer list for each day of the week.

6:59 A.M. Time to call my daughter, Linda. Dale already called the boys, and my oldest, Margie, has been up for a while. Margie is a teacher at the school.

7:00 A.M. Biscuits and sausage gravy for breakfast. Have to make the table smaller this morning since we had guests for supper last evening and didn't get it done before.

7:33 A.M. Had our family devotions. We sang a song and Dale read a Scripture. Dale and I each take a turn praying and then we all pray the Lord's Prayer together.

7:40 A.M. Had a phone call from Charity, a friend of ours who is organizing the cystic fibrosis circle letter reunion. Our eighteen-year-old son, Edwin, has C.F. For several years, I have been part of a circle letter with other moms who have children with C.F. The husband of one woman also has C.F. The letters go from one person to the next. When it comes back to me, I take my old letter out and put in a new one. There is a reunion just about every year in Ohio. We have never attended before but we think it may be encouraging to Edwin and to us to go visit with others battling the disease.

7:44 A.M. Need to make Dale's, Edwin's, and Ricky's lunches. Another phone call—thankfully this time it's for Dale!

7:56 A.M. Another phone call. My daughter Margie is at the school and needs us to bring a cup and some change. (This is her first year teaching third, fourth, and fifth grades.) The men's lunches are all packed and ready. Now the next group—the schoolchildren.

8:03 A.M. Another phone call. Malina, my sister-in-law, thought maybe I had listened to the scanner. We do not have a radio or TV. She didn't know if she should hang out her clothes since it looked like rain.

8:18 A.M. Another phone call. My next-door neighbor Jean said I may need to pick up the schoolchildren in the afternoon. We go to the same church and take turns carrying our children to and from school. She didn't know if she would be home by 3:30 when school is dismissed for the day.

8:20 A.M. Karen, another sister-in-law, brought her five-year-old son Nathan for me to babysit while she and two other women go to Norfolk to do some thrift-store shopping. I don't do this very often. When our older children are in school I have to spend more time entertaining him with stories, play-dough, and books. If it happens real often it gets rather wearisome, but I feel like this is one way I can help the busy young mothers.

8:49 A.M. Kitchen cleaned up and it's time to take the children to school. Have to comb Linda's hair yet, then braid it in one braid down the back.

8:54 A.M. Ready to walk out the door. Had to help Anthony (age sixteen) with his lunch. We do not have a cafeteria in our school so everybody packs a lunch.

9:05 A.M. I'm back home. When we were at school, Anthony remembered we have hot lunch today. I wouldn't have needed to pack lunches! I guess out of habit and in our rush to get to school on time, we forgot. And I'm one of the ones to help make the meal! Now to get the potatoes peeled. Nathan wants some paper to write on using the jiggley pen.

9:14 A.M. Dale just walked in the door. He needed the camera to take a picture of a door. Although he is a minister, he is also a partner in a family-owned business that installs overhead doors. He and Edwin are working together today, as they often do. He says he'll stop and get some yogurt and milk for me.

9:22 A.M. Peeling potatoes. Today is my son Leon's ninth birthday and Nathan wants to see the hammer that his teacher gave him for a present. Couldn't find it, but while looking I straightened up the boys' bedroom and fixed Anthony's bed he forgot to make. The kitty is hungry so I fix her some milk.

9:38 A.M. I found the hammer. Opened curtains and shades, fixed Linda's bed. She is twelve and getting into a habit of forgetting. I want to help her with this. Being faithful in little things is important in teaching her to be dependable.

9:40 A.M. Back to peeling potatoes. I have to get them done and into the oven.

9:52 A.M. Yesterday, I spoke to a sister in the church about a concern, so my thoughts are with her this morning. As I am working, I am also searching my own heart. As brothers and sisters in the church, if we see patterns developing in each other's lives that would hinder victorious Christian living, we have a responsibility to admonish each other.

10:08 A.M. Hung the dresses that were in the dryer on hangers. Fixed more milk for the kitty. Fixed a glass of chocolate milk for Nathan. Now for the cheese sauce to go in the casserole.

10:34 A.M. The potatoes and ham are in the oven. I had my pressure cooker too full because the sediment at the bottom burnt and the potatoes taste a little burnt. Live and learn! I like my pressure cooker though! Nathan and I are going outside and check if there is enough fresh mint in my tea bed to make a gallon of iced tea. Check the mail, too.

11:04 A.M. Back from the toy box. Got it straightened up and found some toys that interest Nathan.

11:49 A.M. Everything is loaded up that I need to take for hot lunch. Heading for the school!

12:17 P.M. The twenty children are all served. The menu: ham and potato casserole, cream cheese Jell-O salad, butterhorns, éclair dessert, and iced tea. Sharon did most of it. Very interesting to hear the children's conversation. Each one made a special effort to thank us for the meal. Now they are out for recess and it's cleanup time.

12:45 P.M. Stayed and visited Margie's room. They are having English class. Third grade is up to the class table first. They are writing paragraphs and need help finding some hard-to-spell words in the dictionary.

1:20 P.M. Miss Margie is having class with the fourth grade—only two girls in fourth grade. The class rule is only one student out of their desks at a time. Sherwin was returning his dictionary to the bookcase. Denny needed to also return his and almost forgot the rule.

1:40 P.M. Home from school. The cotton pickers finished picking the field right next to the house while we were gone. Nathan helped himself to some mint tea and had a spill so I best clean that and wash the dinner dishes.

2:32 P.M. Kitchen is cleaned up again. I'll sit down and have my devotions. Brenda, at the sewing, came up with a list of ways that we can pray for our prayer partner. I'll see if I can come up with some ways too, taken from Colossians 1: 1. That she would have grace and peace. 2. Give thanks to God for her. 3. To pray always for her. 4. That she would have faith in Christ Jesus. 5. That she would have love to all the saints. 6. That she would have her hope in heaven. 7. That she would hear the word of truth. 8. That the word would bring forth fruit. 9. That she would love in the Spirit. 10. That she might be filled with the knowledge of His will in all wisdom and spiritual understanding. 11. That she might walk worthy of the Lord unto all pleasing. 12. That she would increase in the knowledge of God. 13. That she would be strengthened with all might, according to His glorious power. 14. Unto all patience. 15. And longsuffering. 16. With joyfulness. 17. That in all things Christ might have the preeminence.

3:22 P.M. Looked at *Nature Friend* with Nathan—found the hidden pictures. We talked about the hippo's mouth. Being braggy, loudmouthed, and boastful looks just as ugly in God's sight as the hippo's open mouth.

3:30 P.M. Time to get the schoolchildren. The conversation coming home was about Fords and Chevys, which is a common conversation with the children. Karen's children and Garret are here 'til their mothers come back from thrift-store shopping.

3:47 P.M. I need to make a GVS order. (GVS is a mail-order catalog that caters more to the plainer people.) Margie wants me to order a sticker book for Michelle, a missionary schoolteacher and a dear friend. I'm almost finished, but Linda Tyler, our eighty-six-year-old neighbor, is here and needs someone to help her light her stove. I'll let Anthony help her with that.

4:30 P.M. My mom is calling. She wants to e-mail Leon a birthday card but Margie's laptop that she uses as a grade book at school seems to have some problems. My mother rather enjoys working with computers and is giving some helpful advice.

4:50 P.M. Linda brought us the Saturday *Virginian–Pilot*. I need to make sure there are no unacceptables before letting the children look at it.

5:05 P.M. Need to clean up the house.

5:25 P.M. Dale and Edwin are home from working. They heard that a lady, while getting groceries last night, was shot by the sniper. Anthony is leaving with his bow to hunt deer 'til dark.

6:00 P.M. Karen came and got her children. I let her take some of the potato casserole and rolls leftover from dinner for their supper. She found a pot for my coffee maker at the used store which looks almost new.

6:20 P.M. Ricky (our nineteen-year-old foster son) and Edwin were all ready to leave for the volleyball game at the church and hadn't heard it was called off because of the rain. Since it was raining Edwin thought they might be able to play Yard Blitz instead of volleyball. Edwin called Margie at the school to find out where the Blitz game was and she told him that it had been called off. Edwin was upset at Margie for not letting them know sooner.

Anthony just poked his head in the door wearing a pleased smile. He shot his first deer ever! A doe. Ricky went with Anthony to help him bring it home, taking his hunting equipment just in case he gets a shot, too. Edwin was going along too, but Jason, another boy from the church, called to say they would be practicing their songs for the youth retreat at 7:30. Edwin didn't want to get all dirty again so he's taking a nap until supper. After Karen left, Leon and Linda went to help Dale empty the feed pans in the chicken houses. Leon was hoping his cousins would stay to help him eat his birthday cake. I need to decorate that and finish supper.

6:30 P.M. Margie is home and worn to a frazzle. She enjoys her students very much but has had some challenges to work through, disciplinary and academic. It seems like it takes time for the younger ones to get into studying, having lost some of their skills during the summer vacation.

6:50 P.M. The children and Dale just came in from the chicken house. Margie was looking at the Cabelas catalog that came today. She is having a hard time deciding what to get Ernie (her special friend) for his birthday and Christmas.

7:11 P.M. We're sitting at the table. Everybody is here. I'm still working on finishing Leon's cake.

7:38 P.M. Sing Happy Birthday. The cake has a big "9" candle. Our youngest is nine!

7:51 P.M. Supper is over. Now to clean up the kitchen again.

8:30 P.M. Linda cleared off the table and Leon rinsed while I washed. He practiced his Bible memory while rinsing. Now Linda and Leon both want to hold the kitty. Linda wants the kitty to stay sleeping so I have to take care of the squabble. The boys are skinning the deer and Edwin is at church singing. Dale has a conference call tonight and Margie is expecting a call from Ernie anytime. The troubles that young people have seem so big. Sometimes it is hard to know what is the best for them. What would we do if we couldn't trust God for wisdom in guiding our children on the right path?

This evening when Ricky came home, he was singing. He hasn't done that before that I can remember. Ricky has been in our home since February. Just recently he became dissatisfied with his boss's truck, loaned to him for transportation. He's been searching the Bargain Trader for some good deals and thought he found just the truck for him! Money was the problem. He would have had to borrow most of it. After being advised to wait 'til he has more money saved, he gave it up. To surrender our wills brings joy. He sure did want to buy that truck, though.

Leon had to sit quietly on the rocking chair because he squabbled with his sister and now he's sleeping. I guess too much birthday! Guess I'll wake him. He needs to read tomorrow's reading lesson yet.

9:03 P.M. Listened to Leon's reading lesson. Now he's getting ready for bed after playing with kitty for several minutes. Edwin is back, the deer is skinned and Anthony is mixing up a batch of deer jerky. The boys have made up their own recipe and like to sell it to their friends for a small fee. We have a meat grinder they use after the meat is cut off the bones. They mix sauces, spices, and salt, then with a jerky shooter (like a caulking gun) spread it into the dehydrator trays where it dries for six to eight hours.

9:27 P.M. Finally finished that fax for our missionary friend in Mexico. Time to give Edwin his chest percussing therapy, which we do every evening for twenty minutes.

9:56 P.M. To pass the time during Edwin's therapy we finished reading *The War for Mansoul*, a very interesting allegory, picturing the conquest of God to gain the rightful rule of our hearts. Time to call it a day. I didn't get the ironing done or my apples but, Lord willing, there is tomorrow.

10:26 P.M. We had a little pow-wow about who should go to the circle letter reunion in Ohio this weekend. We decided that Edwin and Anthony will go, Linda will go with Margie, visiting some friends, and Leon will stay with his cousins.

It's been a good day but busy and a little unusual because my turn to take hot lunch only comes around about twice a year, and I am not called to babysit real often, but God gave grace for this day.

ON THE JOB

Eva Kaminsky, 28
New York, New York
stage actor (starring in national tour of one-woman show, *The Syringa Tree*)

9:45 P.M. Just got home from doing the 8:00 performance of the play. Tonight's audience looked like they would rather have been at the dentist. It amazes me that people come to the theatre and immediately fall asleep—sometimes in the front row. I'm up there with sweat pouring, literally drip-dropping down my body, and people are looking at me with this "Honey, why did you drag me to the theatre?" face. "You mean I might actually have to feel something? This entails listening and learning?" And it just made me sad and tired. And since I am the only one up there, it doesn't really matter if I am sad and tired, because there is no stopping once it's begun. Everyone backstage said the show went really well tonight, but I felt so disappointed. Mainly in myself for letting it get to me so much. The relationship with the audience is just as important as lights and lines and the other people on the stage with you. And it can sometimes feel like you're dating some imbecile who thinks you're a pain in the ass when you say, "Can we talk?" I wish Gin was home so I could tell her about it. Who would think that being these twenty-some characters every night could make me feel so lonely?

Living with Parents while Applying to Culinary School

A pantry chef, she prepares salads, appetizers, and desserts for "a pretty much standard nice place, y'know, white tablecloths, candle-light." She dropped out of college midway, after struggling on the pre-med track. A mutual decision made with her parents. Someday, she would like to own her own restaurant. She grew up in the Midwest in a one-stoplight town ("it's the flashing red kind") with a Filipino mother and a white father. Her mother taught her how to prepare chocolate banana *lumpia, pancit,* chicken *adobo;* her paternal grand-mother passed down Southern Fried specialties. Before the pantry chef gig, her first job after leaving college was selling vacuum cleaners. She lasted a week—"It was the whole going into people's homes and trying to hawk things they probably didn't want." A hopeless romantic, she loves sappy movies ("I like the really cheesy ones where you know they're going to end up together because it's so obvious, but it's good fun anyway"). Until she hears from culinary school, "I'm pretty much either at work or at home." Her friends from high school are mostly married with babies. Her college friends are still in school or starting new jobs. Meanwhile, she's living back home. "Really weird. Rules rolled back like in high school."

MARIA HENSON, 21, *Norris City, Illinois*

12:00 A.M. I have just finished watching the *Caroline Rhea Show* on ABC Family and have switched to Lifetime so I can watch *Mad About You.* Well, per-haps . . . I hope it's not a boring episode. If so, I'll prolly channel surf. Writing this down makes me realize that I watch an awful lot of television. Oh well, sitting around my living room watching late night TV while everyone else is asleep is not an unusual habit of mine.

12:11 A.M. Semi-interesting episode, but switched to *Martin* . . . will watch this and *Living Single* on USA. These are quality shows and I try to tell everyone to watch them so that the channel does not cancel the syndications. If they do, it'll just be a BIG FAT BUMMER.

12:14 A.M. Wonder if what they say about late night snacks is really true. Apparently, if you eat after, what is it, 10 P.M., it's not all that good for you. But what if you're really hungry, shouldn't you eat then? . . . like maybe you missed supper or somethin'. I don't care, I'm gonna eat my raspberry yogurt and enjoy it.

12:25 A.M. Just checked on my laundry. Really shouldn't let it pile up so much that it takes me like two days (sometimes more) to finish it all. This is my last load for tonight. I'll put another in before work tomorrow. Fun and excitement as always.

12:43 A.M. Ow! Ow! Just bit thumbnail down too far. Seriously, this habit is not working out at all. Tried several times to stop munching the nails. Was able to stop for lil' bit but always started back up. Guess this is my equivalent to an addiction, eh? Well, since the mani and pedi stuff is already out, may as well give self quick pedicure as I finish watching *Living Single*.

1:04 A.M. Time for bed. Dump the junk off the bed, set alarm, pop in *Notting Hill* and fall asleep. Don't forget to set sleep timer on TV so it will go off after I'm asleep . . . hopefully I'll get a good six and a half hours before my week starts. Tuesdays are usually my long days at work.

9:05 A.M. Ugh! Mornings. Am so slow in mornings. Perhaps if I didn't stay up 'til almost 2 A.M., waking at 7:30 wouldn't be such a pain. Was five minutes late to work. Hate that. Working at the Red Geranium (restaurant) is the first job I've actually enjoyed. Working the cold pantry of the kitchen is fun . . . of course, hopefully soon I get to play at the hot end and get to do some cooking. This would be quite beneficial, since I want to go to culinary school. Most schools look favorably on people who have actually worked in a non–fast food type of restaurant. Reading the notes left me—list of prep work to be done, locations of ingredients for today's cold special, etc. Apparently today's cold special will involve lychee nuts . . . interesting. Yup, curried chicken salad topped w/ lychee nuts and chopped green onions.

11:52 A.M. Just finished convincing one of the bakery ladies to try a lychee nut. Only took two minutes to badger her and a simple "I dare you." One would think that after grade school the whole "I dare you" concept would no longer work, however, it's still quite a useful tactic. She didn't seem too thrilled, she thought they looked like rocky mountain oysters. Can I say YUCK?! After she took a bite, I said they looked like sheep eyeballs, which probably didn't make her feel better. However, she didn't seem to hate it. Cool thing about working in a restaurant is trying new foods and making other people try them. I personally enjoyed the lychee.

11:54 A.M. Better check the schedule for this week. Gotta love planning your activities from week to week. The excitement never ends.

11:57 A.M. Grr. Hate it when the servers don't stab their tickets. (Tickets are the lists of items the servers order up. When they pick up their order they stab the ticket to make sure I don't make it again.) It takes like half a second, what's the deal folks?

12:11 P.M. Why is it the hostess never tells me when we have walk-ins (customers w/out reservations)? Sure, it's not as hugely difficult for me as it is for the hot end, but it is annoying if I get slammed w/ a bunch of orders and I had no idea we had that many people in the restaurant. At least the hot end was considerate enough to give me a heads-up about the eleven-top walk-in.

12:52 P.M. "I don't wanna grow up, I'm a Toys "R" Us kid ... there's lots of toys and games that I can play with ..." Love it when random tunes run through my head.

1:40 P.M. OK, that server is workin' my last nerve. I don't know why ... there's just something about him that grates on my nerves. Maybe I'm just being unnice. He's always polite, maybe I think I find him bothersome because he's always asking questions about ridiculous things and he just takes my Hershey's syrup for his stupid coffee ...

2:27 P.M. Face still feels swollen ... onions will do that to my sinuses. Funny thing is, I wasn't even chopping 'em, they were just being cut in my vicinity.

2:49 P.M. Getting some flashes of heat. Running up and down the stairs trying to put stock away in the stockroom upstairs is a pain in my butt. But, at least it's a quick task that I can finish up before Amber gets here to take over. Don't think she'll be too busy. I think there's only about twenty reservations tonight.

4:21 P.M. While driving home from work I hear No Doubt's "Just A Girl." Haven't heard that in a looong time. Reminds me of high school weekend nights. *Sigh* Reminisces. Wait, did I spell that right? Nevermind.

4:26 P.M. Now being back at home, I have to check on my rabbit in his little hutch. Archimedes is sooo cute. When I scratch his little bunny nose he always gets this look of contentment. He seemed to enjoy the sweet potato Dad put in his cage. There seem to be like a thousand mosquitoes out here in our backyard. Hope they're not spreading the West Nile virus. Wonder if rabbits are killed by it. Certainly hope not. Need to winterize Archimedes's cage. I know he has a fur coat and all, but he's still got to be getting pretty chilly lately.

4:35 P.M. How annoying. My father decided to do his laundry today after he got home from fishing this morning. Since some of my clothes were in the dryer he dumped them on the couch so he could dry his. Now my clothes are wrinkly. Can't complain, 'cuz he's off somewhere else now. It's weird, I live with my 'rents but I don't see them all that often. Our schedules are all crazy; I don't even think we've had a supper together in two weeks.

4:53 P.M. Oprah's doing a show on dating after thirty-five. Some chick was tweakin' about marriage and offspring and her lack of them at age thirty-one. "What if I never marry?!?" Apparently now she's accepted and dealt with it (age thirty-six, I think). I hope I'm married by thirty-three. I'm only twenty-one . . . I don't need to be married right now. I so need to get my life in order . . . or at least on its way to being in order before I consider marriage. I would really like to move out of my parents' home and have some sense of independence . . . y'know, paying bills and just being a real grown-up first. But I think it would be nice to grow old with someone. Have someone there to share your life with. To have the type of love where you sleep better just b/c he's sleeping beside you and you know you can reach out for him when you need him. Wow. I'm such a romantic sap . . . sometimes.

4:59 P.M. Ooh, time for *Sister, Sister*. Am so loving they're showing it on Disney. Disney is a great channel. They've got *Sister, Sister*; *Boy Meets World*; *Kim Possible*; and *Smart Guy*. They used to have *Pepper Ann* and *Doug*, but sadly, no more. I miss Pepper Ann, she was fun. Perhaps watching all these shows may make me seem a little juvenile . . . but I don't care. Still love 'em.

6:07 P.M. Just happened to glance at the calendar and it's my friend/sorority sister Santa's birthday. Should send her an e-card. Since haven't talked to her since July don't know what she's up to or even if she's OK. A lil' concerned 'bout her. I don't think anybody's heard from her in a bit.

7:00 P.M. While watching TV, I notice they are showing Botox commercials. This whole Botox phenomenon is disturbing. Are these people aware that Botox is a derivative of botulism, which is a TOXIN. Hello, that's where they get the name. Essentially, in order not to have some laugh lines people are willing to paralyze the muscles in their face with poison. Poison! Hellooo!?! Plus, it's not even permanent. People are willingly injecting poison repeatedly into their faces. I just don't get it. OK, so we don't wanna look older. I can appreciate that. Facelifts, eyelifts, OK. They're kinda frightening and may make one look like plastic. People put more consideration into them b/c it is surgery and all that. But, REPEATED INJECTIONS of POISON!!! At Botox parties! People, come on!

7:40 P.M. Debating whether or not to call Joaquin tonight. He'll prolly be home, since he's on duty tonight (he's a resident's advisor at Eastern Illinois University) and is not supposed to go anywhere. But did talk to him rather recently and don't want to seem too stalker-ish or a super-clingy girlfriend. Hmm . . . needs further thought. Long distance is a pain in my eye.

8:14 P.M. Oh no. Just channel surfed to Disney channel, only to realize the Disney original movie, *Gotta Kick It Up!* is halfway over. I've missed this movie like four times that it's been on. I really want to see this one too. Grrrr . . . maybe next time. Should get that TiVo so I don't miss stuff but no money for it.

8:35 P.M. Final load of laundry! Now, lots of clean clothes for me! "Do a little dance . . . washing my clothes . . . they're so clean!" OK, so not a quality song. Guess I shouldn't write jingles for laundry detergent commercials.

8:40 P.M. School, school, school. "When are you going back to school? ARE you going back to school?" I hear this more frequently than I would enjoy. Hopefully, this time next year I'll be outta here and in culinary school. Hopefully. Hopefully. Save up the cash and all that business, right?

9:00 P.M. Gonna call Nikki. See if we should make plans to go out this weekend.

9:03 P.M. Almost woke her up. She's been having to work super-early in the mornings lately and was about to crash. Felt bad and apologized, but she said I didn't wake her. Didn't finalize plans. Will depend on the lateness of her working. Sadly the two and a half years away at college has left me with few friends in the surrounding area. Actually, Nikki is the only person outside of work that I chill with socially. Most other friends are far away. Sheesh.

9:20 P.M. 'Bout to read my daily devotional in Bible. Hmm, better go to my bedroom and find it first. Lately have been doing better with daily devotional time with God, especially since I've been doing them daily, instead of sporadically as in the past. It's calming and I'm growing spiritually closer to God. It's funny, I had to pause about whether to include this entry, but when I think about it, it's ridiculous for me to feel that way. I shouldn't be ashamed of my faith b/c my relationship with God is what helps me through the rough spots . . . when I'm scared or worried or whatever. Saying that Jesus is my Savior doesn't make me a freak, it's simply a statement of fact. And I'm thankful for that and all the blessings God has granted me.

9:30 P.M. Debating again whether or not to call Joaquin. Yes? Maybe.

9:31 P.M. Maybe not.

9:34 P.M. Oh, why not? Stop being so neurotic, chick, just call him! Fine. I will.

9:52 P.M. Better jet outside to open the garage door for Moms before she gets home from work.

10:05 P.M. Wonder if Sheila and Lerice (sis and bro-in-law) are having fun on their cruise. Wonder if Sheila got her birthday card and gift before they left yesterday.

10:10 P.M. Tried calling Joaquin. Left a quick message on his machine telling him he could call me back tonight if he had time. Guess he's on rounds.

10:20 P.M. Mom just called. Guess they're running late at the store but now she's on her way home. The whole grand opening of the Super Wal-Mart has made all the workers a little cranky and Mom's hours a little crazy.

10:37 P.M. This episode of *Boy Meets World* is a good one. It's a Halloween episode w/ guest star Candace Cameron. Very funny.

10:50 P.M. Do I hear "Hava Nagila"? My phone! Where is it? I bet it's Joaquin . . . yup. Nice.

11:50 P.M. Still talking w/ Joaquin. He makes me laugh. It's not like we even discuss pertinent topics, just day-to-day stuff and randoms. I think I really like this guy. First serious relationship since . . . um, well . . . ever! I think that would be a yes, eh?

11:56 P.M. Oh, for the love of cheese! Sitting here on the floor, chatting on the phone, pick up magazine from floor and set it on the table. In doing so, knock over my root beer and it hits me in the head and spills all over me. What a way to end the day, cleaning up spilled root beer and having my bf give me a hard time about being a klutz. Plus, I'm all sticky. Lovely, just lovely.

11:59 P.M. Still cleaning, still sticky. Put Joaquin on hold to clean up the mess and had to take a moment and write final entry at final minute of my day diary. G'bye folks!

ROSIE'S PLACE

11:30 A.M. The dining room opens and we let in a hundred poor and homeless women and children. We offer all of our guests a bowl of soup, a cup of fruit, and a hot meal. Today the meal is ziti and meatballs with a garden salad. As I greet the women there is a crying baby who is holding her arms out for me. I scoop her up and she stops crying. She looks like she is ready for a nap and she is coming down with a cold. Greeting the women is one of my favorite things, as you get that unique opportunity to offer a smile and a hello to a woman who has very little human contact. Lunch hums along nicely. It is loud, but everyone appears to be in a good mood. A baby has gotten away from her mother and I scoop her up right before one of our tray carriers trips over her. She smiles at me and I melt. She is adorable. I love all of the children at Rosie's Place. They have the amazing quality of seeing only the bright side of things, and I learned early on at Rosie's Place that this wonderful quality is both priceless and precious.

CHRIS NIETHOLD, 29, *Quincy, Massachusetts*;
food program manager, Rosie's Place (shelter for homeless women)

Not a Vampire, but Plays One on TV

*A*s a kid in a family of doctors, she was determined to be a surgeon. She soon found out she couldn't stand the sight of blood ("even fake blood!")—ironic indeed for an actor who would make her mark as Darla in *Buffy the Vampire Slayer*. Switched her sights to ice dancing, competing professionally until she was injured at age sixteen. Applies the lessons from skating ("There are no overnight successes; it's all perseverance and hard work") to acting. Approaches every audition as if she's perfect for the job, then lets it go. On the big screen, she plays Ursula in *George of the Jungle II*. Married to well-known character actor and voice-over talent John Kassir. "We're complete opposites. I'm this anxiety case. I'm packed three days before a trip; he packs at the last minute." A crafter addicted to home decorating shows ("I'll hot glue anything"); presently negotiating a truce with her sewing machine ("We had a fight and we're not talking"). Always has a backup plan ("the Oops factor!"), whether it's cooking, or acting. "It's the seventh take and the well's run dry so you need to dig into your training, your craft, and give them what they want. At least it's not brain surgery."

JULIE BENZ, 30, *Los Angeles, California*

5:00 A.M. Alarm goes off. Make way to bathroom. Weigh myself. Move scale to different area of floor and weigh myself again. Number stays the same. I guess scale is working correctly. Feel fat. Climb into hot shower. Spend next fifteen minutes thinking about day and when I can climb back into bed. Run lines in my head for upcoming scene. Shit—why can't I remember them? I knew them last night. Need coffee. Contemplate never leaving shower.

5:15 A.M. Out of shower. Trying to move around quietly so as not to wake husband. He always accuses me of being loud in the mornings. I will prove him wrong.

5:17 A.M. Shit! Drop hairbrush—sounded really loud.

5:24 A.M. Leave upstairs bathroom. Kiss sleeping husband goodbye. Hope I didn't wake him. Stumble down the stairs in the dark. Have to make coffee and pack my breakfast. I make my usual Kashi GoLEAN cereal and protein powder mixed with vanilla nonfat yogurt. Try to start the day out healthy.

Look to see where dogs are sleeping. Gracie is under the dining room table and Elvis is on his bed under the pinball machine. They don't even wake up. It's too early!

5:35 A.M. As I am leaving, my husband walks naked down the stairs with a flashlight. I smile for the first time today. Last night, I told him of my irrational fear of being attacked by coyotes in the early morning hours as I make my way to the car. He remembered. I love him. He walks me to my car—naked. Thank God it's pitch black or the neighbors would get an eyeful! Kiss husband good-bye. Start car—favorite song on radio (Norah Jones's "Don't Know Why"). Today will be a good day.

6:15 A.M. Make it to work in record time, forty minutes. One of the benefits of getting up early in L.A.—no traffic. I've been working as a guest star the past six days on a television series for NBC called *She Spies*. I play the very spoiled, wealthy daughter (Elaine) of an ambassador who is getting married to an Arab prince. Someone is trying to kill her and the *She Spies* team is sent to protect her. However, Elaine is extremely self-centered and doesn't care at all about the death threat. Comedy ensues. I love playing characters who are so horribly mean because it is a challenge to try to make them lovable—you know, the villain that you love to hate. I've had a lot of fun playing Elaine because I get to tap into certain energies that I don't normally live with, and be very annoying. Today is my last day. I have one quick scene to shoot this morning. Hope to be done by noon. Climb into my little, dark trailer—I'm in what they call a three-banger, meaning there are three separate rooms in one trailer. The rooms are really small and consist of a couch, desk, chair, TV and radio, and bathroom. Each actor has their own room. This has been my home away from home for the past six days. I turn on the news and eat breakfast. I have fifteen minutes before I have to go to hair and makeup. I look forward to having my hair and makeup done. I find it very relaxing and it gives me some time to get focused on the day ahead of me. Plus, if I'm still a little tired I can try to catch a few *zzzzz*s while my makeup is being done.

6:20 A.M. Shit! Forgot to take birth control pill. Seems to happen more and more these days. Maybe it's my subconscious telling me it's time to have a baby. I don't know if I'm ready. Must remember to take pill when I get home.

6:35 A.M. They are ready for me in hair. My friend Monica is working on the show as a hair stylist. She sets my hair in rollers and we talk about the upcoming birthday party I'm throwing for my husband. It's going to be a casual gathering of his friends and I'm planning on cooking all his favorite food from when he was a child. John is of Middle Eastern descent so I am making kibbeh, spanakopita, hummus, *lebneh*, tabbouleh salad, and red velvet cake. I've never made any of these dishes before except for the red velvet cake so I am very nervous about how it will turn out. The news is on in the background.

7:10 A.M. Back in my trailer waiting for makeup to have an open chair. Natasha Henstridge is currently in the chair having her makeup done. She has been so much fun to work with all week. Not only is she beautiful but she is so down-to-earth and funny! She has a little scene to shoot before me so I have some time to kill. Watch news. There has been another sniper attack in D.C. area. When are they going to get this guy? Doze off.

7:50 A.M. Loud knock on trailer door jolts me out of sleep. They are ready for me in makeup.

7:51 A.M. Denise does my makeup. She applies the usual heavy artillery—foundation, concealer, powder, eyeshadow, blush, eyeliner, lipstick, and lots of mascara. The scene takes place in the evening at a formal dinner. Too early to look so glamorous.

8:30 A.M. Called to set for rehearsal. Usually, rehearsal is a time for the actors and director to get together and work out how the scene will physically and emotionally play out. However, in television, shooting schedules don't give you much time for rehearsal. It's really more about playing out the scene for the camera and lighting departments. It's important then as an actor to already have made strong choices regarding the emotional life of the character before you even walk out on set. Thank God I know my lines!

8:45 A.M. Back in trailer. Hair still in rollers. When are they going to take these things out? Pick up knitting. I am working on a baby blanket for a charity that my friend Kim runs. The charity is called Binky Patrol and we knit, crochet, and quilt blankets for children (preemies through eighteen years of age) who are in crisis. We have a delivery coming up of six hundred blankets to some local hospitals in the L.A. area so I am furiously knitting whenever I can. Turn cell phone on.

9:15 A.M. Call manager to discuss upcoming press events for miniseries *Taken*. *Taken* is a multigenerational show following three families through fifty years who are dealing with aliens and alien abductions. It mixes alien myth and lore with fiction. It is the largest miniseries to be made and it is produced by Steven Spielberg for the SCI-FI channel. I still can't believe I am part of such an amazing, history-making project! I have to remember to schedule appointment with manager to show him new headshots. I like to get new headshots every couple of years because I feel I change emotionally as an actor and like to have pictures that reflect that change. PA (production assistant) knocks on trailer door—they are ready for me in hair. Get dressed in wardrobe. I am wearing a heavily beaded evening gown for this scene. The scene takes place at the rehearsal dinner the day before Elaine's wedding. I swear the dress weighs a ton.

9:45 A.M. Hair is combed out and twisted up into a fancy "do." I feel like I'm wearing a helmet!

9:46 A.M. Called to set. They are ready to shoot scene. It's a funny scene and very short so it should go fast. Feel a little sad that this is my last day on the show. I've really enjoyed working with everyone.

11:30 A.M. Scene is finished! It went great and I am really pleased with how it played out. They announce it is my last day and entire cast and crew applaud. Feel embarrassed and almost start to cry. Goodbyes are hard for me. You would think I would be used to them by now since they are a common occurrence in my line of work, but they never get easy. I love working in the entertainment industry. There is an amazing sense of community and I find it hard to leave any job because of the people I get to know while I'm working. Everyone comes over to say thank you and goodbye.

11:45 A.M. Back in trailer gathering up my stuff, eating a sandwich provided by catering and getting changed. Call husband—he reminds me we are having friends for dinner tonight.

12:30 P.M. At Ralph's grocery store in Calabasas. People are looking at me funny. Realize I still have glamorous makeup on from filming earlier. Try to rub some off but just make it worse. Oh well!

1:30 P.M. Arrive back at home. I walk into the kitchen and notice that the dishwasher has been emptied and the laundry that was on the dining room table has been put away. Looks like the rugs have been vacuumed as well. Walk upstairs and see that the bed has been made. Did my husband do all of this before he left for work this morning? Wow! I am a lucky, lucky woman.

1:45 P.M. Call folks for my once-a-week call as I put groceries away. They are going out to the movies so conversation is short and sweet. Let dogs in the house and give them some much-needed love.

2:00 P.M. Change clothes, wash face, go for three-and-a-half-mile mountain run. Running helps me clear my head. Also makes me feel not so fat. Am very tired today. Find running very hard. Hope I make it back in time for Oprah.

2:56 P.M. Back at home in time for Oprah. Have to start preparing cornbread for dinner. Never made cornbread before. Seems pretty easy.

3:10 P.M. Screw up cornbread. Why do I always confuse baking powder and baking soda?!? Have to start over. Thank God I have enough ingredients for another try.

3:35 P.M. I love Oprah! She is amazing. I don't know what I would do without her show. I don't watch it every day but I try to catch it at least twice a week. I think I am going to ask husband for TiVo for Christmas so I can watch more Oprah. I feel inspired. Make stuffing for pork roast.

4:00 P.M. Jump into another hot shower. Sometimes I feel like I am constantly showering. Wish I could schedule my day better so I don't have to shower so much.

4:15 P.M. Remember to take pill.

4:16 P.M. Shit! Drop pill down the drain. Is this a sign? Take tomorrow's pill instead. Hope it doesn't screw up my system too much. I have to remember to tell doctor when I see her this week for my checkup. Also need to discuss when I should go off the pill if I want to get pregnant next year.

4:32 P.M. Publicist calls to talk about upcoming press events. This week, I have two functions to attend and a talk show to film, to promote *Taken*. I have to figure out what I'm going to wear. Start feeling anxiety. Remind myself to breathe. I get very nervous when I go on a talk show. It's such a weird experience. I feel really awkward talking about myself on camera in front of an audience. I feel a lot of pressure to be funny and witty and I forget important bits of information like what show I am there to promote. Usually, my heart is racing so fast that I find it hard to focus on what the host is even asking me. They don't teach you this stuff at acting school! Also find out that I am going to NYC in November to do the press junket for *Taken*. I love NYC especially in the fall. Can't wait to go! Try to get dressed as I am talking. Drop phone. Hope she didn't hear! She reminds me I have a phone interview tonight at 6:00 P.M. My guests are arriving at 6:30 P.M.

SHIT!!!

4:56 P.M. Throw hair up into messy twist. Run downstairs to start dinner. Making a stuffed pork roast which I have never made before. What was I thinking? Butterfly the pork roast the wrong way. Don't worry too much about it—it will all taste the same.

5:10 P.M. Stick roast in oven. Husband calls—he is on his way home, is there anything I need? Tell him everything is under control and thank him for cleaning up this morning. Once again, I am lucky, lucky, lucky!

5:15 P.M. Check e-mail.

5:35 P.M. Husband arrives home. Make out for about five minutes.

6:00 P.M. Baste roast with apple cider. Call interviewer. Shell peas as we talk about *Taken* and *Angel*.

6:45 P.M. Our friends Anthony Crivello and Dori Rosenthal, and Anthony's sister and her family who are visiting from Wisconsin, arrive for dinner. Check roast—still not done. Make apple cider glaze. Everyone stands around in the kitchen. Start to feel nervous. Wish they would leave so I can figure out what I'm doing. Husband is making salad. He looks very relaxed. Why doesn't he ever seem anxious when we have company over? Why do I feel like I'm crawling out of my skin?

7:00 P.M. Take temperature of roast—it's done. I hope.

7:15 P.M. Dinner is served and everyone is eating. Have a glass of wine. Time to relax and enjoy company. Dori tells me about new yoga class she is taking. I think maybe I should start taking yoga to help deal with anxiety.

8:30 P.M. Husband starts to clear table and do the dishes. Anthony's sister says her husband would never do that. Once again feel very lucky to have wonderful husband. Have urge to take him upstairs and make passionate love but must wait until everyone leaves.

9:00 P.M. Everyone leaves. Feel very tired. Husband and I spend time goofing around with dogs. I love my dogs so much. They are so sweet and smart. Look around home and am very thankful for life I have.

9:30 P.M. Try to finish dishes—end up leaving them 'til tomorrow. Snuggle on couch with husband and watch tape of *Sopranos*.

9:50 P.M. Fall asleep on couch.

11:00 P.M. Husband wakes me. I wash my face, brush teeth, climb into bed. Read *The Lovely Bones* for ten minutes.

11:15 P.M. Hear noise outside. Look out back window and see family of raccoons on hillside. Husband and I joke about how we have our own personal wildlife zoo in backyard. Watch them for about five minutes before they wander off into the night. Feel strangely at peace.

11:30 P.M. Turn off light. Husband and I lay in dark talking about day. I love the feel of his body against mine. We are too exhausted to make love. Fall asleep in each other's arms. Today was a good day.

Physical Therapy

7:45 A.M. Look at clock, decide to get out of bed. Go to the bathroom. Begin exercises prescribed by the physical therapist to strengthen back muscles. I have a bulging disc which is sitting on a nerve between lumbar 4 and 5, which gives me much pain on the sides and calves of both legs. Both the physical therapist and I do not think the exercises will alleviate my problem but it can't hurt me either, I hope. Husband gets turned on watching me exercise, so exercises are interrupted for sex, which I am amenable to. Exercises continue after sex.

LENORA S. SCHUR, 72, *Chicago, Illinois*;
retired speech/language pathologist

Lily

3:20 A.M. I am in my hospital room attempting to breastfeed my new daughter, Lily. After a few awkward false starts, she latches on. I am remembering the three months of nursing hell I went through with Sophie Jane, my first daughter, before we got it right. God, I hope we have an easier time. I am very sore, very tired, but it is so peaceful in my room, overlooking the city, lightning flashing periodically. My husband is home with Sophie Jane so Lily (it feels weird to say her name) and I have a lot of alone time. She looks amazingly like her big sister did at birth. I wonder if she'll have the same temperament (like her daddy's) or if she'll be more like me. I don't know if I want to see myself mirrored back at me in the form of a toddler, teenager, adult!!! Yipes!

KIMBERLY C. KNOTT, 38, *Birmingham, Alabama*; **graphic designer**

6:00 P.M. I was hanging out at the 50-yard line and the ball was down at the other end. A little JV game player distracted me. She smiled at me and said, "I saw you on TV." She was so excited. I smiled and asked her how I was and she said the games were awesome, along with the TV coverage. Later in the half, she scored a goal so I waited and whispered that she had a great shot. I love being a role model for these kids. I hope that I don't make them nervous by officiating their games because I really enjoy watching them play and might as well make a little extra money! As I walked to my car, the coach stopped me and told me I made that girl's whole season.

TRACEY FUCHS, 35, *Virginia Beach, Virginia*;
captain, U.S. Women's Field Hockey Team, and Olympic athlete

BEST PALS

10:00 A.M. I call my best pal, Joan. "Joan will you do me a big favor on Thursday?" "Sure," she says, because she is my best pal and never says maybe or no. Joan is my beautiful friend who made me a lifetime fan of hers twenty-nine years ago when she showed me her silicone-filled breasts. She was a go-go dancer from L.A. We were cocktail waitresses together in a disco. Now we are both grannies and we both still have great breasts.

LAKE BOGGAN, 56, *Beaverton, Oregon*; **book publicist**

COWORKERS

I take my coffee to my office, which I don't call an office. It's my "reading room" and where my spirit guides, teachers, and healers convene with me every day. This morning, as I get ready for my reading, I enter the reading room and light my candle and a stick of incense as a good morning gift to my guides. I pull the blind at the window next to the table to let the morning light in and wish the angels, saints, and guides a happy "good morning" and ask them if they are ready to go to work. I talk to my guides out loud, and no one in my home gives it a second thought. Feeling a beautiful rush of light and love, I sense them filing in one by one. Rose, my constant companion; The Three Bishops, my high master teachers; Joseph the Essene, who provides practicality; and the Pleidean Sisters, two angelic beings who came to me five years ago. I am happy to see everyone in place as the room fills with their gorgeous and powerful presence. They are ready and so am I.

SONIA L. CHOQUETTE, 45, *Chicago, Illinois*; **psychic and author**

HEJNICE, NORTHERN CZECH REPUBLIC

9:40 P.M. Our study group participants are from Estonia, Latvia, and Lithuania. Two of the countries are represented here at this gathering, seeming to confirm our initial concern that the group might end up divided along cultural lines. The socializing got off to a slow start, but now it feels like we've got a critical mass of people who are overcoming the somewhat austere surroundings of this former monastery. One of the Lithuanians shares a bottle of some sort of alcohol that is a national specialty. I wasn't planning to drink tonight, but I'm a sucker for the cultural aspect of this, so I share in the laughter and toasts. Everyone has switched to Russian. It's frustrating because I can get the basic context of a story, but then I usually miss the more complex details and punch lines. The banter is friendly and I feel a wave of relief that the group seems to be bonding well. This is another key aspect of this program, allowing the participants to get to know each other better, hopefully laying the groundwork for future cooperation within the Baltic region.

STEPHANIE TUXILL, 32, *Ipswich, Massachusetts*;
international program coordinator

ZUMBA!

1:00 A.M. I'm watching TV again—big surprise. No new shootings today, thank God. And thank God also for Breyer's Mint Chocolate Chip ice cream. It's just me and Conan O'Brien now. I feel lonely, content, hopeful. Late at night is my favorite time of day. The hours are mine to use. There is nothing I am supposed to be doing (except maybe sleeping, but that's no fun). The rain sounds nice pitter-pattering on the roof. ZUMBA! It's a new form of Latin aerobics, a cardio-workout that guarantees I'll burn fat AND learn some great dance moves if I buy these three beginner videos. Maybe I should order them. They're free for the first three months. I can learn the moves in that time and then send the tapes back. Look at the abs on those people! They must be actors, chosen specifically for this commercial right? I didn't get any exercise today. I have to go running tomorrow. ZUMBA! Makes me want to go to Miami right now. I bet life is easier there.

RACHEL CLIFT, 29, *Saxtons River, Vermont*;
independent filmmaker

Married a Long Time...
but Not Long Enough

A widow for the past year and a half. She and her husband had just moved into their dream retirement house—on the coast of Maine, beautifully decorated, with plenty of room for the kids and grandchildren. "We were looking forward to having some great times." Two months later, he was diagnosed with lung cancer. Six months later, he was gone. Reluctantly, she joined the Newcomer's Club. Right before the first meeting, she got cold feet. Her daughter and daughter-in-law both phoned to badger her. "OK, OK, girls." She made herself go . . . and it was a beginning. "Little by little, I'm forcing myself to keep busy." She's joined book and theater groups, attends a monthly ladies luncheon, volunteers at the Historical Society. "People mean well, you get so much advice, but it's always from people with mates." Lonely, but capable. "I'm not as fragile as people think." Domesticity is important to her. A grandma who snuggles with the grandkids in her bed, staying up late and chatting. A classic Greek beauty—her real name is Thalia but she's never liked it. "I've always gone by Binky... and now I'm an old Binky."

BINKY CHAMBERS, 66, *Kennebunkport, Maine*

6:20 A.M. I have been awake since five so I may as well get up and start my routine. Brush my teeth, weigh myself, then go into the kitchen and start my coffee. Take my vitamins and Coumadin and make an English muffin. Then sit "alone" and have breakfast, staring out the window to the backyard and the woods.

6:45 A.M. It's light out now . . . if only you were here. You would be getting ready to go outside as soon as you had breakfast. You loved your backyard and the woods so much. You did not have much time to enjoy them. Oh, how I miss you, my love. You died over a year ago and I still can't come to terms with it. My grief is with me all the time.

This should be titled "The Boring Day in the Life of a 66-year-old Widow." Even the word "widow" is foreign to me! I never ever dreamed I would be in this situation. Of all our close friends and relatives, we were considered the "young ones." Well, they are, after all, in their seventies and eighties. How can this be??? YOU, GONE and ME, THE WIDOW! I better snap out of it. I don't want to have another horrible day like last Wednesday. I had not had such a bad day in three or four months. The anger, rage, and misery all came back. What set me off? Oh, I know—Ginny called and mentioned that she and Nick were leaving for St. Thomas this week. Then, coincidentally, Cynthia called telling me all the plans she and John had for the holidays. I know they mean well and it's nice of them to keep in touch, but talking to them just makes me feel more lonely for you and more despondent. It was all going to be so perfect—our retirement, our new house, our new town, our new life. Finally—rest, relaxation and fun. But, before it really started, our life—as we planned it—came to a screeching halt! How unfair!

I've tried so hard to reinvent my life. Sometimes I think—if it weren't for my children and grandchildren—I almost feel as though I dreamt my whole life with you. That it wasn't real. WHERE ARE YOU? MY LIFE IS CHANGED FOREVER.

7:05 A.M. Phone rings. Who will be calling me this early? It is my daughter, Leslie, telling me not to leave the house. A sniper just killed another woman outside of Home Depot in Virginia last night! The kid is such an alarmist. Oh well, what would I do without her? She calls me every day, thank God! The 9/11 thing is what jolted me into reality. It was only six months after you died and I had to stop feeling so sorry for myself. That tragedy woke me up. I had to keep telling myself, Binky, you are not the only one with a loss. Hundreds of people just died in their thirties and forties and they have left loved ones and small children. So, pick yourself up and go on. It's not all about *you.*

But, then again, to each individual it has to be about "you." I guess "you" is who you are and you is you.

8:10 A.M. Deb (my neighbor) just called and said she won't be running over for her usual cup of coffee and visit. She is waiting for some repairmen to show up. It's a good thing I have her, too. She, along with the kids, has saved my sanity these past few months. She makes me "laugh."

8:20 A.M. I better go and shower and get dressed. I need to go to the bank and get some gas and also to the market. I need to get ready for George and Gloria's visit tomorrow. They are flying in from Texas and, as much as I am looking forward to seeing them, I am also sad. To think that I am entertaining your West Point roommate and best friend and you won't be here. Once again my mind races to the fact that I am now Jack's widow. Not Jack's wife.

Even to myself, I consider myself Jack's wife (or Plato's wife—his real name), or Mrs. Chambers. That is, after all is said and done, who I wanted to be. I did not want to be Miss or Ms. I loved being "Jack's wife." I guess the young generation of women would consider that losing your identity. Well, I like to think that I was secure with who I was, and who I was . . . was Jack's wife, and mother to Johnny and George and Leslie.

He would have been so proud of me. I've tried to become an extrovert, getting involved with the Newcomers Club. I know I never would have done this if my husband were alive. I was so content just being with him. Even working with him in the insurance agency every day was so comforting and so natural to me. Our friends would often say, "How can you two work together all day and then go home together at night?" We would look perplexed that they would even ask such a question. Oh well—enough. My thoughts are beginning to ramble.

9:08 A.M. Watched the Weather Channel. They are predicting torrential rain for tomorrow. How am I going to drive to the airport to get George and Gloria? I hate driving on the highway in great weather, let alone a Nor'easter. Oh well! Showered and dressed. Then made a call to the bank to double-check my balance.

10:00 A.M. My eighty-year-old sister called to tell me she just spoke to our ninety-seven-year-old mother who has pneumonia. Mother told her she is doing OK. She lives in Massachusetts and reluctantly moved into a nursing home this past year. I try to visit her one day a week but the drive is an hour and three-quarters.

10:15 A.M. My daughter-in-law, Betty, called to update me on the kids' activities, etc.

10:30 A.M. I better get going on my errands.

1:30 P.M. Just finished putting my groceries away. I should make some kind of menu for the next few days. I should have done that before I went shopping, not now. No wonder I spend so much money. NO PROPER PRIOR PLANNING.

2:00 P.M. I check the weather again and the stock market (so I can get more depressed). People are getting shot left and right by this insane sniper and I'm worried about my stocks and my IRA. Binky, you are an idiot!

3:30 P.M. Walked down to get my mail. The usual, plus half a dozen catalogs. I look over my mail, then go through the catalogs before tossing them.

4:30 P.M. After spending so much money on groceries (mostly for my guests this week), I am too lazy to cook something for myself and pop a Stouffer's Macaroni & Cheese in the oven. Oh well, I can display my culinary accomplishments the rest of the week. Just thought of the grandchildren in Vermont. I wonder if they received the "Halloween junk" I mailed to them. I don't understand why the mail takes so long to get there.

4:45 P.M. Leslie just called again. She is still nagging me to go there on the 25th so I can come to her Halloween party. I tell her I just cannot drive for over two hours and especially on 495 and then the Mass. Pike. I refer to it as "the ride of terror." I'm still not a very confident driver after all these years. My husband usually drove us everywhere. What can I say? In the first place, I would feel out of place even attending a Halloween party of thirty- and forty-year-olds. I know she is just trying to cheer me up and trying to give me something to do. As I've told her before, "Honey, you can't be my husband."

5:10 P.M. My brother calls to tell me he visited with our mother today and she is doing fairly well. As well as can be expected at ninety-seven. Oh dear. How I miss her too. I miss her AND SHE IS ALIVE. Sometimes I just want to be able to pour my heart out to her so she can comfort me—but the poor thing is so stone deaf she doesn't hear what I am saying. Even the hearing aid doesn't seem to help. She has her own issues now—how can she possibly give any of herself to me???

5:30 P.M. My mac & cheese is ready. I'll have it with a Coors Light and turn on the TV for company while I eat.

6:05 P.M. Finished eating and cleaned up the kitchen a bit. Lowered the heat and took a cup of reheated coffee to my bedroom with some cookies. I shall read for awhile.

I just read a couple chapters of our book club selection, *Mohawk*. I find it boring and ordinary. I have not cared for most of the books! They are not usually what I would choose to read, but I make an attempt to finish most of them anyway. The book club group of women (we call ourselves "the bookies") are wonderful and fun, so I participate more for the socializing and camaraderie.

8:00 P.M. I turn on the TV and flip channels awhile. Nothing interesting. I guess I'll go in and brush my teeth and set my hair (yes—I still do that 1940s thing) and get myself ready to retire.

8:45 P.M. I won't try to sleep yet or I'll surely have insomnia in the middle of the night. I'll have to find something to watch on TV. I end up watching HGTV and the Food Network.

10:00 P.M. MUCH ADO ABOUT NOTHING.

KIDS

11:41 P.M. Hear my four-year-old son Brett coming out of his room. He goes into the bathroom. What a good boy! He gets up in the middle of the night to go. I am so proud of him. I go in to see how he is doing. Brett!! What are you doing? He has gone poop on the floor. He said the toilet was too cold. I wipe him and tell him to go back to bed. Pick up the rug in front of the bathtub and take it down to the laundry. Switch the load I started earlier and start a new load.

EMILY A. ALAIMO, 27, *Lancaster, Pennsylvania* (TWO SONS, 4 AND 16 MONTHS); **staffing company branch manager**

7:15 A.M. Cecily and I begin our morning negotiations. She says she wants to wear a dress with rickrack. Yes, rickrack. I tell her I'm counting to ten, then she decides or I get to pick. In the nick of time, she settles on last year's Christmas dress, which is red plaid with black velvet ribbon. It has a matching coat. Her panties have to match, as well, which is not so easy. Saturday, for our trip to Sam's Club, she insisted on her Easter dress and hat and she had to carry her Easter basket. I "couldn't find" her gloves. She makes the rest of us look like slobs. I know she's mine but this froufrou stuff bewilders me.

SUSAN C. ANDERSON, 38, *Vestavia Hills, Alabama* (A DAUGHTER, 3, AND SON, 5); **magazine copy chief**

4:05 P.M. My six-year-old son D. W. and I discuss his day. He got a smiley face for behavior. I am so proud of him. I had promised him before school started that if he got all good reports this year (unlike last year) I would buy him a television for his room. The consequences of one bad report would be that I would not buy him a television. The one time he did get a bad report these past six weeks was because he wasn't listening to the teacher when she told him to stop tickling another kid in computer class. I mean, how bad is that? He received consequences by having his computer taken away for the rest of the week. So if he keeps up the great work, I think he could be watching Rugrats in his room this summer.

JEAN NESSER, 33, *Gonzales, Texas* (ONE SON, 6); **administrative assistant at Baptist Children's Home, and NASCAR driver**

8:00 A.M. My daughter Rebecca has gone to school. It's a fabulously gray, wet day! I think I may actually get some things accomplished today. This past weekend was so good for me. We stayed SO BUSY that I didn't have time to be melancholy. Being at a Girl Scout camp, I didn't miss my son Michael. He didn't belong there. I could talk about him without it hurting. We hiked, did crafts, climbed Fairy Rock, cooked on a fire, learned some first aid, and worked our tails off cooking and cleaning up for all the meals. The girls worked so hard! I'm so proud of them. It felt really good to have that much fun, without hurting for Michael. It's been a long time. Here at home again, I walk into his room and see his picture and it doesn't hurt so much. It's weird. It's as if some of the hurt has been erased.

CAROLYN R. CROCKER, 37, *Birmingham, Alabama* (ONE DAUGHTER, 10; AND A SON, 7, WHO DIED IN AUGUST, 2002); **part-time Spanish instructor**

6:42 P.M. My husband John picked up our son Jack from the soccer game and we have all been telling each other about our days. The main topic of conversation that prevails through the hellos, dinner, and cleanup is Jack's insistence to shave his "lip shadow." When Jack turned thirteen last week, I took a deep breath and hoped his adolescence would be less painful than most people tell me. Now... a visible sign that he is indeed growing up and away from me. I do not want him to shave. I extol all the problems of doing so—cuts, rashes, constant upkeep—but the boys just pass it off as a mother's overprotectiveness. So, while I'm at the sink washing dinner dishes, they are doing the deed. John comes down to tell me it is a fait accompli. When I ask how it went, he says they only made one nick on his lip. He called it his initiation. I call it—I'm not ready for this leap into adolescence! One more milestone reached. Oh, I feel old.

DEBORAH A. McKEW, 45, *Sunapee, New Hampshire* (ONE SON, 13); **marketing communications professional**

4:25 P.M. Karate. We're late. Clinton slips off his shoes and scoots through the door, stopping to bow. He stands between a sweet seventeen-year-old "green belt" girl with CP who is ambulatory and a seven-year-old "orange belt" girl with CP who started with a walker but is now in a wheelchair. There's also a boy, five years old, who just started the class. He is on the milder end of the autism spectrum and has much more language than Clinton. I sit down on a bench and put my face in my hands. One mother is reading a fashion magazine. A nanny stands at the observation window. One of the dads is sitting outside in his SUV making a call. Not the usual chatty group.

I go outside to the car to look in Clinton's backpack for his homework. They are learning about the bass clef in music. The aide describes how—when he asks Clinton to tell him a word that starts with "G"—Clinton just reads the same phrase, "Good Boys Do Fine Always." I imagine Clinton trying to give the guy an answer. I've seen that expression on his face when he knows he's supposed to answer but he doesn't know exactly what the answer is. He gives it his best shot, trying to guess from the context. I can imagine Clinton's confusion, thinking the aide must want him to repeat that. So he does. Knowing how he tries so hard makes me lose it. I start to cry.

It would be so much easier just to send Clinton away to a specialized school where he would only be around other autistic kids. But I know in my heart that wouldn't be right. Why can't schools learn to strike a balance? Sometimes I feel like giving up on trying to get him more included. People talk about tireless efforts of parents of children with autism. I feel SO tired. Better to say unyielding.

Therese Ojibway, 46, *Maplewood, New Jersey* (one son, 11);
program coordinator for autistic children

WNBA Forward

An All-Star with an NCAA title, an Olympic gold medal, and a locker in the Basketball Hall of Fame. A knee-wrenching moment: forty-two seconds into the first game of the '99 season—she tore her ACL. Out for two seasons. Surprise! Traded to the Houston Comets in 2002, after five years with the New York Liberty. Then traded to the Connecticut Sun. From injury to insight. "My goals changed. I just want to contribute and play as long as I can. I have a blast on the court." Off-court, she teams up with her mom to promote breast cancer awareness. They also raise scholarship money for Hispanic and African American students interested in health care. She's soon to be a beautiful 6'4" bride, married to a writer from *Sports Illustrated*. Points. Rebounds. Assists. Stats may define the highs and lows of her career, but they don't affect her self-esteem. "While basketball is my love and passion, it's not how I want to be defined as a person. It's up there after my faith and my family."

REBECCA LOBO, 29, *Simsbury, Connecticut*

7:55 A.M. Nothing quite like waking up on a bright, sunny morning and sitting down in my office to get the day started! I don't have that overwhelmed feeling today because my schedule isn't too crazy. I don't have to get on a plane or into a car bound for an appearance somewhere. I enjoy the early morning quiet. I never turn the TV on in the morning but sometimes I like the local DJs keeping me company on the radio. I really enjoy the few minutes where my little world is insulated until I decide it's time to open it up.

I'm guessing it's pretty cold outside because the neighbors' chimneys have smoke curling out of them like a genie from a bottle. Today, like all good days, starts with reading the Bible. Nothing brings me peace like scripture readings. It's the peak of my "quiet time." I've got to be better about making time for that at the beginning of my day.

11:00 A.M. Doctor's appointment: you've gotta love going into a doctor's office when you are the only person in the waiting room. It is a result of either (1) being in a town full of healthy people, (2) being in a town where everyone has a nine-to-five job, or (3) being in the office of a terrible doctor. I choose to believe it's option one or two. I am at the office for one simple reason . . . to pee in a cup. I have no problem with this because I probably have one of the few occupations in the world where peeing in a cup is an annual occurrence. I'm glad God blessed me with good aim. I'm also glad that this sample is easier than the one I'm used to giving to the WNBA. It's not much fun when we are drug tested for the league and can't close the stall door because a woman from the league security office watches to make sure we don't tamper with our urine. Today, I feel like I'm flying first class in the doc's office. Not only do I get to close the door, but I'm presented with one of those handy wipes when I'm finished. It's better than the flight attendant tong-offering the hot towel before you land after a long flight. Ahh . . . the simple pleasures in life.

12:15 P.M. My appointment with my CPA was at noon so I'm running a little late. No matter, I just need to sign my tax forms and get them in the mail today. Of course, I feel like a bit of a fool when I realize that I forgot to bring my checkbook. I have to send about ten checks to the various states we play in during our season. It is the only time of the year when I write checks for $4, $3, $1. I mean, who writes a check for a dollar? The only person I ever knew who wrote checks for small amounts was a girl I played hoops with in college. The rest of the team (including me) made fun of her. It wasn't until last year that I realized she had a good reason for writing checks all the time—she's from Minnesota. Folks from Minnesota write checks for EVERY-THING. But, it can't drive me too crazy. I'm marrying a guy from Minnesota. However, I will make sure to keep the checkbook in my purse whenever a small purchase is made.

12:35 P.M. While waiting in an absurdly long line at the McDonald's drive-thru, I wonder two things: (1) What kind of nasty, greasy food are these people getting in their to-go lives? (2) What does my presence in this line say about me? Actually, I am looking forward to my grilled chicken sandwich with no mayo and less flavor. While waiting, I scan the radio stations and stop on an old Eagles song. Then, while driving home, I listen to the latest from Eminem. I enjoy both. The Eagles song is mentally noted as a possibility for the wedding play list. The Eminem song is mentally noted as a HELL NO for the same list.

1:00 P.M. The priest called to tell me that he received my fiancé's baptismal certificate and we can meet with him to secure the date for our wedding. I'm really excited. Steve and I have only got six months to pull off this wedding and I've already booked the reception hall. We've been pretty lucky so far because we haven't received too much unsolicited wedding advice. We are also lucky because my mom is being incredibly helpful with the planning without being overbearing in any way. Of course, I'm twenty-nine years old and my fiancé is thirty-six, so we'll be paying for the wedding. As a result, we can plan the wedding that we want.

3:45 P.M. I drive two miles to the local bike path for my afternoon run. I've been looking forward to this all day. I don't have any idea how my body is going to feel because I have been slacking the past two weeks with my workouts. However, I am determined to get back on track starting today. I don't really have much choice since our off-season conditioning program begins next week. I want to return in the best shape of my life this upcoming season. I didn't play as much as I would've liked last year and I want to make sure the coach has every reason to put me in the game this coming summer. My goal is to be in better shape than everyone else and to be the most consistent performer on the court at my position. That goal helps me focus every day on the task at hand. But today, I just focus on enjoying my run since the workouts don't get too serious until the program arrives next week.

Whenever I run I have a song in my head that plays on a continuous loop. Today the song is "My Favorite Things" from *The Sound of Music*. I have a million thoughts racing through my mind during the run . . . my upcoming wedding, a basketball game I am playing in on Friday, work I need to get done this evening. I use my running time as my "quiet time," when there are no phones to answer and nothing going on except what I want to think about. I pass a few other joggers and one woman says to me, "Congratulations on your engagement." I have never met this woman but I'm guessing she read about my engagement last week in the gossip section of the *Hartford Courant*. It's pretty darn bizarre that the local paper finds my personal life worth writing about. I'll never get used to that. God bless this woman though because she gave me reason to smile during the fourth mile of my run.

5:49 P.M. I log on to AOL and the only new e-mail I have carries the title, "Petite teen girls take on gigantic penis." I wonder what the heck is wrong with this world. I also wonder if these girls are Nancy Drew clones who must "take on" some superhuman penis in order to save the world? Is a gigantic penis teetering through Times Square before climbing the Empire State Building? Will the girls save the day? Alas, I won't ever find out. I delete the e-mail and let the petite girls go about their business without my audience.

5:57 P.M. My agent calls to give me an update on the travel arrangements for the speech I am giving with my mother tomorrow in Nashua, New Hampshire. Our topic is breast cancer and how a family deals with the disease. Kenton (my agent) tells me that the folks organizing the event were worried after a "stuttering, unkempt man" came by asking for us. They want to hire a police officer to protect us. I quickly flip through my mental rolodex of stuttering, unkempt men I know but none live in New Hampshire. My mind races. Perhaps the man is John Nash with a bus pass and another original thought that he longs to share with a woman over six feet tall. Maybe the cure for a deadly disease (breast cancer?) is in the clutches of the unkempt man and he wants to share it with the Lobo mother-daughter team. Then again, perhaps not. We quickly decide that the policeman is a good idea.

7:10 P.M. I find my speech on the computer and spend about a half hour making the appropriate adjustments for our audience. My mother and I have given this speech many times so I don't have to tinker with it too much. She usually spends about twenty minutes telling the story of her diagnosis and our family's reaction. My mother was diagnosed with cancer right before Christmas in 1993. She had massive lymph node involvement and underwent a clinical trial treatment that involved large doses of chemo. She is healthy now and many people (including doctors) consider her a miracle. My part of the speech is how I dealt with the situation. When my mom first told me about her diagnosis, I was terribly afraid. I was a junior in college and I couldn't help but wonder if my mother was going to die. I dealt with the fears by saying a lot of prayers and immersing myself in my schoolwork and basketball. While I had no control over her disease, I could control the immediate things in my life. Basketball became my refuge. During her battle with breast cancer, our family became even closer. We prioritized our lives and made sure that God and family always came first. It can still be easy to get caught up in the hustle and bustle of daily living, but we all have had a life-changing experience that helps us remember what is truly important in life.

I try to bring as much humor as I can to the talk. When I first started speaking publicly I would get quite nervous and spend hours preparing for my talk. Now, I get excited and have to spend much less time preparing. I love the adrenaline rush I get when the audience laughs at my jokes and the talk goes well. It is such a feeling of satisfaction! I get a similar rush when I do sports broadcasting. I worked on ESPN for three years doing the in-studio analysis for the women's NCAA tournament. I loved the experience and hope to do more broadcasting when my playing days are over. Of course, my future career (and my current one) will depend a lot on when Steve and I decide to start a family.

10:00 P.M. I crawl into my bed and phone Steve. When we are apart, I try to speak to him before I go to sleep because he makes me laugh and I like to go to bed with a smile on my face. I am struggling to stay awake so the conversation is short. I set the alarm for 6:30 so that I can go for a run before my mom and I take our trip to New Hampshire. I feel pretty good. I got a lot accomplished today and did everything that I needed to do. Sleep comes fast and the morning comes faster . . .

COLLECTIVE GLIMPSES ──────────────

67% of day diarists did housework

67% watched TV

64% said they considered this an average day

9:20 A.M. Get home. I need a breather. Turn TV on. BAD MISTAKE. I tell myself, you really need to clean the house, do laundry, go to the grocery store, your in-laws are coming Thursday. Oh well, there's always later.

10:00 A.M. *Surprise By Design* is on. I have already seen this episode but I might pick up on something I missed the last time. Put a load of laundry on.

11:00 A.M. *Home Matters* is on next. Cute ideas.

12:00 P.M. *Home Matters* is on. I watch.

1:00 P.M. *Surprise By Design* is on again. I haven't seen this one. Put another load of laundry on.

2:00 P.M. The day is almost over. The kids will be home soon. I had better get something done. What can we have for dinner? I'll think about that later.

GAYE G. JOHNSON, 39, *Lawrenceville, Georgia*;
homemaker and part-time bookkeeper

Double Amputee Who Considers Attitude to Be the Greatest Disability

She lost her legs to vascular disease at age twenty-nine. A service-dog trainer—her own dog, Peek, acts as maid, secretary, and elevator operator. Proponent of the concept "pay it forward," she helps other people with disabilities. Former daredevil—bareback riding tricks—turned motivator. "But it took a long time to come to terms with it." Along the way: divorce ("twelve years, put him through school, when it was my turn, he left"), surgery to amputate her legs, followed by a job selling orthopedic shoes. ("It was the most illogical thing I could think of so I did it—and did very well.") Now remarried—when he first proposed, she refused. ("I'm terminal!"). A recent bout with heart disease caused friends to rally, forming the Debifund. "A lot of people gave of themselves. I'm very humbled." She carried the Olympic torch in the 2002 Winter Games. "Queen for a day." She's well aware that life didn't work out exactly as planned, but she's reached a point of acceptance. "It's OK to be the cheerleader."

DEBI D. DAVIS, 54, *Tuscon, Arizona*

6:20 A.M. The puppy wakes me by sticking his tongue inside my nostrils. He's now in the throes of adolescence, which makes him like the perpetual seventh-grader—full of himself. Husband Tim quips, "Best alarm clock we ever had—normally it takes me a half hour to get you out of bed in the morning!"

6:23 A.M. Let all four dogs outside for potty break. The dogs are all neutered male Papillons (the Butterfly Dog): Peek, age 9; Dandy, 6; Cappy, 4; and Harry Potter, 1. They have all been trained as service dogs.

Pup spots a lizard sprinting across the fence, leaps over one of the other dogs taking a dump, lands on the dog, flattens the dog on the ground, right into the pile of poop. I try not to laugh, but laughter spurts out just the same.

6:25 A.M. Still half asleep, I roll into the bathroom, put fecal-covered dog on shower chair in bathtub, accidentally drop shampoo bottle on floor, where the top comes off and sprays the entire room with shampoo. I wipe up shampoo, rinse off dog with hand sprayer attachment. Get out of chair, sit on floor, put dog on towel and dry him with huge doggy hair dryer (shaped like the old canister vacuums).

6:45 A.M. Set up Champion juicer for breakfast drink. Forget to put container under the spout and carrot juice runs all over the counter and under the appliances. Dogs lap up juice spilling over onto the floor. I practice my drunken sailor language.

7:15 A.M. Go outside to my lift-equipped van to get a pamphlet, and find the electric door opener is not working. More sailor's language. Realize I will have to take a bus all the way across town to take Peek (who, as my main service dog, works with me doing animal-assisted therapy) to St. Joseph Hospital's rehabilitation unit, a two-hour trip each way, with three bus transfers.

7:30 A.M. Hastily answer a couple e-mails from students I mentor who are training their own service dogs. Mentoring is much easier for me than training a service dog and placing the dog. After two years of spending 24/7 with a dog, I'm far too bonded to them to let them go. As a mentor, I never have to say goodbye, yet I can still help people to train their own dogs and enjoy their progress. As I'm sending e-mail, we have a brownout in the electricity and the computer crashes. Upon restart, the outgoing e-mails are completely lost. More sailor's language, rewrite both letters, and send.

8:30 A.M. Use old toothbrush to get out dog poop stuck in my wheelchair tire tread, and while on the floor, see I have tracked the poop all the way through the house. I crawl around cleaning it up with white vinegar and using more sailor's language. I'm late! I'm late! I'll never get everything done in time to leave for therapy with the dog. The kitchen is spattered with soapy poop spots. Tim left for work early so he's not around to play "rescue" during this crisis.

9:00 A.M. Quick shower, throw on clothes, leave house with dog. I roll a block to the bus stop, stopping at favored bushes along the way for my service dog to empty out before getting on the bus. Remember I left my ID card for the hospital on the table. I need my ID card or I chance a delay at the rehab facility door while I explain that I am a legitimate volunteer, that the dog will be working, that we both have had all our tests, shots, etc. Go back home to get it. I find the card in the puppy's fleece bed. Puppy had found it on the table, which he was easily able to jump up on because my husband again forgot to push his chair close to the table so it couldn't be used as a stepladder, and I forgot to check its position before I left the house because I was in such a rush. Puppy has chewed up the corners. More sailor's language and a few tears.

I'm so frustrated, agitated and have to stop, take a deep breath, and let it out slowly to the count of seven. This "centers" me enough that I don't yell at the dogs, or just sit down and cry. I envision myself at the rehab facility, with all the patients smiling as we arrive to help them with their exercises, and this keeps me focused on my goal: get it together, get to where I need to be, and put on the enthusiastic attitude as part of my clothing. I can't allow my frustrations to color my attitude. Patients can spot fake enthusiasm quickly. Thus, I need to be in control of my emotions, use them rather than to let them use me.

9:10 A.M. Back to bus stop. Bus arrives, Peek pops up on my lap and we ride the lift up into the bus. Bus driver greets us warmly, points to the back of my wheelchair, says, "You might want to put that in your backpack." I look back, see my lacy bra is still hanging from the handles. I blush crimson, grab the bra, stuff it into my pack.

11:15 A.M. Arrive at St. Joseph's hospital, on the southeast side of the city and across town from where I live. I pin on the card with the shredded, puppy-chewed edges, and in the hallway, pass three people who stop and say, "You must have a puppy! Look, my ID card is decorated the same way!" I smile, feeling a kinship with another person learning how to survive her puppy's adolescence, and doing it with a smile rather than a grimace.

In rehab, my job is to guide Peek through exercises, such as pushing a large therapy ball toward a patient, so the patient can lean forward over a walker or wheelchair, and push it back, thus working muscle groups. Or, the dog may be asked to retrieve items the patient has tossed a distance while toning up arm muscles. As a team, Peek and I are guided by the rehabilitation physical therapist, who decides what particular exercises will most help the patient. Perhaps the most helpful part of animal-assisted therapy is that the patients respond so positively to interacting with a dog, and they try harder and work longer without quitting. It's never boring to do exercises with a dog, but it's often boring and tedious to just do them with a human therapist.

2:20 P.M. Given new patient to work with, a seventy-year-old woman recovering from shoulder surgery. Complained of tiredness and disinterest in doing strengthening exercises. Therapist had her tossing items to my dog, who then brings them back to be thrown again. We work with this patient for about half an hour. Nice to see the disinterest change into enthusiasm. I love animal-assisted therapy work!

3:30 P.M. I leave the hospital by the side door, rush past all the smokers huddled by the communal ashtray, wheel out into the hospital driveway road. I keep turning my head every few seconds to make sure we aren't about to get run over. Finally reaching the main road, I pop Peek up on my lap so I can put the chair in high-speed drive mode and get to the bus stop as fast as possible. With Peek in my lap, I can move into the bike lane and go twelve miles per hour. The bus stop is about a quarter-mile away from the hospital. Missed bus by thirty seconds. Arghhhh! Have to wait half hour for next bus. Then, coming into the bus station for a transfer to another bus to get me home, traffic is at gridlock due to a potential jumper on one of the downtown buildings.

Wait two hours at bus station for buses to be able to get through. Peek is wiped out after therapy and wants only to sleep on my lap. I think about the dogs waiting for me at home, and how much they probably need to get outside to eliminate, and remember to take a moment to praise myself for putting out the puppy pee pads on the floor just in case I was delayed in arriving home. This takes the edge off my irritation, and I remind myself that getting upset won't get me home any quicker.

4:00 P.M. Dogs ecstatic to see me, and no "accidents" in the house, not even from the puppy. I let dogs out in backyard, do a few training tricks with all of them. I use my pointed target stick to guide one dog into a spinning circle on his hind legs. I work with the puppy on capturing his charming little "puppy bow," with thoughts of how these behaviors can be worked into a "dog dancing" routine I'll eventually present at schools, for civic groups, and canine freestyle competitions, to show that service dogs can wear many hats. I guide another dog through trotting backwards as I roll towards him.

4:15 P.M. I take the puppy for a one-mile walk to Wal-Mart, using the city sidewalks and street crossings to practice automatic stops, sits and starts, and to ignore distractions—squirrels, skateboarders, backfiring buses—along the way. Meet adorable child in Wal-Mart who can't stop calling the puppy's name, "Harry Potter." Harry the puppy manages to contain his enthusiasm and keep four paws on the floor. I beam with pride!

In Wal-Mart, I'm hypervigilant, watching the pup closely. Lots of distractions. Dogs in a store are always people-magnets, so I have to be prepared for people rushing up to pet the dog at any time. The pup has to learn that people may be wonderful, but that his "job" is to learn how to remain focused on me, until I give him the signal that it's OK to "make friends." On the way home, puppy manages to pass fence with four barking dogs, and puppy doesn't react.

YES! To see Harry Potter maintaining eye contact and focus on me amidst all these wonderfully tempting distractions helps me realize he is well-suited to being a service dog. Only a small percentage of dogs are able to handle these kinds of distractions continually while working in public. Some are just too stressed at having to ignore everything, so it takes an exceptional dog to be able to "make the grade."

5:45 P.M. Return home with puppy. Husband arrives home from work, leashes the other two dogs and joins me for a relaxing dog walk. My husband asks about my day, which I outline in excruciating detail, needing the inevitable warm hug from him that I know will follow. I ask him about his day, and he shares stories of student and teacher interactions, and how much the janitors enjoyed the Krispy Kreme donuts he brought in for them steamy hot that morning. I stop to show Tim a new dance routine step I'm working on with the puppy, incorporating his "puppy bow" with a quick spin and rollover for a particular part of the music phrasing we've been struggling to develop. Tim offers a great suggestion to change the routine to let the bow be the ending note, instead of the beginning. I squeal with delight, having missed the obvious.

6:30 P.M. Both Tim and I are too tired to make dinner and clean up. We opt for Japanese takeout. I take the puppy in my chair for another outing to pick up the takeout. My good powerchair is in the shop getting a drive belt replaced, so I'm using my old house chair, which has no headlight on it. In the dark, I hit a pavement eruption on the sidewalk and get thrown out of my chair. Puppy stops and waits while I pull myself back into chair, and sop up blood on my skinned knee and hand. Puppy waits patiently while I fish out Band-Aids and antiseptic from my backpack and apply them. Sailor language for the lack of care for sidewalks, but happy praise for the puppy who waits quietly and responsively, instead of running off.

7:30 P.M. Finish up late e-mail, shut down computer, watch TV with Tim and dogs. During commercials, I clicker-train the dogs. Sometimes I just toss down an object on the floor, such as a small box, and start letting the dog interact with it. The goal is nothing specific, only to "capture" a movement or behavior I want to see repeated. It might be touching the box with a paw, or pushing it with a nose, or trying to put two paws on the box at the same time, or to retrieve the box. I'll pick one behavior offered, ignoring the others, and the one I want to be repeated will be noted with a CLICK at the exact time it is offered, then I'll give the dog a treat. The click marks the moment to be remembered, like a camera's click captures a "freeze frame" in time, and the treat reinforces the behavior. It's hard for me to watch TV without doing something at the same time. So I end up grooming the dogs, trimming nails and feet, while watching the program.

10:00 P.M. Last nighttime outing for dogs, and then a rousing game of fetch with each of them from bed. Tim screeches as puppy accidentally steps on a very tender piece of his anatomy. Puppy interprets screeching as invitation to play, and steps again on Tim's tender parts, eliciting even more screeching. I try not to laugh, and distract puppy to allow husband to catch his breath.

10:30 P.M. Lights out, we all go to sleep. Dogs find places on the bed between us, and puppy tunnels under the comforter for his favorite place between husband and me. Fortunately, they are small dogs, only ten pounds each, so they don't take up much space. And, there is extra space where my legs would be, as well. However, my husband often quips that if we get one more dog, we'll have to take out the bed and just have a wall-to-wall futon to accommodate the dogs.

11:30 P.M. Puppy is barking wildly in the living room, and Tim and I both get up to see what's causing all the racket. The cat is in the living room playing tag with the puppy. Cat is sitting on puppy's favorite toy, refuses to budge. Outraged puppy vocalizes his displeasure, barks rapid-fire in his high-pitched alert barking manner. The cat yowls back with a long, breathy yowl, so that together, they sound like two singers—one singing the melody, one doing the harmonizing. I cue puppy by a voice signal of "Harry, come!" to follow me back to the bedroom. But I don't trust him, so I tether him with a soft leash to my arm, in case he decides it's playtime again during the early hours of the morning. Life is good! I'm so exhausted.

Tips

3:00 P.M. I discovered a very simple technique for meeting men! Simply walk around inside Home Depot with a confused look on your face! Of course, this works best if you happen to be of the female persuasion, but it works!!! I had four male Home Depot employees asking me if they could help me find something! One was an old guy, one was short and fat with really thick glasses, one was way too young, but one was kinda cute in that rugged sort of way. I highly recommend this yet-untapped resource for single females everywhere!!!

SHANNON E. BUCKELS, 34, *Brea, California*; **patrol officer**

The rest of the day was spent helping people resolve problems or resolving the problems for them. This always makes me think that the first words we should teach little girls are, "No, do it yourself." Teach them how to say that sentence to other people. We grow up thinking it is somehow our job to fix everything or make everyone happy, to make everyone satisfied. It isn't our job to make everyone happy. We need to empower them to solve their own problems. I think teaching little girls how to say "NO" is probably very important.

PENNY JESSOP, 53, *New Orleans, Louisiana*;
program coordinator, Tulane University School of Public Health

9:47 A.M. Board bus at 127th Street and Harlem. I do something I've never done before. I take notes on two older women's conversation. I learn from them how to grow old: Get an executor who cares about you. ("Georgina's executor can't even take time out to take her to the grocery store. Now that's not right.") Don't talk about all your ailments. ("If one more person that I know is going to have some test done, I'm going to scream.") And don't be afraid to plan for your dying. ("Don't tell me that you want me to have that tablecloth in the back of your closet. Write it down!")

LOIS A. ROELOFS, 60, *Palos Heights, Illinois*;
professor emerita in nursing

8:02 P.M. I just sat down and took a breath. I'm drinking my fifth Diet Coke for the day. I should titrate the caffeine with some red wine. Life is all about finding balance, is it not?

KAREN L. WILLIAMS, 44, *Mt. Pleasant, South Carolina*;
director of home healthcare services

5:00 P.M. Leave office for BART Station. Swing by bookstore to pick up *First Break All the Rules* for work research. I'm so tired of every leadership book being written by a white guy. Where are the women in this field? At least I don't have to read *Who Moved My Cheese?* Eve Ensler should write a book on leadership.

MICHELLE GISLASON, 33, *Berkeley, California*; **conference director**

11:30 A.M. I love my hairdresser. Her name is Ivy Leaf. She does a fabulous job but most importantly she always makes me feel good about myself and about life. She's got great energy and a positive attitude that is infectious. Everyone should have an Ivy Leaf in their life.

KATHARINE KITCHEL, 28, *Norwich, Vermont*; **mediator**

Thirty-Five Years a Teacher and Still Looking for Classrooms

Always running into former students. "'Mrs. Rubenstein! Mrs. Rubenstein! Do you remember me? You taught me math in eighth grade'—I never remember their names but I can always remember where they sat." Active in her synagogue. President of a local chapter of the Labor Zionist Alliance. Treasurer of her stock club. Caller at Yiddish bingo. "I seem to take over when other people sit back." Very organized. Direct. Peppy. A season-ticket holder to five theater companies. An avid reader fascinated by detail. "I get interested in all kinds of crazy subjects. I love forensic medicine—how they use all the modern scientific things to catch up with the criminal." One son. Two long-time Mah Jongg groups. Sam's widow for the past twenty-three years. "I met a few others along the way but nothing like him." Sam was quiet. She is a people person. "I'd say to Sam, 'We're going somewhere tonight.' I'd say, 'Talk, talk to people. They think I don't let you say anything . . .' but I always felt him standing at my shoulder with a little smile on his face. He'd say, 'You're my pretty dolly.' Those are the things you miss."

LILLIAN RUBENSTEIN, 78, *Skokie, Illinois*

12:37 A.M. Really tired, but can't sleep because I can't warm up. Must be my metabolism. I always joke that I've always been cold, and now after menopause, I'm either hot (hot flashes) or cold, but never comfortable. Have socks on, but still can't warm up. The socks are the slipper-socks that hospitals give you so you can scoot around without slipping and falling. I like these better than regular socks because when I do warm up, they're easier to slip off. So I keep getting leg cramps when I change position (which I do a lot) or stretch, and have to jump out of bed to alleviate the pain.

Also I'm brooding about problems at my synagogue after attending a board meeting this evening. We are an older and declining congregation. A few months ago a decision was made to accept a merger with a somewhat younger congregation, also having membership and monetary problems. Should be good, yes? Not so. Our philosophies are quite different. It's difficult for the younger people to adjust to our ways, and many of us have problems accepting change. The new people I have met seem very nice, and I hope to make new friends; however it will take a great deal of understanding and perseverance to work out our differences so that finally we will become a cohesive group. AMEN.

And this afternoon I heard a talk from a man from the ACLU. Far from a rosy picture was painted by him. He seemed to think that the Bush administration has been planning to make our country into a right-wing totalitarian state from the moment of his election, or should I say his appointment or anointment by the Supreme Court. Although I believe George W. Bush is a patriot, I had felt that he and his administration were using the disaster of 9/11 for their own devices: primarily to assure his reelection. And this afternoon, the man from the ACLU reinforced my opinion. Here were other people who are probably more knowledgeable than I agreeing with me. And don't we love when people agree with us? Makes us feel so righteous. I worry so about our country.

And now WAR WITH IRAQ!! A lose-lose situation for us, and I fear a win-win situation for Saddam Hussein.

And to top everything off, my hot water heater is leaking. In the last month, have had to repair my air conditioner, the fan in my furnace. And now the hot water heater. Money, money, money! I'm a product of the Depression, and out of habit try to live on a budget. Thank goodness I can pay for these things without really altering my lifestyle, but at the same time, I find that I must complain. I think I better stop this train of thought, settle down to read a bit to calm me so that I can try again to sleep. Reading a Belva Plain novel called *Her Father's House*. Good for distraction.

3:55 A.M. Off to the bathroom. Where-oh-where are those wonderful nights when I was younger and slept through the night without interruption?

8:25 A.M. Called about my hot water heater. Can't be done today. They need to order and pick up the heater that they had recommended. Tomorrow is impossible for me. Too many other commitments. I have a Hadassah meeting and luncheon for which I have prepaid and faithfully promised a few friends I would definitely show. Then I'll have just enough time to come home, change, and report to usher for a play at one of the local theaters. The workmen need at least two hours, maybe as many as four hours to work. It will have to be left for Thursday. My days this week are completely filled, but I could cancel my Mah Jongg game on Thursday (not that important, and these women are very understanding). I usually play twice a week: Tuesday evenings (except when I have opera tickets) and Thursday afternoons. This week an extra Mah Jongg game was thrown in on Tuesday afternoon.

Must hurry. My Bible class is this morning. We meet with our Rabbi (also our teacher) in the library of the synagogue. I pick up three people on the way, two of whom never learned to drive (they thought their husbands would live forever to chauffeur them around) and a dear man in his nineties who is no longer allowed to drive. Last year when I was on radiation following a breast lumpectomy, the staff would arrange my schedule so that I could pick up my passengers on Tuesday mornings. We're studying the *Pirke Avot* (Ethics of the Fathers) this year, a departure from our usual Bible studies. Very interesting! It amazes me how these ancient rabbis, who were respected leaders in their communities and lived in a mostly agrarian society, made commentaries on life, politics, employer-employee relationships, domestic tranquility and disputes, and interrelations between all kinds of people. And these commentaries still hold true for our scientific, electronic world today. I always learn something new, and often not about the Bible or the particular subject at hand. Love my Bible class and the Rabbi who teaches it.

4:10 P.M. Attended my Bible class. A little Bible, a little Talmud, a little Gemorah. We had a pretty full class. I have been urging people for many years to attend the class. Last year we had dwindled down to about four or five each session. What a pleasant surprise to my urging. We were fifteen people today! And they all seemed to love it. At least two of the newer attendees said, "Rabbi, I'm so glad to be here. I wish I had come sooner." Thank goodness my recommendations came out so well. And of course, I could see that the Rabbi was pleased. He is a wonderful teacher: always courteous and extremely patient. Sometimes he gently says, "Haven't we discussed this before?" Sometimes, someone will remember. When I remember, it may not be the entire story or explanation, and he encourages me to proceed, trying to hint and unplug the obstacle in my mind. If no one can remember, I am usually the one who has the courage to say, "Tell us again!" And patiently he does. I depart feeling that my head is being expanded with new exciting thoughts. I have this same kind of feeling after I have attended a really good Elderhostel. I come away energized, excited, peppy.

After dropping off my passengers following the Bible class, I went to that extra Mah Jongg game. We met at the home of one of the women, and were treated to a light, but delicious lunch. Can't go wrong with that. During the game, always a few jokes, a little discussion on politics, what new businesses have moved into the area and out, catch up on our families, and where we have been and going, and of course, a little gossip, but never have I heard any sniping or snide remarks. Another pleasant surprise, I won! $2.45 winner! A bonanza for a usual loser. We play for $4.00, which means if one player goes broke, she plays without money (called playing "on charity") until she is able to win a game. And she doesn't pay back her losing during the time she was "on charity." Therefore, the most that a person can lose is $4.00. Makes for a nice easy afternoon. I'm playing Mah Jongg again this evening. Don't really like to play twice in one day. We tried to set a date for the next time we would meet. Could not come to a conclusion today. Almost impossible to find a date acceptable to five busy people.

Spoke to the people who will replace my water heater. Very expensive. We can't get together before Friday. So be it. I'm stuck with a wet laundry room until then. This will take care of any surplus I have managed to accrue the last few months. On the other hand, thank goodness I can pay it and there is the surplus. Always the good news and the bad news. I had been saving the surplus to do some investing. Now that will have to wait. With the stock market the way it is, I'm probably saving money. My interests at the moment are water and nanotechnology. I've been reading and hearing that water will be our next resource to experience a shortage. As our world population continues to increase, we may find ourselves looking for alternative ways to make fresh water. Sounds like a good investment to me. And nanotechnology, working with such tiny, submicroscopic particles. It's in the wave of the future, but I will have to be careful. So many startup companies go broke. I will have to do a lot of research, talk to my broker, read, and use my computer. I am a good research person. I love going from one place to the next trying to dig out the details, and hope when I'm finished I will understand it all.

5:20 P.M. I'm home for a short time before going out again to the second Mah Jongg game of the day, and the phone doesn't stop. At this time of day, there are so many calls from solicitors trying to sell something. I try to be polite, but firm. Also, this is the time of day that my family and friends know that I am usually at home. I live alone, and a few of my friends make it their business to touch base with me, to check on me, though they never say. I am truly blessed with wonderful friends. I have to find a few minutes to make a little dinner before going out.

Everything takes time. Must get to my mail and at least sort the important ones from the advertisements. Good that people call, bad that I can't find the time to do what needs doing. Want to find a few minutes to check my e-mail. I'm always interested in that because I look forward to maybe having a letter from my cousins in France and Argentina. I'm the one in the family who keeps in touch and keeps track of as many as I can. I love doing it but I also think it is a duty.

Had a quick snack, and drove to my friend's home for my second Mah Jongg. Our game for the evening is much like the afternoon was, same kind of kibitzing, same kind of discussions. The only difference is that we play for $5.00.

11:15 P.M. Wonder of wonders! Can't believe it! I won again! This time $3.15. Should take off for Las Vegas. A day to remember: two wins in Mah Jongg, a wonderful Bible class, so many great relationships to sustain me. I'm grateful that I still drive, that I'm not afraid to drive day or night, and on any expressway, and am able to have so many activities. How difficult it would be not to be able to get out or to have to depend on others. However, we never know what the future holds, so I am so grateful for what I still have.

Finally, I'll take a few minutes to check my e-mail, and off to bed. Good night.

Getting Dressed

5:45 A.M. Arrive at the station. I'm in the women's locker room getting the rest of my uniform together. First is my bulletproof vest. I know, why do I need a bulletproof vest when all I'm doing is going to the local high school? Well, remember Columbine? I'm not going to make myself a victim if I can help it. And for some strange reason, there are people out there that really don't like me for what I wear. How ironic, huh? Next my police shirt, which already has the badge imprinted on it, otherwise I always put my badge on last. I kind of feel my badge is what makes people notice me. You know you've heard those miraculous stories of how little things have saved lives, well I pray that it will be my badge if, heaven forbid, anything happens to me when I'm on duty. Now gun belt, radio, and, last but not least, gun. I carry a Glock 22, which is a .40 caliber semiautomatic pistol. Fifteen rounds in the magazine and one in the chamber plus two extra magazines with fifteen rounds each. As you can imagine, what I carry around my waist weighs approximately twenty pounds.

IRENE CREWS, 25, *Brea, California*; **police officer**

Knock Knock

10:00 A.M. Cece is in my office talking about a summary of intervention activities. I get NO peace when I'm trying to pump, it's no wonder I can't achieve letdown sometimes. First Sarah was, "Can you open the door?" Then Pam was tapping to come in, then Cece was knocking. Suddenly, there are four people in here and I've got my boob hung out! ZERO privacy! And they don't seem to care. I sit at my desk and pump so as not to take an hour away from my workday twice per day so that I can put in the nine or ten hours that I need to so that I can take Friday afternoons off to be with my baby Eli.

CHERYL BUSH, 33, *West Lebanon, New Hampshire*;
research assistant, Dartmouth College

Separated at Birth

NOON. Working on a few site updates, I notice *Robot Wars* is on TV. What a bunch of geeks, building robots to fight each other in an arena. Geez. Hmm. I look up their Web site. I send the info to my friend Andy in San Francisco.

Andy and I met each other when we both worked for public broadcasting. People who know us say we're separated at birth. This concerns me as a Filipino woman, because Andy is a big, white, gay man. But I know what they mean and it explains why after ten or more years and living on opposite sides of the country, we're still good friends. Andy's interests include Renaissance/Dickens Faires and *Star Trek*, so you can see why I sent him the *Robot Wars* site. He is what we call in the business an Uber Nerd. This also concerns me since everyone thinks we're so alike.

LYN NIERVA, 37, *Stone Mountain, Georgia*;
Web designer

BUDAPEST

10:11 A.M. Program Day has started! I am noticing again my coworkers, and I am once again amazed at the team of people with whom I work. American, British, Macedonian, Greek, Armenian, Hungarian, and Turkish people are represented in this office. We must speak over twelve languages, which is amazing to me. I am really proud to be a part of this group and to do what we do. Did my parents ever dream that their little girl would grow up to live in other countries, learning about other cultures, eating different foods, learning different languages, all while being a volunteer with a house building organization? I doubt it. But, my life has been changed and I will never be the same. And, I don't want to be the same.

TANYA A. WEAVER, 33, *Budapest, Hungary*;
volunteer trainer, Habitat for Humanity International

CARVING CLASS

8:00 P.M. I am taking my fifth folk-carving class at a restored farm museum, taught by a forensic chemist. It is a small group, as usual, with only one fellow student I recognize from an earlier class. These classes aren't really classes but more like a quilting bee. We sit around a long table and follow the lead of the instructor. It doesn't take long to realize that we are a truly disparate group, socially, economically, politically, but the common charge to carve a soda-pop-drinking Santa has us all on track.

MARY ANNE HUNTINGTON, 64, *Cutchogue, New York*;
newly retired

ℒUNCHTIME

12:10 P.M. I come into my office at the preschool to eat and my usual two lunch companions are not here. About a week ago they started eating in their room. They go to the Black Sheep Deli and then to their classroom. They don't ask if they can get me anything at the Sheep (even though I often ask when I go out) and they don't invite me to join them for lunch in their classroom. So I eat alone. I could feel sorry for myself or feel rejected or lonely . . . but all of the self-help books I have been reading say that no one can make me feel that way. I am responsible for my own feelings. So I stay out of their business and enjoy the momentary peace and quiet. But that doesn't keep me from wondering what has changed. I miss them. For years we ate together, shared our days, or food, and talked about places we had gone. Is cancer catching? Is that why they are distant? Or is it just my imagination, my paranoia.

BETSY MOYER, 55, *Pelham, Massachusetts*; **preschool director**

Shy Kid Who Went Haywire

By age twenty-four, three baby daughters, one divorce, and a couple of Mr. Wrongs. None of her daughters lived with her until recently. Spent over a decade on the road, working construction and pipefitting. She liked the job—"being outside, working with my hands, showing the boys that girls don't have to stay home makin' biscuits." She liked the partying. "If there was a bar between the job and the house, I was going to be there." A drunk. A drug addict. A realization. "Just in the last four or five years it hit me—Hey, you're screwing up. You need to change some things in your life. And so I did." Living with her fiancé in a trailer on his folk's farm in Louisiana. Together four years, they hit rock bottom, then cleaned up their act. Sober. Settling down. Quilting. Applying for stay-put jobs with benefits. Looking forward to having all her daughters at home with her—a first. Saving for a five-bedroom doublewide. Regrets? "Tons. A life full of them. But if I could go back and change any one thing, I couldn't cause I wouldn't be the person I am now. I wouldn't have the same kids. And that's something I could never give up."

JUSTINA M. EVANS, 32, *Farmerville, Louisiana*

4:55 A.M. He's up . . . (my fiancé, Tracy). Bathroom light shining right in my eyes . . . thanks dear. I need to get up . . . nevermind . . . wanna go back to sleep.

5:15 A.M. "I love you too . . . be careful" . . . he's on his way to work. Thanks for waking me up . . . again. I would be mad if he didn't though.

6:51 A.M. My oldest daughter Amanda's up . . . bathroom light in my eyes . . . again. At least she heard the alarm today. God it's cold in here! And I gotta pee. I don't wanna get up. OK, OK . . . I'm going! (Talking to my bladder.) Four-wheeler fired up. She's on her way to catch the bus. Note on the computer? From Tracy? Nope . . . Manda. "Took a dollar off the table, hope you're not mad." No, that's fine, but you were supposed to wake me up before you left. Oh, you did . . . "several times" . . . sorry.

7:00 A.M. Step 3. Two more weeks and I can officially call myself a "non-smoker." I'm sick of these patches. Doesn't seem like it's been six weeks already. I've done this all by myself, and this is something I can be proud of! Yeah right . . . whatever.

7:11 A.M. Patch in place, last night's supper dishes put away, little heaters turned on. It's actually cold enough for me to enjoy a cup of tea. I could just run his coffee grounds back through . . . nah. His coffee is nasty anyway . . . seconds is almost as bad. Tea's better. What's for breakfast? Eeeww . . . not that awake yet . . . too early for breakfast. Let's see what's goin' on in the world . . . good morning CNN.

What am I gonna do today? Ummm. Have to replace the brakes on the truck, need to insulate under the slide-out, retape the plastic on the windows, redo the weather stripping on the back door and check the front, finish the laundry, pay the light bill and that hospital bill, need to go to the feed store and get some lime for the sump. Air conditioning system on the space station? I thought it was cold in space? God it's cold in here!

7:18 A.M. Need to check e-mail.

7:21 A.M. I hate waiting on this stupid computer . . . huh . . . no mail.

8:29 A.M. More tea . . . and more bad news. Why is this sniper guy not behind bars? They can round up "possible terrorists" in a matter of hours from all over the world, but they can't catch one lunatic in D.C. in a week? What's wrong with this picture? I feel so sorry for their families. I just hope he stays in that area. Would hate to see him move south toward Auntie's.

8:35 A.M. Dog's out . . . still cold out there. Nobody keeps an eighty-five-pound black lab in the house. Great . . . now he's gonna bark.

8:42 A.M. Done with mail and message boards. Do-it-yourself decorator message boards. Why do I bother? I live in a 36′ travel trailer . . . I have no house to decorate! One of these years . . . if I'm lucky. I know he's workin' his butt off, but it's just not going anywhere! Now that they've cut his hours back, we're losing ground. I don't dare tell him that . . . it would crush him. I can't deal with both of us being depressed. I have GOT to get back to work! Why couldn't I have been born into money? Then I wouldn't have to deal with this crap. And why is it that any time you mention anything about being Native American to anyone on a message board, everyone has a Cherokee grandmother? The only ones that might have are the ones that tell you they're Tsalagi . . . not Cherokee.

8:53 A.M. Here it is, almost nine o'clock, and I haven't done squat. Too cold to work on the truck, so I'm stuck inside 'til it warms up. Sick of the news . . . not time for my BBC shows yet. Great, now the satellite's out! How the hell did it get to the weather channel? Oh no . . . another tropical depression. I hope it moves into the Atlantic like they think . . . we don't need another one this season (sigh). Old black and white movies . . . thank God for Ted Turner and TCM. I don't feel like a mystery though. Need to work on the quilt today if I get time. If I can get that one done, then maybe I'll have enough time to do one for Mother. She needs a lap quilt for Christmas.

I suppose I should get dressed . . . nah . . . why bother. My comfy sweats and his old denim shirt . . . I'm fine the way I am . . . comfortable and warm.

9:14 A.M. Pop-Tart and a Dr Pepper . . . breakfast of champions . . . no wonder my butt's getting so wide!

9:30 A.M. Back to the Internet . . . if it ever connects (sigh). Bad thing about small town "podunk" . . . can't get cable, and nothing high speed (sigh). Not gonna connect, so now I have to restart. I swear sometimes I HATE this computer!

9:39 A.M. Yay . . . I have mail . . . big deal. Oh shit . . . this is a big deal . . . it's from Rae. Rae Evening Earth Ott is the founder/caretaker of the North American Wolf Association in Conroe, Texas, a dear friend of mine. Her wolves are dying from an unknown cause and they are racing against the clock to save them. Oh, I feel so sorry for those babies. I hope they find out what's wrong before it's too late. Donation money didn't make it? Hmm . . . have to call Visa later then.

9:50 A.M. Back to the message boards. Man, am I starved for conversation or what?!

10:15 A.M. Checked the mail . . . damn . . . forgot about (my soon-to-be stepdaughter) Amber's pictures. I need to go get those today. Gotta get that hay out of the big barn for the calves too and pick up some more sweet feed when I go get lime at the feed store.

10:31 A.M. OK, one more trip to the message boards, then I have GOT to get started on the laundry and get OFF my BUTT!!

10:43 A.M. Hmm . . . Miss Bonnie (my future mother-in-law) callin . . . easy recipe? Great! Looks like it's gonna be chicken and dumplins for supper. They'll LOVE that! OK, gotta get dressed, then fix the truck . . . can't put this off any longer. Have to get biscuits when I go to town too . . . I have so much to do today. Ain't gonna' get NUTHIN' done if I don't get off my butt!

11:34 A.M. (Whew) Dressed, one load of laundry in the wash, two loads folded and put away, breakfast dishes done (just noticed no bowl . . . did Amanda eat before she left this morning?), cats fed and watered, bed made (one of these days those silly cats will understand how hard it is to make the bed with a cat on top—or maybe not), teeth brushed . . . again (can't seem to get 'em clean enough today), and now the dog wants back out (sigh). Such is the life of glamour! Time to start on the dreaded truck. "OUCH! Quit bitin' my feet!" Damn cat.

12:28 P.M. Record time for a female brake job? Probably not. Not bad though. Had forgotten how hard it was to changes tires, brakes, etc., without break-ing a nail! (ha!) Of course, now my nails are filthy. Oh well, they needed to be redone anyway. May do that if I can find some extra time today . . . maybe tomorrow.

12:35 P.M. Another load in the wash, one in the dryer. Need to go get that hay from the big barn, and get it put out while I'm still motivated.

12:43 P.M. (Whew) Chicken on to boil and hay put out. General (the bigger calf) was tickled. Red (the smaller one) on the other hand is still leery of me. I guess if I had gotten him at a day old like I did General, things would be dif-ferent. Oh well, he'll come around eventually . . . I hope. Time for a quick check on my mail and the message boards, then gotta get to town. Need to make a list before I go (sigh). I get tired of having to go to town every day.

12:49 P.M. Oh good . . . Mom's on the message board. I wish the swelling in her face would go down. I know those missing teeth hurt. The new antibiotics should help though. Band teacher . . . she needs to call that lady. I need to know about my eleven-year-old daughter Rebecka's clarinet. We're running out of time on the rental, and it'll take me a few days at least to get her a new one. Need to talk to the teacher too and find out why Rebecka's grades dropped from C+s to Fs in three weeks. That's not like her at all. Bound to be something wrong. We need to find out what it is before it gets worse.

Note: My two younger daughters live just outside Houston with my mother until we get a house big enough for everyone (Tracy and me and four daughters). We're working on that. My oldest daughter lives with me and Tracy in the travel trailer. The condition of me getting custody of her back from my ex-husband was that she be WITH me. Tracy and I both work industrial construction and since we travel a lot for work, we live in a travel trailer. No more traveling though with her here . . . that's why I'm not working. Tracy's daughter, Amber, lives with his parents about a quarter-mile from us.

Oh hell! Now the washer's gonna leak . . . that's all I need! (sigh) I'll have to look at it after I finish the laundry.

1:13 P.M. Perfect timing . . . just signed off the computer, and here comes my future father-in-law Mr. Lee Royce. I've already put the hay out! Ah! Chicken wants its turn too? Boiled over . . . another mess to clean up.

1:30 P.M. Late power lunch . . . Dr Pepper and half a can of fat-free Pringles!

1:56 P.M. OK, chicken turned off, bills ready to pay, house shut up. Off to town.

2:54 P.M. Back from town. Stopped by Miss Bonnie's on the way out to pick up Tracy's wayward mail. She offered me a bag of kid's clothes that she found sitting at the dumpster (sometimes that's our local thrift store! Ha!). They were the ones Manda and I set out there two days ago! HA HA HA!!! My big laugh for the day! Also sent some leftover chocolate cake for our dessert tonight . . . thanks.

Got the light bill and doctor bill paid, garbage hauled off. Got the insulation and the biscuits, picked up the pictures. (Hey, there's some from last Christmas on here! I've been wonderin' about these!) Dropped a 12-pack of DPs in the yard as I got home. (Figures . . . cans everywhere . . . have to put those in the back of the fridge.) Chicken's back on, and I still have to make another trip to town for feed and lime after Manda gets home. One of these days I'll figure out how to get it all in one trip (sigh).

3:06 P.M. Back to the message boards . . . hey, there's one for me! (God I'm pathetic!)

3:38 P.M. Tracy called just to check in. I told him to bring me some duct tape from work so I can seal up the plastic on the windows. Manda should be home in the next few minutes. Dryer stopped. Time to swap out the laundry.

4:12 P.M. Manda's home. I forgot about Kelly, the neighbor's six-year-old daughter. Manda babysits her after school (sigh). I don't want to deal with her today . . . my head is starting to pound. She's a sweet baby, but she's so hyper! Clothes folded, another load in the wash, one swapped to the dryer, and everybody fed . . . horses, my calves, Lee Royce's calves, and the bulls. Time to debone the chicken.

4:45 P.M. Chicken and dumplins started. I hate having to make Miss Bonnie's recipes for Tracy. I worry whether they'll turn out right. If it doesn't turn out then we'll just have Hamburger Helper . . . again. Got a few minutes to get online.

5:43 P.M. Just finished with supper . . . turned out pretty good! Now I just have to get Tracy's opinion . . . he's not home yet . . . not sure when he will be home. Miss Bonnie's leftover cake is pretty good though!

6:10 P.M. *Friends* is on. I love this show. I wish they would show the newer ones though . . . that's the downside of satellite, I guess.

6:25 P.M. Thoroughly bored. Think I'll lay down 'til Tracy gets home.

6:50 P.M. Last load of laundry in. Yay! Never did lay down.

7:05 P.M. Tracy's home. Need to get him fed.

7:20 P.M. Eddie Murray called. Said he turned my name in on a req today! YAY!! Tomorrow I'll start calling the office to find out when they're gonna hire me. GOD I need to go to work!!! PLEASE, PLEASE, PLEASE let me get this job!

8:26 P.M. I don't understand it . . . up 'til 5 or 6, my day drags by. I can remember every detail. After Manda gets home, that's it . . . it flies by! Here it is, after 8, and I haven't had a bath, need to wash dishes up from supper, haven't called the babies, and I'm whooped! And of course Tracy's outside . . . piddling. Well, going to call the babies, then MY turn for the bath. I'm not waiting 'til 10 or 11 tonight like I usually have to.

9:47 P.M. Got the insulation put in under the slide-out . . . that should stop that draft. Need to put a strip in from the outside tomorrow . . . that'll help even more. Still didn't do the doors though. Have to get them tomorrow too.

10:13 P.M. Well, here it is ... after 10 and I'm only fifteen minutes out of the shower (sigh). About par I guess. Becka has no idea why her grades have dropped. She can't think of any problems with the teachers or other students, no problems at Mom's house or with me that she wants to talk about ... understands all the lessons. Why is she failing then? Mom needs to call the teachers tomorrow and set up conferences. Codashti (my eight-year-old baby) was quite happy to hear me call. She's so laid back ... but she watches too much TV. Seems like every time I call and ask what she's doing it's "watchin' TV." I can't wait to get them up here. It's been so long since we've actually gotten to be a family. We ARE a family, but being this far apart is so hard. If we don't get a house soon and get my babies up here, then it's just gonna kill me. I can't do this any more ... I just can't.

10:22 P.M. Coffee is set on auto, his lunch is packed in the fridge, laundry is done except one load to go in the dryer (I'll do that tomorrow), and I just don't care about the dishes. I'll wash 'em up in the morning. Never did get to the feed store. Guess I'll do that tomorrow too. I need to go to bed. Hopefully I will sleep, but I'll probably just stare at the ceiling (like I usually do) until midnight or so (sigh). Such the glamorous life.

10:45 P.M. Finally ... he's coming to bed. I get to spend a few quality moments with him before we doze off.

10:54 P.M. I curl up next to him, and that's the last thing I remember ...

ON THE JOB

HILDA L. SOLIS, 44
El Monte, California, and Arlington, Virginia
Congresswoman, U.S. House of Representatives

I arrive at the Los Angeles airport around 10:30 A.M. Before boarding the plane, I call my staff in Washington, where it's three hours ahead, to ask what was on the week's agenda for the House floor. My legislative director, Jennifer Grodsky, informs me that the House will consider a bill renewing the community health centers program, a particular interest for me. Many people in my community use community health clinics as their primary source of healthcare, so I support bills to bring more resources to the clinics.

I also discover that the Democrats in the House will use this week to focus the country's attention on the growing economic problems facing the country. Unemployment is as high as 10 percent in the district I represent, so this is a real concern for me. I'm also worried about the rising cost of healthcare. I decide to do a "one-minute speech" the next day on the economy. One-minutes are an opportunity for Members of the House to talk about any topic of their choice in the morning, before legislative debates begin on the House floor. I tell my staff to begin to draft a speech for me so I can review it when I get to Washington. I ask them to include economic statistics and personal stories from the community I represent.

My flight is long but I have enough reading material and briefing papers from my staff to keep me busy. My offices in Los Angeles and Washington provide me with memos, letters from colleagues, newspaper articles, speeches to look over, and letters from constituents. I like hearing from my constituents because it makes me feel more connected with my community, since I am away three to four days a week in Washington, D.C.

I arrive at the Dulles Airport at 7:07 P.M. Eastern time. I am very tired, since I have been up since 5:00 A.M. I feel like I can't adjust to either time zone. Members of Congress on the East Coast don't know the challenges that face Members who must fly home to the West Coast every week.

Ardie Hollifield, my Washington scheduler/office manager, picks me up. She gives me some memos from my staff about different issues, like the immigration press conference that Leader Richard Gephardt will hold this week, the situation in Iraq, and an update about what the Democratic Caucus Environmental Message Team is working on. I am a cochair of the Team and have been working to inform other Members of Congress about environmental issues. This week is the thirtieth anniversary of the Clean Water Act. We are sending out a packet about the importance of clean water. You wouldn't think that we would have to inform people about the importance of clean water but sometimes it is necessary to state the obvious, especially with this Administration as they try to roll back environmental policies that have been effective for the last three decades.

I ask Ardie if she knew how many constituents had contacted our office about the Iraq vote. I am glad I voted against the Iraq resolution. Over 90 percent of my constituents are against going to war.

During the car drive, I call my Chief of Staff Laura Rodriguez around 8:00 P.M. to discuss the schedule for the week. We speak about the possibility of two lame duck sessions in November and December. She tells me what the Democratic Caucus and other Members are saying on Iraq.

Ardie drops me off at my house at 8:30 P.M. I call and check in with my husband who lives full time in El Monte. Many Members of Congress have their entire families in Washington, D.C. But I think that it is important for me to always make sure that my home is in my district. I speak to him every night.

I am going to relax and watch CNN to start winding down and get some rest. The flight was long. I finally go to sleep about 11:00 P.M.

Tomorrow, I will start my day at 7:00 A.M.

CEO and President, Frederick's of Hollywood

The company was on the skids when she came aboard three years ago. "Some people say I'm masochistic or naive, but I'm neither. I said no several times to this job, but when you're a marketer and love brand names, certain things ring your bell." Before Frederick's, she took a two-year sabbatical from high-powered jobs—living on the beach, working with underprivileged kids, teaching at an entrepreneurial youth academy. Then bam! In one year, she met the man of her dreams, got married, moved, and took on the challenge of reclaiming a failing icon's image from sleazy back to sexy. "Sometimes I really do go over the top! I guess this is what they mean by a Type A personality." She's managed to shatter glass ceilings, without becoming a tough bitch. "I've seen it happen. There's a generation of women who got slammed down and had to pave the way. I do believe a woman has to work twice as hard to get recognition." Secrets to her success? She knows when to speak up . . . and when to keep her mouth shut. It also helps that she grew up with a strong-willed father and four brothers. "I learned at a young age how to handle boys."

LINDA LORE, 48, *Glendale, California*

4:15 A.M. I can't sleep again, too many things on my mind. The responsibilities can sure be overwhelming, always thinking about the company and the people. I'll try to count backwards from 300, that usually works.

6:30 A.M. The last time I looked at the clock was 5 A.M. At least I got another hour of sleep before the alarm went off. Steve (my husband) wants to cuddle, the two kittens want to play, and I need to get ready for work. Always this dilemma! Steve wins!

7:00 A.M. Jump out of bed. Now I'm really going to have to rush. But I can't help it, the kittens are so cute and loving, I need to play with them for a few minutes. I wonder why they always like to sit in front of the shower door and stare. Cats are so funny. I think they lower my blood pressure.

8:00 A.M. Today I feel good about how I look. Since losing weight I can once again fit into my designer clothes. Because it's a big day and I will need to make a public appearance, I choose a fitted designer pantsuit (chocolate color with a tweed jacket and a Hermès scarf). It's an elegant but fun outfit. Leave the house for work. LATE, LATE, LATE. I have a very hectic schedule today. I have to stop at Lindora (weight loss center), weigh in, and get a vitamin B12 energy booster shot. I've lost another two pounds! I'm happy about that. I went on a modified Atkins diet in June and have now reached my goal weight. Lost thirty pounds, YIPPEE. It was really important to get the weight off and get back in control of my body. Control the controllable, especially after the year we've had.

8:15 A.M. Stop at Starbucks, eat on the run (as usual), ice tea and a fruit cup along with a protein bar. Pick up voice mail and return calls on the way in. After thirteen years working in Beverly Hills and Santa Monica, working in the heart of Hollywood is a trip. Frederick's of Hollywood has been in this same location and in the same building for fifty years. The architecture is Art Deco and the building is really beautiful, even if it is somewhat run-down. We have plans for some renovation in 2003.

8:45 A.M. Arrive at office. Take the stairs three flights, need to get a little exercise to get the blood going. My office is really so funky it's almost cool. It's on the top floor of the four-story building; I'm one of the lucky ones as I have a view of the famous HOLLYWOOD sign. Even though it's old it has a warm feeling.

Morning prep. Executive staff meeting today so I prepare while picking up e-mail messages. I usually average about forty to fifty per day. Today's staff meeting will be dedicated to the forward thirty- to sixty-day plan for our emergence from Chapter 11. We are putting together this plan so we can grow this amazing company. In the past ten years there has been no real vision, strategic plan, or formal marketing process (except for the famous catalog). Our charge is to give the company a new image, a new balance sheet, a new culture, and a new structure. Much of the work is well on its way. We are scheduled to emerge from Chapter 11 by the end of the year.

It is also a critical time for sales and receipts right now. Masquerade, Christmas, and Valentine's Day plans must be executed. The dockworkers' strike and the backlog of merchandise sitting in the harbor has us all biting our nails. Our entire silk program, along with other important merchandise, is sitting on a boat in the harbor. Thank God, business is excellent in the stores right now. The store team has done a remarkable job in turning around the way the stores look and operate. With the new merchandise vision and product selection, business is great even in this difficult economy.

10:00 A.M. Staff meeting. Sometimes I feel like a mom; I think being a female CEO sort of puts you in that role. Today is a day when I have to be a counselor, cheerleader, and a business leader. The entire organization looks to the CEO and senior management to feel the mood or tempo. If I am unsure or insecure, the group sees and feels it. Thankfully I've had a lot of practice and we have an excellent staff. Today we have a lot to cover. I think the meeting will run long. And, as usual, I'm interrupted by a phone call from lawyers.

This experience has given me an education I could never have received under any other circumstance but Chapter 11. It is the equivalent of a Ph.D. in turnarounds, in finance, in legal, and in people skills. It is something I'm really glad to have achieved and would not recommend to 99 percent of the population. The work is 24/7 and it is really tiring, especially after over two years. It is the most difficult work experience in my thirty-one-year career.

12:30 P.M. Grab a bite of lunch with Yolie, VP of marketing, so we can discuss the holiday billboards and bus shelter campaign. We will be advertising for the first time in the company's history with a campaign including billboards, bus shelter posters, and radio spots, all tied to the theme "Own the Night." It is really good to work with such capable and committed people. We go to Hollywood and Vine Café and laugh at how much life has changed since we worked together at Giorgio six years ago.

1:30 P.M. Back to the office, returning calls and making last minute preparations for tonight's event at the Hilton. We will be helping out the Men's USTA Challenger Tennis Tournament that is being held at the Burbank Tennis Center. It is also a charity event for the Burbank Center for the Retarded. Steve rarely asks me to do anything where his work is concerned, but this is special, and for a really good cause. So I really wanted to help out. Tonight we have an informal showing of our models in Masquerade, a sexy, fun version of costuming. The outfits we have chosen for the event are Harem Girl, Flapper, Sexy Nurse, and French Maid. These are all complete with fun accessories and hair (wigs) if needed. It should be fun and interesting. There isn't much I wouldn't do for Steve. I consider myself to be one of the luckiest women alive to have him in my life.

3:00 P.M. Meeting with the direct group to go over a system to be installed that will help the Internet and store businesses by creating a new database system.

4:00 P.M. Talk to lawyers again. It's a never-ending process. This is like the movie *Groundhog Day*. Every time we think we've reached an agreement the rules seem to change or we rehash the same issues. There have been so many false finishes that it can be unbelievably frustrating. There are too many "cooks in the kitchen" and it seems like you have to please everyone. Not to mention, this is pretty much a male-dominated industry (bankruptcy professionals) and a lot of egos.

5:15 P.M. Time to leave for the Burbank Hilton hotel to make sure everything is in order. I need to be there at six and traffic in L.A. can be brutal!

What did we do before cell phones? I sometimes think there is too much accessibility. No wonder so many people are stressed out.

6:00 P.M. I'm right around the corner from the hotel, which is across the street from the airport. Since 9/11 they have closed up so many entrances and put up so much security that it makes the process of getting into the hotel parking lot take as much time as it did to get here from the office. To top it off, there are NO parking spaces. I meet this very nice man who is running the car rental drop-off and pick-up from the hotel parking lot.

It never ceases to amaze me how kindly people sometimes react when you are kind to them. He was one of those. The universal accounting system pays off with a very convenient parking space for me!

6:15 P.M. Finally at the event. It's really a thank-you party for the players, with the informal modeling as the high point. The setup looks great with quite a spread of food and an open bar. Steve introduces me to the promoter of the tournament and to the general manager of the hotel. The three of them worked very hard to make this event a success. They all thank me and are genuinely grateful that our company has supported them tonight. I guess they are expecting double the turnout because of the Frederick's models. It should be fun.

6:30 P.M. OK girls, you have only sixty minutes to get makeup, hair, and costumes. There are four girls with a couple of changes each. We also have a hair and makeup person. The outfits include two Masquerade segments, and two segments of innerwear as outerwear. We are showing four different looks tonight. Corsets with jeans, camisoles with evening pants, mesh tops with contrasting colorful bras, and open-weave nightshirts that double as tunics with satin or micro fiber bras. The look is fun, sassy, and sexy without looking trashy. The models love the looks. It really makes life easier when the girls like what they are wearing. It always seems like you are going to run late when it's SHOWTIME, there is an excitement and a flurry of activity that is really amazing. That kind of energy is contagious.

6:40 P.M. A very special treat, I was introduced to Ashley, the seven-year-old daughter of the tournament promoter and one of the most beautiful and sweetest girls I've ever met—I offered to adopt her without any luck. Ashley quickly becomes my assistant and buddy. She hands the girls their outfits and helps them button buttons and fasten hooks. She is so sweet that she actually helps calm the girls by her presence. They have to watch their language and their actions around a seven-year-old, but this is no problem since they too have taken to Ashley. But the best is when we do Ashley's makeup. (All of this was with her parents' permission.) What fun this was! So rewarding for me.

8:00 P.M. Showtime. What an eclectic group of people in this audience—players (twenty- to thirty-year-old professional tennis stars from all over the world), their coaches, sponsors, city officials, umpires, staff, and the Burbank Center for the Retarded. Cameras are snapping everywhere. Steve is the Master of Ceremonies and he introduces me to the crowd and I introduce the models and the fashions. We have some great models and the crowd really loves it. Because this is not a formal fashion show, there is no long runway. When the models are introduced, they walk through the crowd and then mingle with the guests for a period of time. They answer questions, have their picture taken with the guests if they like and talk to them. Then they go back and change into the next outfit. I have a great time talking with everyone and teasing the players who are very nice and somewhat shy. My new little buddy Ashley is on cloud nine when I have her help me introduce the models at the microphone.

The event was very memorable for all who participated. The most excited and sweetest response came from the developmentally disabled tennis team, who got their pictures taken with the girls and the pros. It was a really good feeling to help out my husband and best friend. Steve was so grateful and he really seemed to have a good time. He introduced me to many of the people there and really seemed proud of me.

10:00 P.M. I'm exhausted, hungry, and my feet are killing me. (Shoes, a woman's folly. In my years of experience I've learned to try to mix fashion with comfort.

But no matter how hard you try, if you wear high heels and are on your feet all day, they're going to hurt!) Steve and I have a bite at the Daily Grill. We recap the day's events with each other and think about how lucky we would be to have a little girl like Ashley. We are working with a surrogate to create a family of our own. This is a very exciting time in our lives and we are looking forward with lots of hope and prayers to next year.

11:30 P.M. It is the end of yet another jam-packed day in my life. I barely even want to wash my face tonight. Of course the kittens want to play, they have been alone all day just sleeping and having fun with each other. Sometimes I wish I could trade places with them. And then I think of how exciting, full, and wonderful my life is and has been. Through all the good times and the bad, it is a wonderful journey.

12:00 P.M. As I lay in bed I thank God for my many blessings, pray for my family, my friends, and the world.

THE GREATEST SHOW ON EARTH

5:45 P.M. My father called me from the office in Virginia. He just arrived from Denver. We usually speak at least once a day when we are in the country. The first thing he asked me was if I saw any great acts that we could hire for the 134th Edition for 2004. Even though I saw six different circuses while I was abroad, I did not see anything that captivated me. I told him about my trip to Europe and all the people I met there. I let him know I met this woman, Ika, in Warsaw. Ika is an agent for Polish circus acts and she used to take my father and grandfather around Poland looking for acts years ago. Although I had not seen her since I was two years old, she said she knew who I was immediately because I look exactly like my father. Ika told me that she had dinner in Washington, D.C., with my father and mother in April of 1980, and my parents left after dinner and went to the hospital where my mother gave birth to my sister, Alana! I had never heard that story before and I can't believe I had to travel to Poland to learn that. My dad laughed when I told him. He is busy with so many other aspects of the company; it has been a long time since he has seen some of these people. He knows most of them from when he and my grandfather used to visit all these circuses. It is very exciting to walk where my father and grandfather have walked and to be the third generation of the Feld Family to be involved in this extraordinary business.

NICOLE FELD, 24, *Vienna, Virginia*;
assistant producer, Ringling Bros. and Barnum & Bailey Circus
(part of family-owned Feld Entertainment, Inc.)

Aloha with a Southern Accent

A lifelong Tennesseean, she was forty-nine, divorced, and tired of her job when she moved to Hawaii, sight unseen. "I've lived my life in a lot of pigeonholes. I never want to be in a rut." Married to a Methodist minister for twenty years—"You don't have a personal life. People went through our garbage cans to see if we had beer bottles." A secretary for half her life. The more years on the job, the greater the secretarial stigma. "If you're older, you're often overlooked for opportunities, especially if you do a good job. Someone once told me, 'You're too good a secretary; we can't promote you.'" She graduated from college the same year as her son graduated from high school. In Hawaii, she remarried, got her masters in English, and segued from secretary to editor at a federal agency. The position came first, the title followed five years later. Positive. Liberal. Gossipy. "I can keep a secret but if someone doesn't say 'this is off the record, don't tell anybody,' I will." Basically shy, but never afraid to say what she thinks. "I do speak up to extremes about things I don't think are right, sometimes when I should just keep my mouth shut."

JUDITH L. KENDIG, 65, *Honolulu, Hawaii*

6:30 A.M. Hard to get up. Harder than usual because of the three-day weekend. Three days of sleeping until 9 A.M. have ruined me. I always set my alarm (the television set) for 5 A.M., and it stays on until 5:30 A.M. I still don't get up until sometime between 6:30 and 7:00 A.M. My husband doesn't understand why I don't get up when the alarm goes off. That just doesn't work for me. I have severe sleep apnea, which means that I go to bed wearing a sleep mask attached to a CPAP machine and a humidifier. Warm air blowing up my nose makes me sleep very deeply, and I need some warning time to help me ease out of my vivid dream life. Even then, my dreams follow me around through much of my morning routine, at least until the hot water from the shower hits me on the head. I love the shower; I could stay in there all day.

Today I want a new bright red lipstick. I check the top of my closet, which is filled with pink boxes of all shapes and sizes because I just became an independent Mary Kay beauty consultant. I am doing this to help my sister-in-law climb the next step of the Mary Kay ladder of success. I'm really not a very good salesperson, but I promised to give it a try. It's so different here than where she lives. In the South, everyone *darlin'*'s everyone else. It's easy to have a Mary Kay party there. Some women have become millionaires selling Mary Kay cosmetics. I find that amazing, but I will never join their ranks or get my own pink Cadillac.

This morning I'm glad that there are lots of lipsticks. I quickly rummage through a large Tupperware container to find the perfect shade—"Salsa Red." I have a new top to wear today. I bought it on sale Sunday at Macy's. They've opened up a larger department of larger women's sizes. I love that the new department has been moved to another floor, away from the petite department. Why is it that department stores put the plus sizes next to petite sizes? Do they want us fat women to feel bad or the petite women to feel smug? I hope others notice my red lipstick and ask me where I got it. I will reply, "Why, out of my closet. It's Mary Kay. I'm a new independent Mary Kay Beauty Consultant, and here's my card!"

8:00 A.M. Arrive at work after walking several blocks to catch an express bus. During the bus ride, I put on my eye makeup. I've gotten really good at this, even though I know I should do it at home. Which would mean setting my alarm for about 4:30 A.M. Maybe someone on the bus will notice my lovely Mary Kay compact and how much better I look with eye makeup on. Not many folks on the express bus wear much makeup, though. They are mostly University of Hawaii students. I work at a federal agency that's right in the middle of the university area. I like the location because I was able to complete a master's program in English while working here. I still take some creative writing courses now and then and belong to a reading/writing group that meets on campus every Monday evening. It consists of me and three guys who are Ph.D. candidates in the English department. I have thought seriously about doing the Ph.D. program but I'm way too old to be regimented.

On the way to my office, I buy a chocolate-chocolate-chip muffin for breakfast. I cannot give up these muffins, even though Weight Watchers meets today. I don't buy them often, and I do count the points. I am filled with guilt, until I take that first delicious bite. I cannot and will not live a single day without chocolate! I decide that I'll just eat a much smaller lunch and dinner today. Of course, I know better. I'll do what I do every week after the Weight Watchers meeting: eat what I want for the rest of the day, including lots of chocolate and maybe some real chili.

9:00–11:30 A.M. Involved in a mediation meeting concerning a dispute between me and a coworker. This mediation was suggested by my supervisor.

My coworker and I had been unable to solve a conflict on our own because we are both outspoken and strong-willed women. It went as well as can be expected. I just didn't want to be there.

12:00–1:00 P.M. Weight Watchers meeting. I didn't take my diuretic today because I didn't want to have to leave my earlier meeting several times to go to the restroom. I also ate more salty foods than usual over the weekend. I have gained some weight. I have been a member of Weight Watchers At Work since April but have lost only eleven pounds. At first the weight came off as it should, then I hit a plateau. I exercise every day, and my husband and I try to eat right. No fried foods, no meat for him and only chicken or fish for me, lowfat milk, lots of fruits and veggies. I've gotten really frustrated lately, even though Weight Watchers is an excellent weight management program. I have actually been a lifetime member of this program since 1970-something. I reached my goal then and have been gaining ever since. But I can say with pride that I have lost forty pounds in the past eight years.

Most of the members of the group are losing weight and looking really good. But there are few (if any) women close to my age (sixty-five). They are mostly young, with those youthful and efficient metabolisms. My doctor once told me to look on the bright side. With my metabolism should we ever have a famine I'd be the last one standing. There is also a fat-protecting gene in my family's gene pool. I've always been able to lose weight well in a group atmosphere, but this time it doesn't seem to be working. At least not as well. I do know that I think often about the breast cancer I have survived for eight years and how much better my chances of surviving a return of cancer would be if I don't get really thin. This is the first time I've ever admitted this to myself. It's really just another excuse, though.

After the meeting, a group of us discussed "before" and "after" photos we see in magazines and on television. One young woman said she feels that the "after" photos always look garish, some even clownlike. They often picture the "after" women with new hairstyles and hair color that they would never choose on their own and lots and lots of makeup, which they would never wear. She also feels that there are too few older women in advertisements and on television who look natural. When she finds what she calls "an older woman role model" in a magazine, she cuts out the picture. We talked about the women on "Golden Girls" and how they dressed so beautifully and so appropriately for their ages.

I really, really get tired of having to think about food all day, every day. Being fat all your life is such a bummer. And now that I am old, the media's message that the only women who are truly beautiful are young and thin shouts even louder at me. I've decided that either I was a beautiful woman who made fun of fat people in a former life or that next time I will come back as a stunning beauty who can eat everything and never gain an ounce.

2:00 P.M. I'm settled back in my comfortable office chair, one that actually reclines. No, the government does not buy chairs like this for all its employees. However, my doctor requested such a chair because I need to put up my feet several times a day. I once had blood clots in my right leg, which resulted in lifelong phlebitis. The main part of my job consists of editing research manuscripts that deal with many aspects of Pacific fisheries, coral reef ecosystems, the endangered Hawaiian monk seal, threatened and endangered sea turtles, and various aspects of oceanography. I like my work very much. I would just like to have my own office since there's a great deal of traffic in and out of here all day long. Currently, I share an office with two other women.

My good friend, Bonnie, calls from downstairs asking me if I can come by for a piece of cheesecake. Of course I go. This is Tuesday after all. The cake is wonderful, and I enjoy every bite. With no guilt.

2:30–4:30 P.M. My coworker Dave calls with a question about punctuation. We continue our conversation about other things. He sounds really happy because his father has been in the hospital with a very bad infection but seems to be coming around. Dave is from New York and I'm from Tennessee, but we have the same sense of humor. He's the only other person I know (except for my son) who loves the novel *A Confederacy of Dunces* as much as I do. In fact, he's one of the few people I know who's actually read it. What we like about each other is that we are both appropriately irreverent and not likely to take many things seriously. We work with many Asians and Pacific Islanders, most of whom are gracious and kind, but reserved. A psychological test was given to employees a couple of years ago. I was the only person in my work group who tested out as an extrovert. Actually the dominant personality type in the laboratory (more than a hundred employees) is introvert, which makes for an interesting mix. And which means that Dave and I are more likely to speak our minds, something that makes others uneasy. But then we, too, have our admirers.

I receive an e-mail from my son, Jay, who lives in Washington, D.C. I've redone his résumé and am sending him copies tomorrow. I worry about his living in the Washington, D.C. area. Jay would be an easy target for the sniper because he is over six feet tall and shaves his head. He's a waiter who wants to become what all waiters want to become: a Broadway or movie star. He's got the talent and the looks, just needs that one lucky break.

I spend a few minutes sending some Web pages to my brother, Chris, and his wife about beach rentals in the Myrtle Beach, South Carolina area. My three brothers, my sister, and I are planning to take our mother there for her eighty-fifth birthday in June. This was the family's favorite vacation spot when we children were growing up. The first time we went to Myrtle Beach was in 1950. Hardly any beach houses were there then, but two Christmases ago when my mother and I visited my brother who now lives there, we hardly recognized the place. It's become a major resort area and, sadly, has lost its former charm.

4:30 P.M. I go to catch my bus home. I walk past two of the University of Hawaii's dormitories. The students are so full of life; the girls in their low-ride jeans and short skimpy colorful tops and the boys with bulky shorts down to their knees and T-shirts advertising everything from beer to surfing to electronics. When did college students get to be so young? They all seem to be talking on their cell phones. I don't even own a cell phone; I'm not interested in being reachable every minute of my life.

I am so engrossed in the book I'm reading—Carl Hiaasen's *Native Tongue*—that the bus driver has to honk at me when he arrives. Derek, the bus driver, is so good to me. If I am not at the bus stop when he arrives, he will wait and then drive slowly by my building looking for me. I've ridden the bus for so many years that I can't imagine traveling any other way. My friend, Beverly, who works in the University's housing department, misses the bus, so I don't have anyone to talk to on the way home. I continue my reading.

5:00 P.M. I get off the bus, pat Derek on the shoulder and promise to see him tomorrow. He honks as he passes me walking up the street. I arrive at my apartment building about eight minutes later, check the mail, and wait for the elevator.

5:30 P.M. I have sorted the mail, changed my clothes, checked the answering machine and the computer for messages, and turned on the television. I read the paper, eat a couple of sugar-free popsicles, and watch my favorite stress-relieving show, *Designing Women*. I have seen every episode countless times and know most of the dialogue by heart. I love this show because the ensemble of actresses is so perfect. They each represent a strong aspect of the Southern woman (I'm one of those by birth). My favorite character is Suzanne Sugarbaker (played by the wonderful Delta Burke). She represents the in-your-face bitchy characteristics that Southern women don't always let you see. Her famous line, "I think the man should kill the bug," pretty much sums it up for me. It's too bad that she left the show after problems with other cast members. Some of it had to do with her gaining weight, which had to do with her deciding to stop starving herself to become a size she was never meant to be.

6:30 P.M. My husband is usually home by now, but every other Tuesday he works until 8 P.M. After I eat a container of leftover popcorn, I decide to bake some Hungry Jack (reduced fat) biscuits, but the oven has finally died. It's been terminal for several weeks now, requiring us to preheat it on "broil" rather than "bake." The biscuits are already on the cookie sheet. What do I do now? I get out a skillet, put in some oil, put in the biscuits, and put a lid on it. The biscuits come out rather well, and I eat a couple with some pimiento cheese. Have to call the landlady and tell her about the death of the oven.

8:10 P.M. I am watching another favorite television show, *Frasier*, when my husband gets home. Franklin doesn't like sitcoms; he hates the "canned" laughter. I always tell him that this is a live show; no canned laughter. He says if it's not canned, then it's enhanced somehow. I argue that the show is too funny to need any help. He goes to change his clothes and checks out the biscuits. He thinks I've made one of his favorites—potato cakes, which I never make these days. I know he's disappointed, but he eats a couple of biscuits, then packs his lunch for tomorrow. After *Frasier* is over, I answer some e-mails. Then Franklin and I share stories from our day. Franklin works for a furniture company that specializes in Scandinavian and other European furniture. He deals with the day's frustrations by telling me about particularly difficult customers. He's very funny and an incredible storyteller, acting out what he is telling me and sometimes mimicking voices.

9:00 P.M. We watch *Dateline*, and he gets out the card table for me to set up all my sleeping equipment, which usually takes me five or ten minutes. I have to attach a couple of hoses to a couple of machines and then one to my sleep mask. I drink a cup of sugar-free hot chocolate with light whipped cream on top. I throw away the remaining biscuits so I won't end up eating them.

10:30 P.M. I am finally ready to go to bed, which I don't always like. It takes me at least an hour to fall asleep. I once took prescription sleeping pills, but since such medication can make sleep apnea worse, I have weaned myself from them. I've had the going-to-sleep problem my entire life (or at least as far back as I can remember). But it's worse now. I am fascinated, though, about sleep.

I wonder if there's ever a time that everyone who lives in my apartment building is asleep. I wonder why I can't sleep when I need to but yearn to take a nap when I can't. I truly understand what Poe meant when he talked about sleep being "little slices of death." After I do fall asleep, and before I am drawn into my dream life, I am sometimes startled awake by what seems to be a dark presence over me or around me. I feel so vulnerable. My mother says she would like to die peacefully in her sleep one day. I'm afraid I might die every night.

I kiss Franklin goodnight and begin the long process of relaxing enough to get to sleep. If tossing and turning burned more calories, I'd be a really thin person by now.

OOPS

8:30 P.M. In the lobby of a Citibank: I came here for an extremely cautious ATM withdrawal, $20, so I can eat dinner and go to a movie. A date with myself. Out the money spat from the machine, but there was only one $10 bill! Great. What am I supposed to do now? My account has registered a $20 loss and I've only got half of it. I cannot afford this shit. I called Citibank on my cell phone in the lobby. They told me I have to file some sort of report with my bank. It could take weeks to get reimbursed. I need that $10 right now! I want to eat and see a movie, not choose between them. Wait a second . . . hold on . . . oops. It's, um, another $10 bill. They're stuck together. Let's see, ten plus ten is . . . yeah. That would be twenty.

RACHEL CLIFT, 29, *Saxtons River, Vermont*; **independent filmmaker**

5:20 P.M. Milo just woke up and is nursing. His big sister Inky is scouring magazines for pictures of things that start with "S" to glue onto her homework. She has very carefully cut out a pink short-sleeved sweater from an ad for Fabe 208, a boutique in the East Village. The sweater is emblazoned with the legend I ♥ My Pussy. If this makes it to kindergarten it will serve as a nice sequel to the time Inky explained the murder of John Lennon to a three-year-old classmate who had never heard of death before.

AYUN HALLIDAY, 37, *Brooklyn, New York*; **zine publishing author**

2:10 P.M. Oh no, I just checked the shooting schedule and realized I've been wearing the wrong wardrobe all morning! Boy-oh-boy is shit gonna hit the fan. That means none of what we shot today will match what we did yesterday. It's not my fault either, that's why they hire wardrobe people to make sure they are following the continuity. I can't help but feel bad because that's just how I operate. Whenever things go wrong I always seem to feel like I could have done something to prevent it, even if it wasn't my fault to begin with. I break the bad news to the script supervisor, who also feels bad because she feels she should have caught it too. The director gets wind of what we're discussing and in a very calm tone he directs the first assistant director to make the call to the producers to see what he should do. He is instructed to continue as is and the problem will be fixed in the editing room. I feel really sorry for my wardrobe girl cause she made a mistake and she feels like crap, but I hug her and tell her mistakes are what make us human. She thanks me but I can tell she is disappointed in herself. I know that feeling all too well.

TARAJI P. HENSON, *Los Angeles, California*, **actor, *The Division* on Lifetime Network**

9:10 P.M. Most of our friends from VISTA have left, a bit early for a regular Stitch and Bitch, but they are new. The conversation turns to Camp Ten Trees and Carrie's and my gay friends. In the course of the conversation I make a joke and effectively out someone in the room. (But I don't realize it until later.)

KATHRYN E. PURSCH, 24, *Seattle, Washington*;
community resource specialist

4:15 P.M. I'm listening to a phone message, something from my daughter's daycare about her not getting on the van, when another call comes through. "Vicki, do you know where Josie is? She never got on the van and we've been looking for her for the past hour." Dear Lord, in the rush of the morning's chaos—the babysitter, the preparing for class, the usual five-year-old drama—I forgot to call Josie's daycare to tell them she wouldn't be there after school. "A friend picked her up at three," I confess. "I'm so sorry!" The daycare has called my brother, my friends, the whole world it would seem, or at least all those on the emergency list. "Every number we have for you is wrong," they tell me. "We had no way of getting in touch with you." My remorse is end-less. Why didn't the kindergarten teacher tell the van driver a friend had picked Josie up? Why didn't I tell the van driver she wouldn't be going to day-care? "I swear to you I will never do this again. I promise. I am so sorry." For the past hour, half a dozen well-meaning childcare providers were certain they had lost a five-year-old. What's worse than losing a child? Thinking you've lost a child when the parent knows exactly where the child is.

VICKI FORMAN, 40, *La Canada, California*;
English instructor, University of Southern California

6:22 A.M. Oh shit. $2,250 bid sent in for an Amanda Gray outfit on eBay. Do THEY think that is real?! $22.50 correction sent.

ELLIE RICHARD, 42, *Asheville, North Carolina*; **life coach**

Satellite Sister

*J*uggling a nationally syndicated radio show with her four sisters, while maintaining the delusion that she is a stay-at-home mom. On the air, she's the "color commentator," quick with the observational humor. Off the air, it's back to her regularly scheduled life—"trying to figure out the next meal." Married to a guy she knew in college, and vowed never to speak to again. (He allegedly lobbed a beer at her roommate during a frat party). Six years after graduation, they met up again . . . and her previous vow was quickly supplanted by a new one—"I do." All told, they spent thirteen days together before getting engaged. Two sons, ages seven and four; for five years she squeezed in some screenwriting. Then came *Satellite Sisters*, a surprise hit that filled a void in radio programming . . . and in her life. "There were creative things I wasn't able to do through my children. I love the work and I love my kids—I have no problem reconciling the two lives." She's the baby of eight kids. Labeled by sister Monica as "the smartass" (which the *New York Times* misquoted as "the smart one"). Any sibling rivalry? "Never. That's not to say we don't fight. But if one sister does something annoying, you just call another sister to talk about it, and that's that."

LIAN DOLAN, 37, *Pasadena, California*

5:23 A.M. Sitting in LAX in the Northwest Airlines terminal. I am on my way to Minneapolis to give a speech to a hundred women and then do some work for a new sponsor, General Mills. Yes. A product endorsement for Hamburger Helper. My first big endorsement.

Left my boys and my husband asleep at home. I hate to travel now. Travel used to be exciting before kids and September 11th. Now, I am pretty sure I am going to die on every plane ride. I always leave written notes now, something I didn't do before 9/11.

Do kids understand things like, "Mommy has to go give a speech"?

Now, I have to write the speech! Starbucks just opened.

5:45 A.M. I admire people who can brazenly order cinnamon rolls and chocolate crumb cake at this time in the morning with no thought to calorie count, fat grams, or the inevitable 8:45 A.M. sugar crash.

5:48 A.M. Donna Fazzari, my agent from United Talent Agency, has just arrived. She is going with me because she arranged this product endorsement. I have never traveled with "people" before. Must write speech . . .

On the plane: Headed to the Twin Cities, home of Mary Tyler Moore/Mary Richards. I have no shame in saying that MTM was one of the great influences of my life. Mary taught me how to be single, employed, smart, and funny. Other women may cite Mother Teresa or Gloria Steinem, but, for me, Mary was it. When in doubt—either professional or personal—wear a kicky hat. How great is that?

Later on the plane: Completed the speech. This is where having written a book (*Satellite Sisters UnCommon Senses*) comes in handy. Lots of good material in there that I can steal from myself or my sisters who also wrote the book.

One great thing about working with my sisters is that I always have backup. Public speaking or presentations are far less intimidating because my sisters are there. Today, I will be in a room full of a hundred professional women and Liz will be on the speakerphone. If I get in trouble, I can always throw it to Liz.

2:03 P.M. At the hotel in Minneapolis. Beautiful fall foliage as we flew in—one of the weather-related things I miss in California. Just had the most delicious wild rice soup at the world's slowest hotel restaurant. Had to use "my people," Donna, to get some service. Like me, she gets crazy over slow service. But really—it's a bowl of soup. Get on it.

Nervous about speech now.

5:25 P.M. Did the deed. Gave the speech. A tough crowd at first. Cautious Midwesterners? Or just tired lawyers, accountants, and money fund managers? Or maybe, they just didn't like me. How can that be?

After a day of serious topics and lawyers and judges on the agenda, this group of women needed a little time to adjust to my delivery and message: Using Your UnCommon Senses in Everyday Business. By the end, we had 'em. Nice group. Then I signed all the copies of our new paperback for this group. Women loved the new cover, even though Liz hates it. Our faces are the centers of little daisies. You've got to see it.

After these kinds of events, women love coming up and telling you about their sisters or *Satellite Sisters*. They appreciate the fact that we can relate to their lives on a very personal level. Makes me think that we are onto something.

Off to dinner with General Mills/Hamburger Helper team. This is the Central Time Zone, so I guess that's why they have dinner at 5:30 P.M. Fine with me—that's when I eat at home with the kids. Really looking forward to post-dinner, hotel room TV-and-remote-control time. What a treat!

8:30 P.M. Nice dinner with a hardworking bunch of working mothers. We all confessed that sometimes the obligatory work dinners save us from that exhausting bedtime ritual with the kids. Let's order some appetizers and a glass of wine! A getting-to-know-you dinner—we talked about Target, the election in Minnesota, kids, work, family dinners, child care. The usual stuff of women's conversations.

After dinner, made pilgrimage to Mary Richards statue in downtown Minneapolis. Hummed theme song, twirled around and threw imaginary hat into air. We're gonna make it after all.

Called home. Boys brushing teeth. Quick goodnight to husband and sons. I'll be home tomorrow.

9:00 P.M. I'm eating this Doubletree cookie now.

10:00 P.M. *NYPD Blue* is just not the same without Ricky Schroeder.

MOMMY MOMENTS

9:42 A.M. During the ride to school my three-year-old son and I argue about the music's volume. He likes hip-hop and so do I but this morning my mind can only handle the beats moderately. He asks, "Turn up the music, please." I say it is loud enough. He then asks again and I turn it up a smidgen but of course he is not satisfied. So I just give him the ultimatum, "This current volume or no music at all." He asks me again and I give in. He just figures that he will eventually wear me down. But during this short drive, by the time he wins the volume battle, we are at school. I am still the remaining champ.

JAMI JOYNER, 26, *Columbia, Missouri*;
**coordinator, Black Culture Center
at the University of Missouri, and Ph.D. student**

6:00 P.M. When my husband Jarrett goes out, the kids (four and three years old) really test me. They're sassy and out of control. It's obnoxious, and I have to work hard not to let loose a whole lot of rage upon them. Rage that they generate, but also rage that lives deep inside, somewhere. It all gets tapped. I want to be level and loving with them all the time. How humbling it is to be a parent. How much we live with our demons in our faces, with our human limits in our faces. I'm not sorry to be called to accountability on that, just sorry at the accountability that I actually provide. I have a long way to go towards being the mother I'd like to be.

ALISON BODEN, 40,
Chicago, Illinois;
minister and teacher

8:45 A.M. So we're at the bus stop. No other parents yet. A third-grade boy from our cul-de-sac yells to me, "You look weird." I tell him that isn't polite. "But you look really weird and your hair is a mess and your coat is ugly." I tell him that is rude and that I hope no one ever speaks to him that way. Should I tell his mother? I'd want to know, I think. Here's Max's carpool. I load him into the car seat, kiss him, and he's really sad. Off they go, back to the bus stop. Here's the boy's mom. I don't tell.

WENDY SCHERER, 41,
Columbia, Maryland;
at-home mother and business researcher

11:00 A.M. The kids are watching a video. I go through the guilty-mother checklist in my head: 1) It is only thirty minutes of their day. 2) It is educational. 3) I really need to get something done around this house!

ANNE MARIE LEMAL-BROWN, 38, *South Hadley, Massachusetts*;
figure skating professional and coach

4:00 P.M. The bus arrives—my angels (Harrison, ten, and Graham, eight) are home.

4:05 P.M. Honeymoon's over. Harrison asks if he may play GameCube. I say no. No GameBoy either. No TV either. I suggest he consider doing his homework. He flies into a state of high dudgeon. There's nothing, nothing, nothing to do! The doorbell rings. 4:08 P.M. It's John, John, and Matthew, calling for Harrison and Graham. Bodies, skates, helmets fly. They're out the door. Ah, bliss! Old-fashioned, wholesome, outdoor fun! Boys frolicking with their neighborhood friends—no phone calls, no parent-arranged encounters. Steal an hour at my desk, dealing with stuff.

5:30 P.M. Head downstairs to cook dinner, matzo-meal latkes. At this moment, Graham and Harrison return from old-fashioned neighborhood fun, not even bloody. Go upstairs to Graham's room to play.

5:50 P.M. Fighting breaks out. Harrison won't help clean up mess he allegedly helped create in Graham's room. Shouts, screams, imprecations. "You're an idiot!" "Shut up!" "I hate you!" "I hate you!" Thudding, grunting, bones breaking, perhaps. I bound upstairs, pull them apart—they're getting bigger and stronger, soon I won't be able to get near them when they're like this. I demand they remain apart, remand them to their rooms to do homework. Trudge downstairs, return to latkes.

5:52 P.M. Hostilities erupt again. "Clean up!" "No!" "Stupid!" "Idiot!" Sounds of boy flesh rolling, pressing, crashing to ground, rattling glassware in kitchen cabinets around me. Something in me snaps. I bound upstairs. I'm a lunatic. I scream. I stomp. I pull them apart. I drag them into their rooms. I bellow that they are to remain there until I say they may emerge!

5:55 P.M. I walk downstairs, pick up my wooden spoon, and stand motionless at the counter, trying not to cry. I lost my temper . . . again. I'm a horrible mother. I screamed. I bellowed. I lost control. I'm horrible. Horrible.

6:05 P.M. Bill comes in, all smiling and cheerful. He sees my face. Adios smile and cheer!

6:15 P.M. Dinner is ready. We call Graham and Harrison. Graham sits down and Harrison comes and stands beside his chair. He speaks so softly, I can barely hear him, "I'm sorry Graham. I'm sorry I called you an idiot." He pats his brother's back. Graham leans toward Harrison, puts his arm around him. "That's OK. I'm sorry, too." They come to me as I stand at the stove, put their arms around me. "We're sorry, mommy. We're sorry that we made you so angry." I hold them and try not to cry. I tell them I love them very much and I'm sorry I screamed but I cannot bear it when they hurt each other. We sit down at the table, tired and drained. Graham, who professed to hate latkes an hour earlier, serves himself three. Harrison says he thinks Graham dislocated his jaw and it may hurt to chew (he is mistaken). We eat.

ROBIN CANTOR-COOKE, 50, *Williamsburg, Virginia*; **writer and editor**

Author/Celebrity Interviewer

*H*ost of the nationally syndicated radio show *Between the Lines*, and audio interviewer for Barnes&Noble.com, she has interviewed thousands of writers. "One of the best reporters covering books anywhere in the world," attests mega-author James Patterson. Her basic premise for a good interview—"I actually read the book." A truth seeker with a big heart, she connects through words and smiles. Her third job is morning news anchor on local radio. Key the microphone and she's in her element. A fearful, difficult childhood didn't subvert her innate optimism. "About twenty-five years ago it hit me, there are only two forces: love and fear. So I decided I'd rather live on the love side." An uncanny ability to will herself a good parking space. "And, if you can do that, what can't you do? I use that as a reminder when I want to achieve bigger things in my life." Reads about ten books a week—virtually all of them on the treadmill. Dancing is a passion. Married with two teenage sons. "I love my life, and careerwise I'm just getting started. My dream is to inspire people to be their best." She exudes vibrancy. "I think walking your talk is really key."

DIANA P. JORDAN, 49, *Portland, Oregon*

2:30 A.M. The alarm goes off and I'm up! Today's the day I've been waiting for—I keep my day diary and—bonus—it's also payday. I flash on the bank balance in my mind and checks to be paid, and I know it's nearly all going out. I pray for financial freedom and zero debt. Oh, I should call today about the loan conversion rate—if it's in the fives, we should do it. I pray my husband has a better month selling cars—a much better month. I can't think of any more ways to cover our bills if his income is short. It is all commission, but I believe that we attract what we put out—and, I'm sure he can attract the right combination to bring our income up to above breaking even.

Case in point about making things happen: I know I had angelic assistance—I got the only (that I know of) one-on-one media interview with Mayor Rudy Giuliani during his few hours in Portland yesterday. I am so jazzed (this interview will be edited down for *Between the Lines*). I began working on it several months ago when I saw that his book *Leadership* would be coming out—finally ended up with a PR guy who kept me up on the progress. I read Rudy's book Sunday, and I finished it Monday on the treadmill. I made about eight calls between 3 A.M. and noon until finally "You can meet him at the bookstore and do the interview with him there." Yeah!

2:54 A.M. Shower. Man, I'm running late. What I'll do is pray to hit work at 4 A.M. and the time will likely fly appropriately.

3:00 A.M. Wonder why my husband's up. He says he's "checking football scores." I'll carry on independently, as I always do. On go the face creams. In go the pills. All toward vitality. I breathe to keep a brief anxious thought of "time" at bay—nearly every time I get anxious while blow-drying my hair, the power goes out just in the bathroom. True! I think my energy is too intense when I am focusing on fear not love, so I consciously switch it—and breathe and set mini-deadlines.

3:04 A.M. Still blow-drying. It's all about Intentions. I intend to be on time. I intend to finish reading a book by the time the hour or two is up on the treadmill. Intentions end up 100 percent true for me—like a magic wand. I put the power into an unseen force's hands and let go—it's a fun ride! That reminds me of one of my other interviews yesterday with Dianne Martin, who wrote *The Book of Intentions*. We look like sisters, and I told her I felt like my words were coming out of her mouth. She felt that energy, too. Another hint, though, girl—time to write your book! Gotta finish taxes today first.

3:21 A.M. I turn the radio on and hear Celine Dion's song—"Because you loved me . . ." It's how I feel. So blessed. Hair is straightened and sprayed—ready to go.

3:28 A.M. Hardly any OJ—darn! I'll have to go to Costco. No interviews today. Yesterday I had three. The third was with Thom Steinbeck—John's progeny—with a prayer for all of us to write our family stories. Another "hint" to write my book!

3:30 A.M. I check my in-box—111 e-mails. OK, I'll forward the news ones to K-Lite, the local station where I'm the morning news anchor. I'll do those when I get to work and the rest when I get home. Last night, I skipped some cuz I went to kickboxing class straight from Giuliani. I had so much energy!

3:40 A.M. I feel great, happy, full of energy. Eating a slice of eight-grain bread with honey. I go to Tarot.com and Voyagertarot.com. Yesterday, when I asked Voyager if I'd get to interview Giuliani, it gave me the Success card twice out of a seventy-eight-card deck. I love that. Tarot: What do I need to know today?

Queen of Swords. A relationship is about to change. Voyager gives me Two of Crystals. Be self-aware. I am!

3:45 A.M. Gorgeous morning. Star-studded sky. Radio comes on, "What a feeling!" True! A marquee states: "Why not?" I love that open feeling of "yes." And, all the lights are turning green for me on the drive. Thanks, angels!

4:03 A.M. I'm @ work. Out of twelve lights, I sailed through ten greens. The last two lights—when I knew I'd be at work on time—I had to wait for just ten seconds apiece.

4:14 A.M. "Tiny dancer marries a music man"—this song makes me wistful. I'm still the tiny dancer, but I am saddened that, somewhere along the line, my husband's music seems to have died. Checking EW, NYT, *USA Today* e-mail newsletters, also MSN, KGW, KOIN.

4:28 A.M. In the studio, after culling through the faxes, getting *USA Today*, *Oregonian*, and *Portland Tribune* downstairs—ready to rock!

4:45 A.M. AP—weather, national news, state news, entertainment—choosing my stories and rewriting them as swiftly as possible. I think it's funny how often we change what I say, and it keeps things fresh. I read on KGW.com that Giuliani had talked of not being sure it was fate that he was mayor when the Twin Towers were attacked, but he was prepared. I'll have to listen back to my tape, because that's what I wanted—some thoughts about our place in the Universe, destiny.

5:10 A.M. On Air! I love this! Key the mic—and I am full of joy that goes for miles! . . . despite the quirky computer that didn't work seconds before.

5:27 A.M. Third break on air. I didn't have all the rewrites in that I wanted. There's a moment of disappointment. The *NY Times* has more interesting information about the meat recall than AP—and I can beef up the Giuliani press conference story with information I got from my talk with him.

5:58 A.M. I tested that newscast to the max. I rewrote so many stories that I hit the last paste just as Andrew said, "Ten seconds." I shrugged off my sweater—having heated up—and I began. Voice needed a breath first. Ah, well. I'm so self-critical.

6:08 A.M. There's hardly any local news worth repeating. I have four articles from local e-newsletters to rewrite. I love making news interesting—it makes it interesting for me, to choose and rewrite good stuff. My boss Chris once said that he thought I'd invented a new kind of news—all the content, but not depressing. That's my intention. I'm surprised it became obvious so soon! That pleases me to get people going with a smile in the mornings. News is brutal right now. It needs some leavening with lifestyle stories, studies, and polls.

6:53 A.M. Computer froze. Great. Major frustration. Andrew, my producer, put another song on. I fixed it! Another lesson—print! I'll print my 5:25 and 5:55 newscasts from now on so I'll have something to read if the computer freezes again. There may be a bug in this computer.

7:11 A.M. I fired off another e-mail to engineering and to Chris. Sometimes, I'm too nice. Nice got me Giuliani. Nice is not getting results for me when things are wrong or off-balance. It's a question again of voice, speaking out. Oh, I'm not shy, not anymore, and given a particularly rough spell and a safe environment, I'll let off a string of profanities that can embarrass a sailor, but I'm way too patient with computer problems at work and with my husband at home. I rarely have fits of anger since I've healed so much. I ride the emotions and release them easily, usually with appropriate words. Otherwise, I don't like myself. So, I'm calm . . . and I will be insistent.

7:39 A.M. A moment of crabbiness—I feel I haven't been as much of an "artist" today as I'd like—with the tech problems. Let it roll out. Newscast is in thirty seconds.

8:08 A.M. I'll rewrite a few features for tomorrow. During the aircheck session when Chris and I listen to samples of my on-air work, I'll bring up the computer problem.

8:20 A.M. I'm glad I don't have any interviews today; I need a little break. I will have to do IRS stuff, though, and go to Costco, clear 100+ e-mails, and decide on a few more author interviews. I wonder what's up with my contract for the Barnes & Noble deal—I'll call my agent. We're finalizing a deal for me to do audio interviews with authors for Barnes&Noble.com, as part of the company's "Meet the Writers" feature. Quick blast of anger as I think about money-in-the-bank situation.

8:37 A.M. Chris just nailed me for mentioning my feelings in the e-mail to engineering. Engineering just has too much to do. Bummer, the first time I'm not careful to excise emotions. Now I feel small. I apologized. He says, "Don't be sorry; it's just advice." Oh. Clean. I like this guy.

8:40 A.M. We're listening to my aircheck. It's OK. I just told Andrew that it's dangerous for me to focus on feelings in this day diary I'm writing. It's too easy to stay in feelings when instead I prefer to roll through them. Pretty darn good aircheck. I'm tired now. And, I need to refuel by being nice to myself. My weekly latte may do the trick. I'm still sad that my son lost his job at Starbucks.

9:10 A.M. Really cool—Chris says that Dave, the station general manager, was on the phone with the consultant and said that mornings sound "slicker than snot." That's high praise, Chris says. It makes me laugh—I love guy language.

9:44 A.M. I am so honored. Chris was hugely impressed that I was able to get the only media one-on-one with Giuliani in Portland. At the same time, I chasten myself—I know well the high cost of getting high on myself—so easy to get shot down. Stay humble and appreciative. That's a much easier way to live—not so many highs and lows, and the gifts are many. In some part of me, I believe that I "accidentally" knocked my diamond stud out of my ear getting into the car when I left work for my home studio, partly as penance for letting my ego get out of balance. Of course, as soon as I sent up a little prayer, my hand went right to the diamond, nestled in a crevice under the seat. Can't find the earring-back yet, but I'll look when I get home.

I feel "in a hurry," although I'm not sure of my priority rankings yet. I guess the IRS, then read two books on the treadmill, then e-mail. So amazing—I'm at the bank and suddenly a car pulled out where it was easy for me to just slide in. I believe life is truly magical and that small miracles come sailing in more swiftly still when they are recognized with gratitude. I found a check for $200 from AP while at the bank. It was tucked into a small section of my wallet. That will help with this month's bills. Awesome.

9:56 A.M. Gotta go pick up blank cassettes on the way home, and I'll have a latte. I'm not sure if there is such a thing as Instant Karma, but I use it as a behavior mod mechanism—to grow more swiftly as a human being—as pure as I can be.

10:19 A.M. What a gorgeous day! Blue skies—it'll be warm. I feel so blessed! Even if I am going to Costco now. Just called home and my husband is in a grumpy mood. He won't say why. It could be because he wanted steaks and I said no. The money's too tight this month. I spoke the truth, but maybe it hurt him. I'm sorry. I know he tries; trying isn't the same as doing.

10:30 A.M. Hey, this is not too bad. The store just opened, it's not crowded. I love it!

10:50 A.M. Adding it up as it goes in the basket, I feel a healthy sense of self-control. Thanksgiving foods are appearing on the shelves. I feel wistful. My family feels so small in number. I wonder whom we can invite—my older son's friend, Mark, for sure—he's been living with us for about three months now. I like how he noticed that I was feeling stressed last week and bought me purple daisies. That relieves all my tension, and even now makes me mist up. Yikes, better hurry.

11:00 A.M. It should be around $182.76. That's my guess. Missed. It was $202.73.

11:26 A.M. Pass the dentist's office. Yes, I remember the phone number. I call to get my younger son in soon. No dice. I feel good about how I manage the "small things in life" although I imagine that the expression "God is in the details" has more to do with the joy I feel as I drive home in the convertible, warm sun beating down on my bare shoulders.

11:56 A.M. My older son is mad at me because he's short of cash and he wants to borrow money earmarked for education. I calmly refuse to either lend him my money, which is tightly budgeted due to past stupid spending on credit, or his education fund with Smith Barney. I say, "I believe in your ability to come up with a creative solution, for example, by asking the guy next door if he has work for you." He says, "I hate manual labor." That makes me sad.

12:06 P.M. Via e-mail, I see that the contract revisions for the Barnes&Noble.com deal have been made. It was sent at 6:46 A.M. Let's see . . . I wondered about that @ 8:20 A.M. I'm evaluating my intuitive abilities again.

12:25 P.M. I'm heading to the gym. I need a break. My son yells at me for leaving just when he needs help filling out a financial application. I say that I'll help him when I get back. He is furious, but it's right to set limits, however strange it may seem to me. I'll do treadmill and read two books. I didn't eat—just couldn't—I feel sad that my son and husband are both upset. We're seeing karma here, unattended needs are seeds to later despair.

2:27 P.M. On the treadmill, I read *The Camera My Mother Gave Me* and half of *Everything Is Illuminated*. I need a joyful book right now! I think what I really need is food. I should have known better, but I wanted to escape. I read in a sea of shifting energy. Certain guys come around and we talk. There was a drifting sensation with two of the guys, as if to balance off the intensity of our previous conversations. One guy, whom I've known for years, is a bit standoffish. His energy flittered over me like a wistful breeze. He works in the same industry as me. Earlier, I'd told him of scoring the Giuliani interview and his jaw dropped, his eyes asking, Had he missed something about me? I have to put words to his expressions, because he never says. I really want him to be proud of me. When I want people to like me, or I guess what they're feeling because they know my career is exciting and they are tentative . . . that's difficult. I like when I simply appreciate people for who and what they are, not how they react to me. That is false.

The other guy at the gym I haven't seen in a week. We'd fallen into the custom of my walking fast/reading and him running next to me. Very peaceful and nice. We missed that connection. He keeps saying he missed me, glad to see me again. Is it friendship or flirtation? I'm notoriously bad at that. I acknowledge everyone I know, so no one will feel left out. I need their friendly faces. That is so supportive, I feel cared about, and I so need that. It's kind of an unconditional caring thing, and I don't know what to do when these relationships—even with women at the club—turn a bit more intimate in tone or conversation. Today, I really needed a hug, but I didn't get one, and I didn't feel right about asking anyone for a hug. So my emotions are drifting a bit. Oh, darn, I'm sure it's that I haven't eaten since my yogurt at 9 A.M. I'll eat a decent meal now. Oh! I have to deal with the IRS.

I just got home. There are forty-nine pieces of snail mail and thirty-seven new e-mails to open, and bills to write. I'll go outside and do it in the sun. I need the light!

3:29 P.M. I ate an apple and I'm on hold on the phone with a tax expert . . . in the sun, with my dog Java nearby. I feel sunnier inside, too, and one of my guy-friend's smiles comes to mind. Ah, that feels better. God, I am nurtured by the sunny spirits of friends.

3:52 P.M. My older son just got home. He's a little down. I tell him that it's fascinating to me that by dwelling on my feelings today, I, too, felt a bit lower in spirits than usual. Ride your emotions like waves, I say. Give credence to each emotion, acknowledge the feelings, and let them ebb and flow. And, we need to have plans. He's down about money, so I say why not live at home for a few extra weeks to save up and also apply for college scholarships. He seems cheered, a bit lighter. That makes me feel better, too. The silly song from *Cabaret* comes to mind: "Money makes the world go around." Except I recall it as "Love makes the world go around." Yes, Love does. Each time I connect with someone—an eye sparkle, a smile—I am nurtured, I grow lighter, more of me is helium, like a hot air balloon, and I feel I am lifted off the ground, and connected to the earth at the same time. My spirit grows until it rests lightly around everyone and everything around me.

4:33 P.M. I'm such a wuss. My younger son needs a ride home from school, and the older one who wants to nap until 5 P.M. refuses. I'm too tired of this long argument to bother. I go. Then, I'm reminded I go because I look forward to being with my younger son. And the sun soaks into my skin as I drive, brown leaves flutter by in contradiction to the summery day. We are so fortunate. And, the music reminds me that my body wants to dance. I feel/see the choreography as I listen.

4:55 P.M. Tax advisor says it's OK to wait—relief! Now I'll make dinner for the family, and since they all will eat after activities and work, I'll make my quesadilla. Sounds good! *Oprah* was about "older" single women—wish I'd seen that show. But, I got to talk with my younger son and ease him into a better mood—he was angry about another student's unjust claim that she had to do a project alone without the team. I like that Justin is so aware of justice—he's so aptly named. We talk it through and now he's happy again, talking about an impressionist painting he did that the other art kids praised, "You'll be the next van Gogh, or Monet, or Wolf Kahn." I'm warm in my heart again. He's smiling and buzzing about, happily fixing a snack.

5:33 P.M. Make that fifty-six pieces of mail—the UPS guy just left. I have to laugh. I'm making chicken breasts and rice, quesadilla, chicken strips, and a smoothie. The TV news is on—and I feel that journalist pull toward the sniper story in D.C. Chief Charles Moose is on, and I fire away questions at him in my mind, as if it's one of the news conferences he used to run when he was Portland's chief. I feel wistful, sad for the threatened residents of D.C., and I wonder about the Tarot card for drama. I see Moose's emotions rise and fall, like I'd seen so many times before, with a detached compassion.

5:41 P.M. Ten pirouettes from the counter to fridge to put food away. Dance is good for the soul. I want to call my husband. I haven't heard from him for four hours; that's unusual. Hubby is on a test drive. I sense his eagerness, and say "good job."

6:06 P.M. Three hours after deciding to eat, I'm devouring my quesadilla—homegrown tomatoes, avocado, kalamata olives, and shredded cheeses. It is so good and calming, even with the hot salsa on top. Dinner's done—chicken and rice—and the boys are scattered. Oldest son to work, younger son and the boy who lives with us on errands. I am breathing to send peace through all my muscles. I open mail while I eat. It's relaxing, almost hypnotic. I'm thinking lycopene, the word riffs through my mind. I probably need that—and the tomatoes taste fresh and delicious. I let my hips relax, sitting cross-legged on the chair. That feels better.

6:26 P.M. Bloomie's catalog and TV news both highlight Christmas. I don't know about gifts this year. We don't have a lot of extra, but I can be sure my family is happy. It'd be fun to take the boys to the Kilnmanjaro studio and paint ceramics at that store again.

6:44 P.M. My husband just called back and I updated him on the tax problems. I said I wish he had taken care of this years ago when he was supposed to. I am exhausted when I consider all the work I do on behalf of both of us: everything, except for errands to the dry cleaner—he does that. Oooh-ee. Suddenly, I feel lonely. The only noise is the TV. I hope my younger son comes home soon. Family matters, and we are too few.

6:57 P.M. Elie Wiesel's book *After the Darkness*. I turn the pages, stunned at the images of such barbarism, knowing, knowing, all too well, that such cruelty still exists in some people, summoning supporters of their insane evil . . . and, I know that those of us whose hearts beat with love—not fear or hate—must breathe that love into the air around us. I pray I can do more, with my words, with my news, with my smiles to strangers.

7:28 P.M. Time for e-mails. I'll hit the biggies and do the others tomorrow after my two interviews. Then, I'll finish reading *Everything Is Illuminated* in bed. Jasmine, my cat, just leaps in, giving me a lift in my heart.

8:27 P.M. Done with e-mails. I am so relieved. Say goodnight to my sons and husband, mostly by phone, and it's time to take a book to bed.

8:43 P.M. My younger son just got home. I wonder what he's been up to because I'm just getting to know his new friends, but he's been OK and honest. I like the way we talk—he's much more forthcoming than he was even six months ago. My goal has been for him to put words to his feelings instead of shoving it all down, and he does that very well now. Consequently, dealing with tougher issues in conversation is usually straight, fast, and finished soon, because he has no baggage. It took me years to dump all my toxic garbage out and torch it. Now, feelings can roll through without stacking up and damming my life.

I live my life not as a giant To-Do list, but as a series of connections from person to person. On the air, it's my smiling words reaching out to touch listeners . . . in interviews, it's my smile and encouraging energy—and I know my material. Like Giuliani says, know your work and then operate intuitively. I believe that, totally! On the streets and in stores, I smile, connecting, too, with my eyes. Like Giuliani says, I like people, and I want to connect with them. It makes me warm inside, and it connects me with the whole world. (I'll listen to the tape for an exact quote later.)

9:10 P.M. I must read for a few minutes. Jasmine's on my bed, camouflaging herself, black fur on a black blanket. True, she only lies on that—and thinks she's invisible!

9:30 P.M. The boys' cell phones keep going off . . . and, I am turning off the light.

Thank you for a wonderful journey today. Sweet dreams!

FIFTH ROW SEATS

I don't know how Sheila did it (and after asking her, she didn't know either), but she scored us seats TO SEE DAVID SEDARIS in the first five rows. Unfortunately, they were sandwiched between the girl with long blonde dreadlocks who was sitting in front of me (who kept slinging her hair back and forth . . . I felt like I was getting a lashing every few minutes) and a guy behind me who insisted on yelling "BRAVO!" and "THAT IS SO GOOD" and other thoughtful insights. Nevertheless, the show was excellent.

LYN NIERVA, 37, *Stone Mountain, Georgia*; **Web designer**

CURVES

5:10 P.M. Curves for Women is such a stupid name, thought up by some guy in Waco, Texas. But it suits me. Most of us who exercise here are either dumpy or gray-haired, or both, and I love seeing this circle of women stretching, pulling, jumping to the oldies music. Curves or not, doing this I think we all look great. Today I don't know any of the others. Sometimes I do. I come at different times. We can take our half hour anytime the place is open. It's a No Big Deal commitment that is easy to keep. A woman across from me must have done aerobics; I copy her dancey moves. Walk in, do three circuits, walk out. That's it. Dr. Sachs said I should exercise. She will be pleased. Everything I do is for approval. I still haven't outgrown that.

AGNES ANNA ZEPHYR, 60, *White River Junction, Vermont*;
library assistant

BROWN IS THE NEW BLACK

8:48 A.M. Woke up. I really did not want to get up. I had to drag my feet out of bed, it's not good, I am not wanting to go into the office. Took a longer shower than normal, also lingered in the closet for a while looking for brown. I am tired of doing the black thing in NYC. I want to start wearing more brown.

MARIA CONCEPCIÓN, 27, *New York, New York*;
associate producer

THANKSGIVING

3:05 P.M. Mom calls. My blood pressure goes up as she waffles over whether we (her kids) should spend Thanksgiving with her or my father (who has remarried). This is the same argument/discussion we have had every Thanksgiving and Christmas for the last ten years. Remind her that as my in-laws will be in town I'll be having Thanksgiving at my house. I get snappy, hang up the phone, and immediately feel guilty and call back. She doesn't pick up.

SUSAN A. CLANCY, 34, *Cambridge, Massachusetts*;
Harvard researcher

SOWETO

At the HIV/AIDS clinic, we go through the waiting room where women sit on benches waiting for the results of their tests. They are silent, graven-faced, unanimated. In a room, the counselor sits in front of the seventeen smears. Above four of them are little white plastic triangles that have three colored sensors. The center sensor is gold-colored. Positive. Robin says, "That's lower than usual. Sometimes half of the group is positive." That doesn't make me feel any better. On the wall, the stats for the clinic for 2001 are posted. Thirty-one percent of the women tested that year were positive for the virus.

BARBARA FISHER, 65, *Johannesburg, South Africa*;
senior social science researcher, Perinatal HIV Research Unit,
University of Witwatersrand

AMBITION

2:00 P.M. Going through another guilt phase about not earning enough money. Should I be doing more with my life/career (such as it is)? My husband, Jeff, says he doesn't mind being the main wage earner but I know he'd like to take time off to write more songs and play more. After being away from corporate life for six years, don't know if I'd be marketable anymore, especially with the job market now. Any job I could get would be nine to five, the standard two weeks vacation, and certainly wouldn't be here. Jeff says we should just enjoy our lives the way they are now, for as long as it lasts. Maybe I should be more ambitious, but why change a life-time of sloth? No kids, no major debts or responsibilities, and I'm totally content. "Here lies Beth—she was good at Trivial Pursuit." Good thing I'll be cremated.

BETH L. THORNEYCROFT, 43, *Nashville, Tennessee*;
personal assistant, NashTrash Tours

GLORY DAYS

4:43 P.M. "Hey Yolanda." "Hey Bill," I say every day around this time. Bill is the person that does a great job cleaning our offices. Bill and I have a special connection—we are both avid Steelers fans. However, I must admit, he's got me beat on just about everything from trades to the stats. We lament over quarterback Kordell for about five minutes and then celebrate over every minute of our seventies/early eighties reign in the NFL, and then on to our recent victory. Bill makes my day! "We'll be alright," he says. He always ends our conversation with that proclamation of truth.

YOLANDA M. SCOTT, *Homer City, Pennsylvania*;
assistant professor of criminology

CYBERPRAYER

6:20 A.M. I turn on my computer and feel strangely comforted by the electronic hum. "The sound of technology," my son Brendan calls it. Prayer changes everything, says a devotional in my inbox, and I thank God that it's true. How miraculous that so many believers are linked by the Internet, that we have all "cast our nets" on the troubled waters.

LAURIE BARCLAY COLLETT, 49, *Tampa, Florida*;
neurologist and U.S. Amateur Champion ballroom dancer

Detective Investigating Juvenile Sex Crimes

She's got two young kids of her own. One rule of the job: "I never put my children's faces on the faces of my victims." Toughest aspect of being a detective? "Knowing who's telling the truth." A born cop, following in her father's footsteps. Intense. A workaholic even in high school—student government, soccer, band, prom queen. She still does it all. "If Conner's preschool needs a mommy, I've got to do it. I always have to do my best. I've got to get that A. Everyone says, 'You're running around with your head cut off,' but I thrive on it." Recently separated from her detective husband of six years. "He thinks I got hardened because of the job. I don't see it that way. We both got really, really busy and forgot about each other in the process." Striving to do what's right for her family and the department. She has a great nanny, a sister around the corner, and a best friend across the street—"Without the support, I couldn't do it." After the separation, she and her husband bought houses just two miles apart. "We did that for a reason. I'd like to keep our family intact."

KORTNEY K. DODD, 32, *Anaheim Hills, California*

12:17 A.M. Awoken again by the sound of my three-year-old son coughing. Where did this come from? He wasn't coughing this evening. Should I try to wake him up again and give him the cough medicine? No. I'm not up for another wrestling match—screaming and getting the cough medicine all over the carpet, bed, and our pajamas. I'll wait until he wakes up and comes into my room.

4:30 A.M. Wake up and the house is quiet. No coughing. Is he all right? Did he wake up and get into bed with the nanny instead of me? Am I insecure or what? I walk into his room and his head is at the foot of the bed and he has no covers on. I reposition him and cover him up, relieved that he is finally sleeping peacefully (and he didn't choose the nanny over me). Can't get back to sleep because I have millions of thoughts going through my head ... Start watching the clock and stressing that my window of opportunity for sleep is slipping away.

5:58 A.M. My son walks into my room and gets in my bed, coughing. I ask him if he wants some medicine and he tells me people woke him up last night, not realizing it was me. He then asks me to scoot over on my pillow so he can lay next to me and puts his arm around me telling me, "You a good friend, Mommy." These are the little things that should reassure me that everything is going to be all right and I am a good mommy.

6:20 A.M. Finally get out of bed to get ready for work and I turn on my TV for my son to watch in my bed. Shower and get ready for work. My son asks me where I am going, like he does every day I go to work. He tells me he will miss me and I reassure him that I will miss him too.

7:20 A.M. Walk out of my room and see the nanny and my son sitting on the couch watching the Disney Channel. I give my son a kiss, ask the nanny how the baby slept and she tells me fine. I tell her that I'm going to be late tonight and I will stop by the store to get bread on my way home.

7:25 A.M. In my car, cell phone call to my mother. She is always a sympathetic ear when I need it. Tell her about my restless night and my worries about being a single parent. As if on cue her pump-me-up speech makes things better.

7:40 A.M. Arrive at work and walk into the office that I share with my two partners. For once there is no message light on my phone. My sergeant comes in and briefs us on a robbery and assault with a deadly weapon that occurred the night before. Thank God it wasn't a sex crime or juvenile crime. I'm not sure I would have had the energy for a call-out in the middle of the night.

8:20 A.M. Go back to talk to the robbery/homicide detective about the case. Hear that the suspects are in custody and that they were part of a "white power" group. I check the suspect list because I am working a case where the suspects were also yelling white supremacist remarks before the attack. I did not recognize the names.

8:27 A.M. Take two Hydroxycut pills and eat a rice cake with peanut butter at my desk. It is amazing how much willpower you have to lose weight when you are single again after six years of marriage.

9:21 A.M. Call a video company in New Jersey to order the child abuse documentary film *Close to Home* by the Discovery Channel. Saw portions of the documentary on *Oprah* in September and thought it was great. They tell me it will cost $95.00. (It better be embossed in 24 kt gold.) But I need the film for a presentation on child abuse I am doing at Cal State Fullerton on Tuesday, so I bite the bullet and give them my credit card number. It's a tax write-off.

10:23 A.M. A Children's Social Services worker telephones me regarding a case where a mother's boyfriend beat her up and was arrested for domestic violence. She wants to make a home visit to interview the children but doesn't want to show up if the suspect is back at home. Verify that the suspect has not yet posted bail and is still in custody.

10:43 A.M. School resource officer calls to notify me that a fifteen-year-old assault victim who I worked with before was just transported to the hospital for alcohol poisoning. Apparently she and a friend took rum to school and proceeded to get drunk. The school resource officer tells me that the victim and her friend have been provided with alcohol by the victim's father. I ask her to submit a report so that I can call in a child abuse report and file misdemeanor charges of contributing to the delinquency of a minor. Father is currently out of the house so the minor is protected.

10:51 A.M. Hate crime district attorney calls me and we discuss the case where a group of boys approached a group of football players. One of the suspects hit a boy in the head with a bat while another suspect pepper-sprayed the crowd. "White pride" and "fucking nigger" were yelled prior to the assault, making us think that it was a hate crime. I notify the district attorney that re-interviews of both suspects and victims revealed that the suspects were looking for "football players" and not African Americans. He refers me back to the juvenile court district attorney. Another hoop to jump through to get this case filed and make sure these kids know that they are held accountable for using weapons in my city.

11:28 A.M. Call in child abuse report to Social Services for general neglect and domestic violence for fifteen-year-old girl.

11:41 A.M. Leave for lunch with partners . . . as usual the local taco joint. I think Dave might melt if he doesn't have a taco a day.

12:54 P.M. Return from lunch and learn that the Citizen's Academy class that I am in charge of does not have a speaker for the court-system topic next

Wednesday. I scramble and call the judge we used last year, leaving a message. I hope he can fill in on such short notice. I e-mail the other two speakers as a reminder. What did I do by committing to that assignment? Some people say I have a hard time saying no. I think they are right and now I'm feeling overwhelmed. There is way too much on my plate!!!

1:32 P.M. Driving to the local junior high to interview a fourteen-year-old suspect who fought another kid and won. The victim's parents are demanding prosecution because their son was knocked out and his tooth punctured his lip.

2:04 P.M. Driving to another fourteen-year-old suspect's home to interview him about a burglary that occurred in his apartment complex where a Nintendo video game and remote control car were taken. There is no answer at the door. Is he looking through the peephole? I leave thinking I'll call his mom later at work.

2:27 P.M. Arrive at the Yorba Linda substation where an officer briefs me about a report she just took about a man walking around naked in an apartment complex. When the manager went to talk to him, she witnessed him through his open windows naked and masturbating. We are interrupted because the radio gives her a code-3 call of a head-on traffic collision and she runs out of the station. I told her I would follow up on this when her report was complete. Is this guy a registered sex offender that has sneaked into our city?

2:33 P.M. Make the phone calls to the fourteen-year-old suspects. The suspect who got in the fight swears that the other kid threw the first punch and both victim and suspect met at the school to fight. He said he won the fight because he took boxing lessons. I guess the victim will think twice about meeting other kids to fight. Even though I feel this case is a mutual combat situation with no clear suspect or victim, I will submit my investigation to juvenile probation for review so the mother of the alleged victim will not cry foul.

3:07 P.M. On my way back to the station I decide to stop by an Internet café that I have received complaints about from parents. Apparently minors are staying at this café until one in the morning on school nights. As I pull up, fifteen kids are waiting outside for this place to open.

Intrigued, I start asking them questions. I see parents just dropping their kids off right and left in front of this business. One of the kids tells me that he can play on the Internet for three hours for $5.00. Even though he has a computer at home, he likes to use Red Zone's because he can be with his friends. I ask him if he looks at porn sites at this place and he says no, you will get kicked out for that. I then see about five adults waiting in the shadows for this place to open. They are tatted up and down their arms and I wonder why they aren't at work. My cop cynicism sets in and I immediately think they are parolees.

The doors open and the kids pile in, followed by the adults, to get assigned to a computer station. Inside this café the ceiling and walls are painted black with small halogen lights sporadically spaced. It reminds me of a dungeon, the perfect place for sex offenders to prey on little boys. PARENTS DO YOU KNOW WHERE YOUR CHILDREN ARE, AND ARE YOU MONITORING THEIR ACTIVITIES?

Mental note: Never allow the kids to go to an Internet café when they are older.

I talk to the person behind the desk. He reassures me that he asks everyone at 10 P.M. if they are eighteen years of age and they all tell him yes. I can't believe my ears . . . Of course they all tell you they are eighteen, you idiot!!! But instead, I remind him that it would be better to check everyone's ID and I obtain the owner's telephone number to contact him when he returns from Taiwan.

3:44 P.M. Return to the station and walk past the watch commander's office where the corporal yells, "Dodd, why are you always so serious?" I just laugh. Why am I always so serious? I need to just relax and enjoy life more and quit taking the world's parenting problems on my shoulders.

3:46 P.M. Sit at my desk and notice the light on my phone blaring at me. Which parent is calling me now to scream at me for talking to their children without first obtaining their permission? If I had a dime for every time a parent accused me of violating their constitutional rights for talking to their children without their permission, I could retire way before fifty years old. I'm not ready to tackle the phone messages yet.

4:25 P.M. Receive phone call from partner telling me that she heard that our sergeant was on his way to the hospital because he just found out his father may have had a stroke. Say a quick prayer for them both and wonder if there is anything I can do. I guess my problems aren't half as bad as I think . . . I'll check those voice-mails now.

4:31 P.M. Six messages, none from irate parents, small fires to put out, nothing big.

5:30 P.M. Touch base with mother of minor who was transported to the hospital for alcohol poisoning. Minor is sleeping and cannot be interviewed. Now mother advises me that, while her daughter was drunk, she disclosed another crime. Might explain the promiscuity issue and alcohol and drug abuse the daughter is experiencing now. She will have her daughter call me tomorrow so that I can interview her regarding these statements and make a report.

5:45 P.M. My ten hours are done. Time to go log off the computer and go home. Friend called earlier and asked me to go to the mall to pick up an anklet for our Mexican cruise this weekend. I had to go the mall to pick up some sunglasses anyway. Will try to make it quick so that I can rush to the store to pick up the bread and make it home in time to kiss the kids goodnight.

5:50 P.M. Arrive at the mall. It is good and bad that I work so close to it. Walk through Nordstrom and am tempted to stop. No, I better not. I'm on a single income now and need to start being more prudent with my money. Pick up a cute pair of Ralph Lauren sunglasses and then head off to find the anklet my friend wants. On the way, I stop at the Disney Store to pick up a Minnie Mouse stuffed animal for my eighteen-month-old daughter for Christmas. Oh no . . . they are having a sale and I pick up a few more items for the neighbor's kids for Christmas.

6:15 P.M. Stop by Victoria's Secret and look around at the pretty lingerie and feel a little sad that I have no one to wear it for anymore.

6:30 P.M. Finally find the booth that has the anklet and, of course, there is only one sales associate behind the counter piercing four sets of teenage girls' ears. They are acting like teenagers and I stand back and watch one of them kick the other for something she said. I'm so glad that I'm not thirteen.

6:50 P.M. I'm still standing at the counter and there is no end in sight. Teenage earlobes keep appearing. The sales associate looks at me, apologizing for the wait.

6:51 P.M. I walk to the Hallmark store and pick up a birthday card for my husband's grandmother. I know he will not remember. Men in general are not good with sentimental dates. Anyway I haven't broken the news to her yet that we have filed for divorce. I'll wait until after her birthday. I also pick up a cheering-up card for one of the district attorneys who has helped me in my career and who is going through a difficult time.

6:59 P.M. I walk back to purchase the anklet and the teenagers are still there. I wait a couple of more minutes and think maybe this isn't worth it. My friend will have to buy her own anklet. The clerk stops what she is doing and thanks me for being so patient. I tell the clerk that I know which anklet I need and point it out to her. She boxes it up and gives me a 10% discount for the long wait. Cool!

7:10 P.M. I walk out of the mall and head home feeling really guilty. This is a regular pattern for me . . . one minute I say I need a little time to myself and the next I feel guilty for taking it knowing the kids are at home. Ever since my husband moved out, I have had very little opportunity for time to myself . . . working a lot of overtime, trying to give the kids even more attention than before. The cruise was actually a gift from my husband before we split up. He had set up the cruise for my friends and me. Why didn't he set it up for him and me? Why didn't I tell him I would have rather gone with him? Maybe that was one of our problems . . . we lost track of each other.

7:24 P.M. I call my sister and she tells me she will have to call me back because she is in the middle of *The Real World*. I act offended that I don't even rate past a TV show and she says, "You're saved, a commercial . . . Hi, how are you?" I make my full report.

7:29 P.M. Walk in through the garage door and no one is in the living room. I hear little voices coming from the hall and sneak down, peeking around the door and into my daughter's bedroom. My son, daughter, and the nanny are on the bed doing a puzzle. My son sees me first and yells, "Mommy," and runs toward me, wrapping his arms around my neck. My daughter then climbs down from the bed chanting, "Mommy, Mommy, Mommy" and tries to move her brother out of the way for her hug. These two little people are my life and they are the best part of every day.

7:34 P.M. Get undressed . . . Do I want to go and work out after the kids go to bed? Oh crap! I forgot to go to the grocery store to pick up the bread. But I can go to the gym before and stop by the grocery store after . . . putting me home about 11 P.M. OK. Screw working out tonight. I'll make it up next week.

7:45 P.M. My son starts watching the Cartoon Network and I tell him, like I have told him before, I do not like the way people act in those cartoons and ask him to go and pick a movie from the cabinet. He chooses *Thomas the Train*. Much better content.

7:59 P.M. The nanny picks up my daughter and she waves at me and says "night, night" and blows me a kiss. I say goodnight to my sweet baby girl and watch as the nanny carries her to the bed.

8:59 P.M. I tell my son it is time for bed but that he has to take his cough medicine. The fight is on! He shakes his head no and refuses to open his mouth. The nanny picks him up and I hold his arms down and try to shoot the medicine in his mouth with the measuring syringe. He bites his teeth together hard and turns his head. I try tickling. Doesn't work. I try threats of time out. Doesn't work. OK, son you win. I go out in the garage and break out the big guns ... HALLOWEEN CANDY BARS. I wave the snack-size Crunch bar in front of his face and tell him if he takes his medicine he can have one.

9:04 P.M. After kisses and goodnights, nanny is putting my son to bed and I leave for the grocery store. I feel this incredible amount of peace. The store is quiet with soothing music and I find myself just strolling down the aisles. I pick up the bread and a few other necessities that my husband will need this weekend as he watches the kids while I go on that cruise. I save $18.20 in coupons ... kind of makes up for the splurge on the sunglasses earlier tonight.

10:04 P.M. Arrive home, dogs greet me at the door. The house is quiet and I put the groceries away. I see the empty Cheetos bag in the cabinet and realize I forgot my daughter's favorite food at the store. More guilt. I'm starving. I put three taquitos in the microwave and sit down at the table.

10:17 P.M. I see the envelope of Hallmark cards I purchased earlier. I write out the birthday card to my husband's grandmother because I know I have a late meeting tomorrow night and it will never get there in time if I don't do it now.

10:28 P.M. Look at the insurance papers on the table. It's open enrollment time and I have to choose an insurance plan since I will no longer be covered under my soon-to-be-ex-husband's plan. I can't deal with this now and put the papers in my car so I can look at them at work tomorrow.

10:49 P.M. Walk through the house, shutting off lights and locking all the doors. It is all up to me now ... the kids, the finances, important decisions, my mental well-being. I am scared but, at the same time, I am strong and my life will be what I make of it.

ON THE JOB

JACQUELINE A. JOHNSON, 41
Lakewood, Washington
Starbucks barista (favorite coffee drink: a French press of Starbucks organic Serena Blend, or a simple Americano)

6:45 A.M. Start my shift as a barista for Starbucks. Working with Sara and Amy this morning. They're both so great to work with. I notice we already have a fairly long line of customers, so I quickly put on an apron, take a quick scan of the back bar area, seeing that we have enough coffee brewed to cover the line, and take a position @ the bar, where Amy is eagerly awaiting a helpful hand in getting these drinks to the customers. Starting a shift @ Starbucks @ 6:45 A.M. can be like walking into a party in full swing. Music playing. Frappuccino blenders whirring. Steam wands steaming. Register people calling drinks to the bar. And a line of people to the door eager to get to work on time. Hurry, Hurry, Hurry. Everyone wanting a tall, a grande, a venti, xhot, not too hot, no foam, xfoam, 1 pump of syrup, 7 pumps of syrup, light chocolate, xcaramel, 1%, 2%, nonfat, breve, 1½ Equals, ⅔ full, double shot, triple shot, ⅔ decaf, etc., etc. All to be in and out of the door within three minutes. Of course that doesn't always happen. We make mistakes, multiple drink orders slow us down, but we try hard to satisfy.

Earning Her GED after Forty-Five Long Years

"The day I get that diploma will be the happiest day in my life. More happy than having six kids. Ha." Now "wonderfully blessed," she's known some hard times. 1982—her youngest is born, her husband leaves, her kidneys fail. The doctors say she's too high risk for a transplant. Five years on dialysis. "The kids practically raised themselves. All of them helped each other." Then a new doctor offers some hope. A few weeks later, she's in line at the welfare office. The cab driver who brought her there comes running inside, "They want you at the hospital now!" That's all he knows. She's sure something has happened to one of her kids. At the hospital, the social worker meets them at the entrance, "Dotty, Dotty! They have a kidney for you!" From the welfare office to the operating room in less than an hour, including a bathroom detour to kneel down and pray to the good Lord. After the transplant—"It was like being born again." Once she's earned her GED, she's going back to that hospital to look for a job in data processing, though she wouldn't mind being an orderly. "I really want to work there so I can give back something someone did for me."

DOROTHY THOMAS, 60, *Roxbury, Massachusetts*

My day starts at 5 o'clock. I wake up but I do not get out of bed. Sit up. Look at TV. The time is 4:59 A.M. Say my prayer. Talk to God thanking him for another day. Lord knows I am tired this morning with pains in my body. It's a rainy day, I don't want to go out today but I promised God if he let me get back in school I would go every day. I miss my high school education more than anything else.

5:30 A.M. Oh well! Let's get this show on the road. I run my water for my bath and I love it when the water in the tub is very hot. While I am in the tub I think about what I will start to do for the day. Will I cook this evening? What are my grandchildren doing?

6:00 A.M. Get out of the tub and dry off. Get a banana for my breakfast. Get my medicine and a glass of water. Take my medicine before I start my day.

6:35 A.M. Turn the sound on to the TV. Pastor Weeks is on. She is a very good speaker for a young lady. There is so much that I get from her before I start my day. Drink a glass of juice.

7:00 A.M. Pastor Joel is on. I love to listen to him speak. Also T. D. Jakes and P. White. These are three of my favorite pastors. I love them. I try to tune into them every day if I have the chance. They are very uplifting and inspiring.

7:30 A.M. At this time I will read my Bible and get my lunch ready for school. Start getting dressed for school. I like all my teachers. They are all very good teachers. Our math teacher Margaret is very good. She is patient. She is one of those teachers they should have in the Boston public schools with the kids that really want to learn. She loves what she does. She gives her all, all that she learned in school she would give back and more. I really look forward to attending school. I guess you could say it took me a lifetime to go to school and try for my GED. I would have finished school but my aunt raised me in Mississippi, and when I was fourteen I went to stay with my mother back in St. Louis. I had to quit school to take care of my brothers and sisters. There were twelve of us.

8:00 A.M. Dressed. Waiting for my ride to pick me up for school. Oh, I forgot to take my insulin. My sugar level has been good for a while.

8:45 A.M. Time to go. My transportation driver is outside. I go downstairs out the door. My grandchildren are out to school. Three of them live here. My daughter Tammy is here getting ready to have a baby. It is raining and my stomach is upset because I didn't drink milk with my medicine.

8:50 A.M. I pull up to the school and get out of the car right in time. Made it to the bathroom where I stayed for a while. After about fifteen minutes I felt well enough to go to class. One of the students was walking over to the class. We get along well.

12:00 P.M. Math class, which I love to go to. We went over our math work getting ready for our quiz which we have every Thursday. Margaret keeps our mind on math. I myself look forward to Thursday. This way I know what I need to work on. Also, we can come in early and stay late and she will help us with the work that we have trouble with. I do take the time out for the help that she gives me in the evening. I also feel confident in my math, but I do accept the extra help that she gives me.

1:45 P.M. We are starting to do work on the board. We work 'til it is time to go home. I like the classes that I am taking. Some of them are easy and some of them might seem to be a little harder for me, but I will stick with it until I complete what I am there for.

2:00 P.M. Class is over. Everyone is getting ready to go home. See you tomorrow. We all leave at the same time. First, I didn't want to go to school. I was afraid of the younger people. I was afraid that they would make fun of me, but I want my GED more than anything. So when I came here the teachers and the students treated me just like everyone else. You see I am sixty years old.

I go downstairs and wait for my ride. Sometimes I wish that I still had a car. I am able to drive but I don't have the money to purchase me a vehicle at this time. You never know, God might just bless me one day with a car again.

2:15 P.M. My ride is late today. Kirshrown, one of my classmates, came over, and we started talking about computers. He stays late some days he told me, starting on Tuesday. If I want help he will help me with my computer work.

2:35 P.M. My driver is here for me. Kirshrown walks me over to the van. Helps me with my book bag. Goodnight Kirshrown, see you tomorrow.

2:45 P.M. Now I am home and I get in. Tanysha, my youngest daughter, and Tammy and my grandchildren are all here. There is plenty of commotion. I try to sit down and start to warm me some noodles, slice a mango, sit at the table and eat my food while I do my homework.

4:00 P.M. My granddaughter and grandsons come into the kitchen. Bobby is nineteen, he is my oldest grandson. He belongs to Gloria. He always lived with me off and on. The other two are Tammy's. I do sit down with them and have conversation about what is going on or what has went on with their day. It's time for me to go upstairs away from the loud noise and rap music. I miss my quiet house but ever since I let my daughter Tammy move in I have not had a minute's rest or quiet.

4:30 P.M. I turn my TV on hoping today they have caught those people who are shooting those poor innocent people. Only God knows who it is at the moment but very soon they will get caught. I pray to God that he let them get caught soon. So far they have not caught anyone.

5:30 P.M. Talk to my oldest daughter, Gloria, who always is saying, "Mom when are you going to stop enabling Tammy. Let her go into a shelter to stay.

The children keep breaking up your stuff. Your blood pressure keeps going up. Your sugar is going down. How long are you going to keep living like this?" God knows best.

6:20 P.M. I wash a load of clothes and hang them out to dry. I then take the time to read my science book for the night. My children are downstairs making the family something to eat. My grandchildren are getting their baths and getting their clothes ready for school.

7:30 P.M. I take this time to do my examples in my math book.

8:00 P.M. Language arts, then I take the time to watch channel 16 (Lifetime).

9:00 P.M. I run my bath water for my bath. Soak in the tub about an hour. When my water starts to get cold, I run a little more water to make it hot again.

10:00 P.M. I go downstairs, get me a glass of milk, apple, mango, peanut butter, and crackers. Oh, well, I guess I will say goodnight. The kitchen and things are all cleaned up and the children are in bed. Don't forget to say your prayers, God Bless All.

COLLECTIVE GLIMPSES

82% of day diarists ate breakfast

51% flossed

34% did thirty minutes or more of aerobic exercise

25% were on a diet . . . 53% of them stuck to their diet

70% had caffeine . . . 26% drank alcohol . . . 7% smoked cigarettes

12:37 P.M. I have an hour before my next meeting. I need chocolate. The department next door has a stash of Halloween candy out for public consumption, but it's in a talking bowl. Very annoying. I have to make my selection quickly or draw everyone's attention after the hand in the bowl keeps repeating, "Thank you" and "Happy Halloween." I try to sneak up behind it. I've been reduced to outwitting a plastic hand in an orange bowl to get a chocolate fix.

MARY B. SCHAEFER, 49, *Amesbury, Massachusetts*;
executive director, Merrill Lynch/MIT Partnership

Law Student Focused on Social Justice Rather than a Six-Figure Salary

"People tell me all the time, 'When you get older you'll realize the reality of making a dollar,' but money isn't the center of life, and I know that's true because that's not my parents' brand of success. It's possible to live a life where you give back and are still just as content." Latina. Born and raised in San Antonio, much of her childhood was spent visiting relatives on both sides of the "Tex-Mex border." Currently studying in Michigan, but her heart remains in Texas. So do her long-term dreams. "Someday, I would love to run for Congress in Texas. That might not happen, but you can still work hard towards the things you dream for yourself. If you make it, great. If you don't, you still have some amazing experiences trying to get there." Her parents taught her she could do it all—"Hopefully, one day, I'll be a good mother as well as a good lawyer." Her own mother helps her keep the faith—"Every time we talk, the first and last thing she says is, 'Are you praying for your family?'"

MARISA BONO, 23, *Ann Arbor, Michigan*

4:12 A.M. My legs are throbbing from the marathon Sunday, my first, and it went well. I qualified for Boston by fourteen seconds, a minor miracle. The price is this pain waking me up in the night. I have a Therma-Pak that I have been strategically moving to whatever new nag wakes me up each time—knee, hip, calf, quad. I don't want to be limping around school like I was yesterday, embarrassing. Friends asked about the race and automatically look down at my leg expecting to see a brace or bandage or something with the way I am woodlegging around. (I am kind of proud of it though, like it is a badge of courage, scar of war—war is what the last two miles felt like anyway.) Back to bed.

7:08 A.M. I am awake and running late already. NPR on the radio—bomb blast in Bali. I'm tripping around because my place is such a mess. Can't wait to get some coffee.

8:30 A.M. Now I'm in class and feeling much more calm. This is Contracts. It is everything you would think a law class would be. We are in a large room that looks like it is straight out of the 1940s. Long wooden tables that come down in stadium seating from the back. They curve in elongated moons towards our professor who is lecturing at a wooden podium. The windows are enormous with long heavy blue drapes, and the hanging lamps lighting the room are roughly the size of my kitchen table. There are maybe ninety of us in here, most of us seated behind laptops and coffee cups. Many are dozing. This is an extra-long makeup class so we aren't used to being up this early.

Prof. Ben-Shahar—he likes us to call him Omri but that's still hard to get used to because he looks more like Prof. Ben-Shahar—is from Israel and has a heavy accent. That, coupled with wise eyes, a clean goatee, and sweater-vest, complete the image of a stereotypical law prof. He looks stern now, lecturing with his arms crossed, randomly calling on the ones who are typing with their eyes closed, half asleep. He was in the Israeli army when he was my age. But yesterday some of us had breakfast with him, and he talked to us at length about the joy of being a line cook in Israel during his sabbatical last year. Imagining him in a tall white chef's hat makes the subject of property entitlements less intimidating. I am starving and just discovered a half-eaten Clif bar in my backpack. Breakfast of champions, haha. I should pay attention now.

9:30 A.M. Sitting in the basement snack bar briefing cases for legal practice. They are constitutional issues in criminal cases, super-interesting and my favorite type of law so far.

10:30 A.M. Now in Constitutional Law. Prof. Hills looks like a bird, pointed nose where his glasses perch. He is hard to keep up with because he speaks so quickly, often breaks into impressions and random subjects, from Dr. Seuss to personal anecdotes. He runs, skips, jumps, he gets red in the face, huffs and puffs. Lets you know when he's exasperated with you as easily as he sings your praise. It's a performance really. He could sell tickets.

I have to bug Hills again after class. The Latino Law Students Association (LLSA) is preparing to write an amicus brief for the affirmative action cases the law school is going to have in the Supreme Court. I am a staunch supporter of affirmative action. Michigan's ardent defense of its affirmative action policy was one of the school's attractions for me. I've heard it said that affirmative action stigmatizes students of color. If my professors or classmates think I didn't earn my place, they have never conveyed that perception, and for any sense of alienation I might feel as a minority, I have never doubted that I will succeed here. This will be my third time asking Hills to give the LLSA's brief-writing team a crash course in constitutional law, which we need since we are mostly first-year students. I am debating whether to ask in front of his young daughter, who he has with him in class today, for leverage.

11:30 A.M. I did end up talking to Hills after class and he agreed to meet with LLSA to discuss constitutional issues regarding affirmative action (over pizza of course) the following week. Now, I'm back at home finishing up my briefs. Lunch is a Lean Pocket. I have been living on these things. My landlord finally turned on the boiler and the good smell of heat is in my room and the kitchen. About time.

12:30 P.M. Criminal Law with Westen. He calls me "Bono," which I get a kick out of because that's what people call my dad. Class just started and I am passing notes with my friend, Rabeha—a little tricky since we sit in the front. We might live together next year. I think she would be the perfect roommate, funny, genuine, and not too intense about law school. Not that intense is bad, it's just that it's pretty easy to get too worked up about the quest for the perfect grade around here, I don't want to have to deal with it at home. Westen is always using me in his examples of criminal conduct. "What if someone were slapping Bono around and she just got fed up with it and shot them?" and "What if I knocked Bono over and she hit Ms. Kamaluddin accidentally—would she have a defense?" I wonder if his use of me in violent scenarios is any indication of my grade. I hope not.

1:30 P.M. Legal Practice. Frost is consistently calm and patient, always smiling—the perfect professor for this class, since it's all about making mistakes. Legal Practice is where we are supposed to learn how to write and research like lawyers, something not many of us have had any experience with. We are discussing the cases I was reading earlier. One of them, *Graham v. Connor*, is a Supreme Court case discussing whether the force a policeman used in apprehending a man was excessive. The man was diabetic, and when he felt an insulin shock coming on he asked a friend to drive him to the store so that he could buy some juice. When he got to the store, the line was too long, so he ran back to the car so that he could get some juice at a friend's house instead. A policeman saw him, thought he was acting suspiciously, and followed him, while calling for backup. The man passed out on the lawn of his friend's house. The police handcuffed him, refused to give him sugar as he went into insulin shock, and called him a drunk. Somehow in the process, his ankle was broken. Not just one but two courts said the force they used was reasonable, even though there was no real cause for arrest and the man was released. I have a sneaking suspicion that the man was black but it is not even mentioned. I asked Frost about this after class and he said that the lawyers on both sides probably felt that it would be most beneficial to their clients to leave race off the record. This reminded me that I will have to be careful about tempering my opinions about race in my profession. I imagine biting my tongue while litigating this case as the defense counsel.

I am constantly changing ideas about what I want to do with my degrees. When I go to lectures on campus, I think I want to write and teach. When I read the newspaper I think I want to be an immigration advocate. In class most of the time I think I want to be a civil rights attorney. I like the feeling that my future is so open and pliable now. Whatever it is, I want it to be different, not the same old thing. I feel lucky and happy.

3:30 P.M. I'm sitting with Manu, Aaron, and Andrea in the snack bar and we are "studying." This is pretense for nonstop chatter and laughing as usual. I love being around them, talking about race issues, politics, life, shooting the breeze. We are actually a diverse little group: Manu is Indian; Aaron is Jewish and from Alaska; Andrea is half white, half Hispanic. Most often we tease each other or disagree just to cut our teeth on verbal argument. Manu and I are sometimes hypersensitive about racial issues and Aaron is affectionately teasing us, pointing out the coffee special (vanilla cream) saying, "See what they are trying to do? They are even trying to make the coffee white!"

As we chat I reflect on how I really feel like myself around these three. Most often around the law school I am more quiet and passive than I have ever been in my life. This is the first time I have ever questioned whether I belong. I come from a place where I am not a minority—there is a huge Latino population in San Antonio and Houston, where I went to college. Here, it's so different. All my professors are white males, all the decisions we study were written by white males, all the portraits in our halls are of white males. I often wonder how I am perceived—a woman or a girl? A Latino or a "spic"? A representative or the exception? Here, when I tell people I'm from Texas, they say "No, I mean what country are you from?" even though I was born here. I hate hearing that I speak English "so well," even though it's my first language. It's hard enough to maintain my own identity while finding a place here. It's even harder when others are already trying to put me in the place where they think I should be. It's bad in that way. But it's good in that it makes me work hard. I feel like I need to prove something. Whether I do or not, it's incentive enough for me. Off the soapbox, the four of us start to study for real.

5:30 P.M. Still reading crim in the snack bar with Manu.

7:30 P.M. Manu dragged me to a lecture dinner at Cottage Inn, a pizza place, with Frank Wu, a visiting professor here who teaches immigration. There were about thirty students there, mostly students of color. He spoke about racial stereotypes, civil rights, and building bridges. He compared diversity to democracy, saying that both are processes that are never completely achieved but should always be worked towards. I am heartened.

My legs are definitely better than yesterday. But I think I hurt my knee. I can't walk down stairs . . . Back to criminal law in the snack bar.

8:30 P.M. Still reading criminal law in the snack bar with Manu. In half an hour I will put my books away in my locker (yes, law school is just like high school in more ways than one), which is marked with a big "Don't Mess With Texas" sticker.

9:30 P.M. Trudged home in the cold to read for Contracts tomorrow. The law quad was beautiful, cold and clear and the moon is so white. The law buildings are architectural wonders. At night they look like a castle with climbing ivy, stone turrets, and stained glass. I was back to feeling lucky to be a part of it all on the walk home.

10:30 P.M. Still reading for Contracts. There is a sorority next door and some of the girls are squealing, literally, in the parking lot.

12:00 A.M. My mother called. I love my parents and get homesick after I talk to them, every time. In this stressful place they make me think of comforting things, like the warm Texas sun on the tile in our kitchen, evenings near the *chiminea* on the back porch, Sunday dinner and a movie. I respect and admire them so much. My mother is a social worker and my dad works for the city. I want to contribute to our society the way they have. They remind me of what I want to work towards here in Ann Arbor, of what I want to dedicate my life to, common good, social justice, whatever it should be called. Tonight, Mom lectured me like a child about going to D.C. for a war protest in a couple of weeks. After all, there's a sniper on the loose. Out of millions of people, I think the odds are in my favor.

After I hung up with my mother, I called Sabah, my sweetheart. We met as seniors at Rice. He was studying there on scholarship from his country, Kuwait. He is a constant source of love and support for me. He doesn't baby me, he's respectful, and he treats me like an equal. I love that. Sabah is an engineer and amateur boxer in New York and lives his life like a soldier. Every time I feel lazy I think about his diligence and get working again. His work ethic is amazing. He spends eight hours at work everyday and three at the gym, seems like he only stops to eat and sleep. He wants to represent Kuwait in the Olympics. We have a singular relationship. He's Muslim, so between his culture, religion, occupation, we are so different. But different in a way that is complementary, does that make sense? We are both big dreamers, have strong emotional links to our families, our religions give us similar ideologies about life and how to treat others. I don't know what's in the future for us. But, for now, we see each other often and talk every day, flirt on e-mail and encourage and love one another, and for me that it is the perfect relationship right now.

I wash my face and pull out another Therma-Pak. An Our Father and prayers for my grandmother, my brother, Sam, and Natalie.

Assisted Living

My mother has always had many medical and emotional problems, and they've all been magnified by age. Some nights, she gets into wild rages and starts calling my youngest brother, with whom she shares a house, at work (he's a newspaper editor, so he works evenings). Call after call, all night long. It's distracting and embarrassing for him. Or she gets out of bed after her home health aide leaves and wanders around the house, tired and foggy, until she falls. So far, she's never been seriously injured, but the paramedics come out to the house every few weeks. My other brother (who lives near me in Boston) and I have found the best way to prevent this is to call in the evening, right after the aide goes home. That way, if mom is going to "go on a nutty," as my brother puts it, she'll rail at us instead of my brother who's working.

Tonight, though, she just wanted to chat for a bit. She wants to know when I'm coming to visit. I told her probably next month. What I didn't tell her is that when I do go, it will be to take the next step toward getting her into assisted living, which she clearly needs. I know she won't like it. I know she'll do everything she can to stay in her own home and, truthfully, I can't blame her for that. I'd do the same. But she's just getting too frail and feeble to be alone and we've got to do this. Just as she did for her own mother.

Anne E. Stuart, 45, *Braintree, Massachusetts*; senior writer, *Inc* magazine

Executive Mom

$\mathcal{V}$ice President of global advertising for a corporate giant. Mom to a two-year-old daughter. In her spare time (ha ha) she started "Executive Moms," a not-for-profit geared toward creating connections and resources for women who are both professionals and mothers. Her approach is fundamentally positive: "The thing is, we're just overly fulfilled." Executive Momorandum: It's OK to create a family and still create yourself. In her days as a twenty-something single, she climbed the corporate ladder, but assuaged her non-exec side with stints as a cabaret singer, freelance writer, and TV producer. Now married to a successful public relations executive, the city is in their blood. "It's funny, I never thought I'd raise a child in Manhattan. Now I've become the poster child for it. At least for now." To those who work for her, she comes across as completely confident and poised (whether she feels that way herself or not). In million-dollar deals, her signature tactic is to negotiate with niceness. She's driven to succeed as a wife, mother, daughter, businesswoman. "Part of that drive is wanting other people to regard me well. I thrive when the people I really care about give me positive reinforcement. A little of that goes a ridiculously long way with me."

MARISA THALBERG, 33, *New York, New York*

7:05 A.M. Awaken without an alarm clock—I haven't needed one since Hannah was born almost two years ago (though in fairness, the days of her waking up with a cry are almost entirely gone . . . now it's more the expectation of her rising that awakens me). Within seconds my mind reaches for an inventory of the day. What do I have this morning? What meetings? Things to tell the nanny.

7:20 A.M. David rolls over and reaches for me, still mostly asleep. I hear Hannah now through the monitor and feel a flash of relief that is just on this side of conscious thought. Somewhere along the line, we determined about 7:15 to be the wake-up norm for our child. A 6:30 morning, and we're a little indignant. But come 7:30, instead of enjoying the extra minutes of rest, we become mildly concerned. OK, mostly me. David murmurs that he'll get her. But I'm doing the mental math on my time with my daughter today, realize that I've got that thing to go to tonight, and jump up myself to get her. I don't know how we'd function—how I'd function—if David wasn't the equal partner that he is, in the household, and as a parent. And yet, I can't help but also feel a very primal need to be just a little more equal when it comes to our child.

7:25 A.M. Hannah is lying awake in her crib, a pacifier in her mouth and another in her hand, which she strokes against her cheek. The room smells of cherry and mentholyptus from the Triaminic patch we placed on her chest to try to alleviate her bad cough overnight. She points to her chest now and tells me, "Hurting?" but it sounds as much a question as a complaint. When I reassure her that, "No honey, it's making you feel good!" she brightly repeats, "Feel good!"

7:35 A.M. After a diaper change, a trip into the kitchen to get her juice (she insists on the blue sippy cup today) and a string cheese, we go into our bedroom—our weekday morning routine. "Wake up, Daddy!" Hannah announces as I place her next to David on the bed. We both still thrill to such little things. I'm guessing one day breakfast in bed will seem a regrettable decision, but this works for us, and our bedding has survived. Hannah predictably and immediately asks for "Elmo." It's been forever since I've watched the *Today Show*, but we have no small measure of gratitude for the lure of *Sesame Street*, and both David and I are keenly aware that the "Elmo's World" segment comes on at exactly 7:40.

7:42 A.M. David's in the shower. I'm next to Hannah on the bed, who is watching her little red friend with rapt attention, while I feed her strips of string cheese like she's the queen of the Nile. And I start writing. I'm late.

7:55 A.M. Really running late. Want to wear these great Alice & Olivia satin striped pants I bought in a moment of entitlement (though even then, on sale), but think perhaps they should be worn by an actual skinny person. Decide to wear them anyway. Black blazers can cover a multitude of sins.

8:05 A.M. Doing my makeup and hair in the bathroom. Hannah usually joins me, perched on the sink so that she can alternately play with the water and with my lipsticks and brushes, but today she is more interested in the bread "and JELLY!" that David just made for her.

David had Columbus Day off yesterday, I didn't, so he was the one to leave Hannah with our nanny, Vee, in the morning and reclaim her at the end of the day. "So did you use your time with Vee yesterday to go over a couple of things with her?" I ask from the bathroom. "Oh, absolutely!" he answers blithely.

The truth is, we both manage substantial groups of people at work, and yet both become wimps when it comes to managing our one employee at home. Of course, this one employee happens to care for our child all day. Vee loves to play with Hannah; she really doesn't love to straighten up around the house. Both are technically parts of her job. But then we see how much she genuinely loves our child and we cannot help but feel a profound sense of appreciation, and relief. And because of this, we fail to have the stomach to keep raising the "cleaning up" part. So some days I wash the dishes with equanimity, other days I stew a bit . . . and other days our apartment is actually together (enough), both she and my child are wearing big smiles, and then my day is really made.

8:15 A.M. "What are you doing?" David yells from the other room." I'm writing!" I call back. "What could you possibly have to say? You haven't done anything yet—you've brushed your teeth and gotten dressed!" I imagine how different the men's version of this would be.

8:30 A.M. David and I are off to work, having left Hannah happily on her way to the corner store with Vee, with the expectation that the man at the counter will give her a piece of chocolate, which we've just found out he often does. Though I don't love the idea of the daily dose of chocolate, I smile at the thought of what a small town NYC can be.

We even get seats on the bus and can read a bit of the paper.

9:00 A.M. My e-mail inbox seems filled with problems already. I am the Vice President of Global Advertising and Production at one of the largest designer fragrance and cosmetics companies in the world. As head of advertising for all of our brands (Calvin Klein, Vera Wang, Nautica, . . .), my job has aspects that most people would consider glamorous—fancy lunches with publishers of magazines like *Vogue* and *Vanity Fair*. An office in Trump Tower with views of Central Park one way and the Empire State building the other. Lots of free perfume. But after that, the glamour quotient takes a precipitous dive. The head of one of our international offices is upset about how an advertising mandate is affecting media plans in Hong Kong and has copied the world on an e-mail telling me so. I decide to send an e-mail back with the intent of explaining, mollifying, compromising a bit . . . and adding a little measure of guilt that the issue was ever handled this way. It seems to work; I later get a very conciliatory e-mail back.

In general, business is rough and our company is heavily rumored to be for sale. I am trying to keep my team motivated, convey confidence in the decisions we've made so far, and yet have enough humility to be willing to question and change any decisions we've made that may not be working.

Quickly go through the junk e-mails, the few fun e-mails about my book club next week, and then deal with the work ones. I soon have about thirteen different e-mails and documents open on my computer desktop, and reply to two while listening to voice mail at the same time.

My mind then shifts to the second career I have recently bestowed upon myself (as if one wasn't enough). In the past couple of months, I launched a not-for-profit organization to provide community and support for working mothers like myself: it is called Executive Moms. It mushroomed out of my own little need to feel connected to other women who were in a boat that looked something like mine. I work because I need to financially and, in reality, I also work because I need to emotionally. But it is a path that can be riddled with particular challenges, not the least of which is guilt—and I wanted more of a foundation for feeling good and supported in this path. I couldn't find it, so I started it. But I suppose I was always a better camp counselor than a camper, so maybe it's not so surprising that it would turn out this way.

We had our first big event last week and it was incredible—over 150 women attended the luncheon. I was able to get *Ladies Home Journal* magazine to sponsor it; they were amazing in their support, and the vibe in the room was so positive, so energetic . . . all the hard work and varying degrees of nervous breakdowns felt repaid. It wound up even being a reunion of sorts; among others, I ran into one old high school classmate and three former coworkers from my very first job in advertising. All of them had heard about Executive Moms from others. At the same time, I felt incredibly bolstered by the presence of friends, colleagues, my own mother, and the one token guy in the room, David. It's funny, too—I had really struggled for days (nights, actually) trying to put together the right remarks; yet when I rose to speak before this amazing group of women, the words just flowed.

I know I tend towards having an idealized vision of how anything I plan should turn out (whether a big party or a little family excursion), and this definitely can be a recipe for disappointment. Reality is just never what we plan. However, last week, reality was better. It has occurred to me, though, that success can be as terrifying as failure. Now I have to keep going! This morning, the e-mail invitation for the next event went out, and I am compulsively checking the Executive Moms e-mail to see if anyone has RSVP'd yet. It's only 9:15 in the morning.

10:30 A.M. One of the things I love most about coming to work, that drives me most, is how much I care about and feel committed to the people on my team. That camp counselor thing again. I was forever the teacher's pet growing up, for better and often for worse; now I wonder if I "manage down" better than I "manage up." But whether it's the most politically astute posture to take, I've come to a point where I cannot help but be honest in my reactions and be as real as one can be in the artifice of business life. In a way, managing a team at work makes me feel parental. When they do well I could not be prouder and when they make mistakes I want them to learn, but I also want to protect them. And yeah, though I am sure I'm highly imperfect in their eyes, I do want to be sort of loved back, if possible.

10:50 A.M. I need to eat something. I've gotten so caught up at my desk that I've forgotten about breakfast, but that slightly shaky feeling I inevitably get serves to remind me. I take a minute to toast two slices of light bread in the kitchen and add peanut butter, for protein.

11:00 A.M. On the phone with the president of one of our divisions. I like that she is smart, sarcastic . . . and appreciates the importance of advertising. A competitor seems to be succeeding at our company's expense and it is causing a lot of panic. We discuss how to protect the new brand we are planning to launch under her division in the spring. She and I both recognize that we are playing in an environment in which there is increasing pressure to be promotional. The entire beauty industry has been complicit in conditioning consumers to expect gifts-with-purchases and hard-sell tactics at the fragrance counter—now we're stuck with having to compete with these tactics that cost a company like ours a lot of money to execute. As a result, there is often less money in the pot when it comes to what was once the undisputed force in driving big fragrance sales— a great advertising campaign, with enough of a budget behind it so that everyone would see it. Even young adults today say they remember that first Calvin Klein "Obsession" campaign, though they could not have been more than preschoolers when it was launched.

As it stands, we've come up with a strategy to make the most out of what we've got. Since this new brand has been conceived to reach young men, and is designed to be very sporty, we put together a plan consisting of ads in targeted men's magazines like *ESPN*, *Men's Health*, *Maxim*, and *Sports Illustrated* (we can't afford TV), plus a radio campaign, and a big sports marketing program across top college campuses tied to the NCAA March Madness basketball tournament. It's a smart, tactical plan. I worry, though, that as the big ticket item in the marketing mix, and one that is hard to quantify, "advertising" might be the first target of blame if things don't go well. For all our sakes, I hope this goes well.

11:30 A.M. People have been in and out of my office all morning, and I need five minutes to send e-mails to all the people who were nice enough to volunteer for Executive Moms. Moment to moment, my job veers from feeling perfectly manageable to seeming completely out of control. (Or could that be My Life that I mean?)

12:22 P.M. Need to just finish writing these e-mails before my lunch appointment at 12:30. I've got time.

12:30 P.M. Why did I think I could get them done in time? Very LATE, elevator not coming, forgot to charge my cell phone. But I do really like these pants, I decide. Wonder how Hannah is feeling but cannot call because my phone is dead.

12:45 P.M. Lunch with a publisher at the Plaza Hotel. Love her and haven't had good one-on-one time with her in a while so I'm actually looking forward to it (though long lunches create their own stress in terms of time away from the office). We order cranberry juice-and-seltzers, dig into their excellent bread, and start talking about the tumultuous life at both our companies. Conversation soon shifts to motherhood, and we *ooh* and *ahh* over each other's baby pictures. A complete "Executive Moms" moment. She has heard of my new venture and is very complimentary.

Then she throws me a curveball and suggests she might know of an interesting job opportunity for me. I am immediately flattered, appreciative, and panicked.

Just the suggestion of another major life change makes my stomach twinge and my head feel light. Literally. I think about how good my current situation is, but then wonder if I choose to stay, will that choice continue to be mine in these uncertain times? I also wonder how much this other job might pay. I could really use a bump in salary, especially thinking about the sickening cost of preschool next year, one of the most distasteful by-products of our decision to stay in Manhattan. I never would have imagined that I would be the one carrying the burden to make more money.

2:45 P.M. Voice mail, e-mail, a line forming at my door. Sometimes it seems that actually thinking is a luxury. Need to review rough plans for the meeting at 4:30 that is a preview for the meeting tomorrow at 4:00. My manager of interactive advertising, who I now consider a friend, bursts in with three new emergencies, including how to handle another glitch with our Web site that has political as well as technical implications. I'm a little short with her, but her good intentions as well as her apologetic look immediately make me feel guilty, and I silently vow to be cooler and more organized to handle such diversions. To compensate, perhaps, I find myself taking a moment to tell another one of my managers how much I like her haircut.

For some reason, the lunch conversation made me miss Hannah. She and I had such a great mommy-daughter day on Sunday while David went to the football game, I think that it really would be nice to be home during the week with her a little more (except for this little two-career thing I've got going). I love that she's becoming a real little girl, that we can now make each other laugh and I can see her mind blossom with new words and concepts every day. I pull "Denial" out of my mental toolkit and wield it like a hammer to keep from focusing on everything Hannah must be doing today without me. Another member of my team tells me she needs a breather and offers to get me a Starbucks. I'm not a coffee drinker but feel touched by the offer.

3:30 P.M. Realize I haven't spoken to David all day, since we parted from the bus. Call him and get his voice mail. Wonder if my sister-in-law has gone into labor yet. Today is her due date and I cannot wait to become an aunt; cannot wait even more to see my little brother become a dad. Though once we get the word, we'll need to figure out how we're all getting down to Washington D.C., including my mom, who lives in Queens.

4:30 P.M. My assistant tells me my 4:30 meeting is now pushed to 5:00, and by this time of the day my eye is already on the clock, trying to figure out how I'm going to get everything else done and make it home on time. I need to at least bookend my day with Hannah. If there is a precarious balance to my life, this is what helps maintain it. An evening commitment, or worse, travel plans, and it all feels completely off-kilter (even when I know it's really not). Most nights now, after Hannah goes to sleep, I'm back on the computer working on Executive Moms. Irrationally, I'll find myself resenting David for falling asleep in front of the TV as I work, when it was my decision to do this. He knows this, and has taken to apologizing for his catnaps to make me feel better.

Tonight I'm invited to go to the VH1/*Vogue* Fashion Awards. One of the "glamour" perks of the job, I guess. Given their late start, my plan is to actually go home, spend a little time with Hannah, and then go back down to Radio City Music Hall for the show. I know I am privileged to receive invitations like these, and I try to enjoy and appreciate them. But the truth is, the days of thrilling to such things have past. Well, maybe there's the glimmer of a thrill in relating such activities to relatives (it's OK if they think I have a so-called glamorous life). But often, I'd rather just be home.

6:15 P.M. It has become my ritual to use the time between work and home to call my mother, and we have our quick catch-up, which in recent years has been as much about making sure she is OK as anything. (She's on a short leash with her children, she tells everyone, but after two near-death experiences when she failed to call for help, it's true.) Plus, I've never gotten over my school-aged need to tell my mother about my day. On the phone now, she is still feeding my insatiable need for her praise with more talk about the Executive Moms luncheon last week, and we discuss when we might be heading down to Washington for the birth of her second grandchild.

6:45 P.M. Home about fifteen minutes later than I had hoped, and I actually get impatient with the elevator in our building for depriving me of valuable seconds. However, when I burst through the door with a gigantic hello, Hannah is too busy imploring David to put on Elmo. As I watch the request grow in desperation: "Elmo? El-moohh? ELLLMOOOHHH?!?" I practically have to bribe a "Hi Mommy!" out of her. David gives me the recap of Hannah's day as best as he extracted it from Vee, and we relent on a video, choosing to enjoy cuddling with Hannah on the couch with the TV on, versus contending with hysteria. I reassure myself with this now well-worn psychology textbook tidbit: that children act out with their parents because of the comfort they have with their parents, which enables them to let their hair down and test their limits. This is all just proof of our parent-child bond, I think.

After a while, I'm able to convince her to play in her kitchen, and I help her use a toy fork to "cut" her plastic fruit, which she works on quite industriously.

I look at the mail and see the cover of *New York Magazine*—it is all about Working Moms vs. Non-Working Moms. Damn. David immediately feels badly that we didn't know and manage to get Executive Moms in the story. "You really should fire your PR guy," he tells me. He is my PR guy. I genuinely don't blame him—I'm grateful for the help he's been giving me—but I'm disappointed. Make a mental note to try to find the time to write a letter to the editor, at least.

7:50 P.M. Kiss David and Hannah goodbye—it's rare for me to go back out like this, but with new lipstick and a smaller bag I'm off.

8:15 P.M. Standing in the lobby of Radio City Music Hall, awaiting the start of the VH1/*Vogue* Fashion Awards, amidst a sea of fashionistas, each one trying harder than the next to exude an air of fabulousness. I want to remind them all that they are not the models, actresses, or the designers who will be on the stage, but clearly everyone felt the need to dress as if it were an audition. There is a tremendous amount of air-kissing going on and I find myself both entertained and a little repulsed by the whole thing.

9:00 P.M. David Bowie opens up. My location is excellent and in the caste system of the seating plan, I feel flattered. When I glance down at my watch and realize that Hannah should already be asleep, it somehow gives me the permission to relax more and enjoy the show. "Why not?" I have to remind myself. I stay almost until the end.

11:00 P.M. David is waiting up for me, lying on the couch. He watched a little of the show but found it dull—so apparently he missed the half-second in which I was caught on camera. He and I head into the bedroom. I have my clothes and makeup off within a minute or two. Though bouts with insomnia have at times made my bed seem like hostile territory, I fall into the mattress we spent two hours picking out at Bloomingdale's and allow it to absorb me.

11:15 P.M. We flip between the news and a rerun of *Seinfeld*. I'm too tired to read. Too tired to do anything suggestive. But we almost always go to sleep connected in some way—usually with my head on my husband's chest. Tonight, I ask him to wrap his arms around me. He obliges, spooning me. I begin to relax and quiet, and feel certain that this won't be a night where I'll end up plodding into the bathroom in another hour or two to swallow a cautious one-half of a sleeping pill.

I don't know when we fall asleep. But as it turns out, Hannah will have an unusually rough night, and we each wind up being able to do no more than grasp for shreds of sleep as we take turns getting up to comfort our child, well into the next morning.

$\mathcal{I}$T'S ALL THE SAME

1:00 P.M. Of course, I had to check the discount rack. Good haul! Two cereals (one sweet and one not) and blueberry toaster tarts. Now we've got lots of breakfast foods (and self-service snacks). It's really a bargain—the box is cut open or torn and I get it at half-price The contents are still packaged in the inner seal. Can't really go wrong. What a mom. So this is the modern version of hunting and gathering? Hunting for bargains, or perhaps it's really gathering at the least energy cost (modern equivalent to energy = $). I don't give a hoot what anybody else thinks. The insides are the same.

F. HELENA DONOVAN, 47, *Amherst, Massachusetts*; **Red Cross instructor**

$\mathcal{F}$IRST TRIMESTER

12:00 P.M. I'm hungry. I've actually been hungry for the last hour. It's so hard being pregnant when no one knows you're pregnant, but it just doesn't seem right to say anything yet. My clients are used to me being focused and having the stamina to get whatever needs to be done, done. But, I'm tired. I feel like a cow. I just want to get to the point where I look pregnant, so that I can wear maternity clothes, be forgiven for being huge. But then I'll be really huge, and I might not be able to travel, and then the baby will come and I definitely won't be able to travel for awhile, and I'll need some time off, and I'll lose touch with my clients, and they'll have to go elsewhere, and my little business will go under, and we won't be able to pay the rent, and we'll be homeless, and this is such pointless brain babble. I look up and realize that the project director must have been talking to me, but I have no idea what she said. I suggest we go to lunch.

CHRISTINA R. MAUTZ, 34, *Missoula, Montana*; **consultant to nonprofits**

$\mathcal{A}$DULT ENTERTAINMENT

7:50 A.M. The paper says the newest rage is home parties to sell adult entertainment items. Hmm . . . would at least be more interesting than baskets, candles, or cooking items. I wonder how one (read, *not* me) would come up with a guest list. Can't really ask work friends. Definitely can't ask church friends. Maybe old girlfriends, but if you haven't been in touch in awhile, it's not really the type of party you plan to get reacquainted at. So, another craze passes me by. Oh well, I don't have one of those fancy baskets either.

LYNDA SAVARD, 33, *St. Paul, Minnesota*; **physical therapist**

Hey, Lady

The phone call I just handled has set me off again. It was one of the workshop leaders for a class I'm coordinating. She was concerned that too many older people would be in her class, and that it was geared toward younger folks who would react and understand. I almost blew her ear off. Older people can't react or understand! How dare she! Hey Lady, how old are you and how come you are not understanding and reacting? Calm down Lillian, I tell myself.

LILLIAN KERR HAVERSAT, 64, *Owls Head, Maine*;
executive director of volunteer organization

Your honor

8:00 A.M. Visit with some coworkers who make the meeting but due to a traffic problem many do not. We call it off and head back to our offices. Visiting. What a misnomer. After seven years as a judge I cannot get used to the deference from others. I want to be one of the girls or the guys and be treated equal, but it appears that no matter how hard I try we just can't get there in my professional life. While I appreciate the intent I do not like it. I try to get people to just call me by my name but they insist on referring to me by my occupation. How cold. I know, I know, it is meant to be respectful. Instead it is an invisible shield.

DEANNE L. DARLING, 49, *Oregon City, Oregon*;
circuit court judge

Harm none

5:00 P.M. We're working 'til eight, ordering dinner from a restaurant, Everything but Anchovies. The low-cal chicken sandwich sounds like it might not be too bad. Oohh. I badmouthed someone—said she was an elephant brain. In a way it could have been a compliment!! OK, so that wasn't how I meant it. Now I'll have to think of some way of making it up to her. Even though she didn't hear it, it wasn't in the keeping of "harm none." I'll have to give it some thought.

WANITA WEBB, 47, *North Haverhill, New Hampshire*;
puzzle cutter, Stave Puzzles

GOODNIGHT, DADDY

11:45 P.M. Why am I still awake? I fell asleep on the couch with no problem. I've been lying here for eighteen minutes and I'm wide awake. I should have taken my sleeping pill. Will I ever learn? Probably not. I thought that since my dad had such a great day that I might get a decent night's sleep. Guess again.

11:55 P.M. I'm still staring at the clock watching the minutes go by. I wonder if my dad is sleeping. I hope he is. He doesn't get much sleep. He's usually in too much pain to get comfortable

11:59 P.M. Don't start crying now. You've gone all day without crying. Something that comes rarely. He had a good day today. Maybe tomorrow will be just as good or even better. I hope so. I just can't bear to see him suffer. He's such a great man. And cancer is so evil. Goodnight, Daddy. I love you.

MELISSA A. DUMONT, 31, *Lynn, Massachusetts*;
legal secretary

Human Resources Professional with a Knack for Mediation

"I like to fix problems. I start by showing human interest, instead of bombarding the employee with, 'You did this!'" A motivator who has had to tap into her own inner resources. When her second daughter left for college a year ago, she was at a loss—and fifty pounds heavier. "My husband didn't seem to care and was doing his own thing. I had to find something to do, so I decided to get out and get exercising." Tae Bo. Spinning. Skiing. "I show people my before-and-after pictures to give them encouragement. I feel real good about myself. I never thought I'd get into size 12 pants again." Raised to work hard. Hates when people are late. Wants things done right. When her company started turning more and more mediation cases over to the legal department, she decided to go to California Southern Law School so she could resolve them herself. High energy. Always being asked to chair community fundraisers, whether it's collecting for a widow in her church or sponsoring skiers of color for the U.S. Olympics. Strong, but not tough. "Because I have a hard exterior, people assume they can say whatever they want and it won't hurt my feelings. But it absolutely crushes me."

ROBYN SHARPE, 41, *Pasadena, California*

4:46 A.M. My alarm screeches its familiar song. As I adjust my eyes to the light, I am tempted to hit the snooze button and turn over. I turn it off, lay back down for a moment and sigh. I must be insane to be up this early. But I must. This time one year ago I was sedentary, and fifty solid pounds heavier. As I brush my teeth and wash the sleep out of my eyes, I can still smile at my image because I feel good about myself, even before the break of dawn.

5:01 A.M. I try to start my Tae Bo tape at precisely 5 A.M. The significance of this ritual places me at the top of my schedule. If I start exactly at five, I'll be able to exercise for fifty-five minutes and have fifty minutes to shower, curl my hair, and be out of the house by 6:45 A.M.

5:49 A.M. I'm exhausted and I didn't finish the tape. But my body feels good and I've got my energy boost for the day.

5:55 A.M. As I showered, I reflected on my conversation last night with my husband. My mind can't seem to erase his expression when he came home from work and I informed him that I had cooked dinner. Since our two daughters moved out, I only cook on Sundays. Though he gets in about 9:30 P.M., I thought that because I'd been out of town he'd be happy to see me and want to discuss my trip over dinner. Usually he fixes himself something to eat, or he stops and picks up fast food. I figured a red snapper dinner and a hug would make him smile. He seemed more irritated than anything else and actually wrinkled his nose. I don't know why I allowed this to bother me but it did, along with his dry, smug greeting. I know he's not happy to see me, and I am used to his pretentiousness.

I look in the mirror and ask myself, as I do every day, Why are we still together? This relationship is so stupid and such a waste of my time. We are civil to each other and respectful to a certain degree. But there is absolutely no passion and we are no longer in love. After only ten short years, he is not even my friend. We travel together, dine, attend plays and concerts, but there is no romance, no spontaneous lovemaking, no laughter, or walks on the beach. Since he revealed several years ago to our marriage counselor that he changed his day shift to evenings to avoid being around our then-teenage daughters, I look upon him as simply a companion and put a wall up around my heart. I exhale and get out of the shower.

6:47 A.M. I never thought I'd be as addicted as I am to coffee. If I forget to prepare the coffee maker the night before, I'll make a detour to 7-Eleven and get a cup. I grab a banana, some leftover tuna salad, and my purse, look at the kitchen clock, and jump in my car.

7:10 A.M. This commute is one that I know I won't get used to. Fifty miles one way in rush hour traffic seems desperate. But at forty-one I don't even want to imagine looking for a job again until I finish law school. I try to drive with the flow of the traffic but I hate driving faster than the speed limit. And everyone is racing over seventy on the freeway. I hate driving. Today I'm going to be nice to everyone who waits until the last minute to cut me off. I'm going to wave them in, smile, whatever it takes. But I refuse to let impatient idiots ruin my day by not exercising caution.

7:58 A.M. I've only been here one week, and it is so incredibly busy! Adelphia, the cable communications company I work for, involuntarily transferred me here but, considering the circumstances and their recent Chapter 11 filing, I'm fortunate that they consolidated some of the smaller systems into one big regional office and moved me here instead of eliminating my position altogether. I'm not happy that they parceled the staff out to different areas, but I really am grateful that I still have a job.

The call center director has totally remodeled this two-story office. It is state-of-the-art, the furniture is high-tech and (with almost three hundred people on staff) she told me she spent almost $30,000 just on Ergo Dynamic chairs. She even caters lunch every once in a while, out of her pocket. But the employees are unhappy and morale is down. This is going to be a tough job.

8:15 A.M. Seventy-eight e-mails, two from the kids. The youngest, at Hampton, is finally learning the value of money, because she moved off-campus this year. Her e-mail has hints that ask for money, but I decide not to respond because we will have dueling e-mails for the rest of the day. She knows better, and I know she hasn't spent all the money she worked for this summer. My recent college grad is far more frugal and sends me an inspirational poem. Both of them always make my day. I answer four e-mails and jump on a conference call.

8:30 A.M. Conference call—organized labor unions are trying to convince our call center employees to "join their team." Our weekly conference call discusses the issues at all of the systems throughout the region. I'm sure it is necessary but I'm kind of hyper, so it's driving me crazy to sit still in this chair for an hour.

11:30 A.M. I'm glad I brought my lunch. I hate spending money on fast food. It's too expensive and the fat content floors me. I reflect daily on how much fast food I used to eat over a year ago, sometimes twice a day, and I might have exercised once a month.

This office has a very nice dining area. What's nice is that if you sit down, people will join you, so there isn't that uncomfortable "new kid trying to make friends" feeling. I know a couple of people here from the office I transferred from; so, although we're in different departments, I always look for them first.

My table isn't empty very long. Two female phone representatives whom I've never met sit down and chat with me. They've no idea how comfortable they've just made me feel. One of the women is crocheting a baby blanket and chewing gum, almost in sync. We launch into the age-old discussion of dieting, cooking, and our children's favorite meals. As I look at my watch and rise to leave, Gloria promises to share her *albondigas* meatball soup recipe with me if I'll share my recipe for quiche lorraine with her.

12:45 P.M. My office is in a high-traffic area near the main employee entrance door. The employees, managers, and phone personnel walk by, take a quick peek, and keep on stepping. I know that everyone is trying to size me up. I just want to do my job and go home every day. I actually feel like people are staring at me all the time. I also hate it when people try to give you the lowdown on everyone at the office. I really don't want to know. I want to try to give everyone the benefit of the doubt and if I have to interview, reprimand, or try to resolve an issue, I don't want to have to look at that person and think about something personal that another individual has told me.

1:00 P.M. My counterpart sits across from me and briefs me on the afternoon issues we are about to address. I massage my temples, open my desk drawer, and pretend to search for aspirin, a gesture at which we both chuckle. Then it's time to get started with conferences. Two employees that sit next to each other are involved in an argument that has to do with money. A dollar! Give me a break. I listen to each side tell their story, issue a written warning to the one who actually hit the other in the face with the dollar bill, and suggest that we move the employee who was slapped to another section in the call center. She agrees.

1:45 P.M. A supervisor wants to terminate an employee because she has been absent forty-one days this year, all unexcused. "There are days when she doesn't even call in," he says. "And sometimes she'll come in and leave and not return." I ask him if he's counseled her on her attendance. He says no, but he's written her up several times. I tell him it's my opinion that she's trying to get fired and since she didn't bother to show up today, we'll send her a registered letter asking her if she wants her job. I also gently remind him that he has failed to follow the company's progressive disciplinary action steps by failing to "coach" her regularly after she reached her fourteenth absence, and so on and so on. I listen to him go on and on about how he tried to be a mentor and good supervisor and I look at my watch. My counterpart and I have three more people to see.

I wish my gym were nearby. At my former office, there was one less than two miles away. I miss my office and my staff there. By cable company standards, my old office of seventy-seven employees was small, and every department, including my little staff of twelve, worked as a team and never complained (except for the one person who ALWAYS had problems with her schedule and not being recognized for the hard work she thought she was doing). We actually hugged each other in the mornings, happy to be in a positive work environment. I like to think that I helped contribute towards that positive energy by being kind, pleasant, and objective, and encouraging them daily to be the same. I was told by a former coworker that when my company transferred me, they cried. Ha! I bawled. I bring myself back to earth and act like I'm really interested in the supervisor bragging about himself. I miss my former staff.

2:20 P.M. I'm late for a staff meeting. It started at 2:00 P.M. I'm glad my manager walked by the office and saw me in the meeting with the supervisor. I want to show her that I do respect time. I hate being late. I walk in, apologize, and get smiles from the management staff that say, "You're forgiven this time. But don't let it happen again, new chick."

4:00 P.M. I dash to get some coffee. I still have two grievances to address before I go home.

4:15 P.M. There are three hundred people in this building and I get assigned to listen to the exciting ones. As I sit and listen to a grownup tell me that her coworker is jealous of her and that the coworker likes her boyfriend, I think about all the college courses I took and try to remember which one more closely prepared me for this level of mediation. I cannot think anymore. I don't want her to see me look at my watch so I nod my head and then sneak a peak. It's exactly five o'clock.

5:15 P.M. The coworker that started the ugly jealousy rumor denies everything. She laughs when I reveal the allegations and states that it is the other way around. I play the psychology game, compliment her on her professionalism, and ask her to be a bigger person, ignore the comments, don't feed the fire, and act as a peer mentor and role model to her coworkers. She gives me a big smile and agrees. She looks to be about twenty-two. I look down at her open-toed shoes and notice that she has acrylic nails on every toe, even her baby toe. And each toenail has a flower painted on it. I control myself, look up quickly, and return her smile. One more conference to go.

6:05 P.M. This one was easy. The employee wants to switch from part time to full time. Her supervisor informed her she wasn't eligible. No problemo. I inform her that I will personally speak with the supervisor, confirm her eligibility, and start the paperwork to change her status first thing in the morning.

6:35 P.M. Back in traffic. I select a homemade CD that has Roberta Flack, Michael Henderson, and the Isley Brothers. I want to be more organized, and I want to be polite to others in traffic. With all of the millions of cars on the freeway daily, I don't know why I think my courtesy will make a difference to a driver's erratic driving behavior. But I pretend that it will. I try to relax and not think about work but I can't help it. I came from a different school. I have a different work ethic. I'm forty-one. I learned in college to respect your managers, dress appropriately, work hard. There is a new generation that seems to think the employer owes them, or that they are doing them a favor by showing up for work. I let the Isley Brothers take over my thoughts and concentrate on singing with them. It's funny how good you think you sound when you're singing along.

8:30 P.M. I'm trying to decide if I'm going to go to the gym and ride the Lifecycle or sign on to the Internet. I sign on. I click on "messenger" and see that I have a couple of offline instant messages from people that I'll never meet. One guy's name is Glen. We have been talking since March. I send him a message back and discover he's online. He is not married, I am. We flirt, make innuendos, tell jokes, and I tell him I wish that he didn't live three hours away. It's always refreshing to have someone laugh at your jokes, even when they're not funny. I think he laughs at my jokes just because it's fun to chat and be silly and not be judged or criticized. Sometimes I dream that I'll get up the courage to leave my husband and then I can meet a nice guy like him who will carry me off into the sunset. I snap back to reality because I know there are no knights in shining armor and, if I attempt to leave my husband, we will be embroiled in a nasty divorce. I used to be a fighter but he took away a lot of my energy and feistiness. I don't have the strength anymore so I stay. I say goodnight to Glen and tell him I'll look for him tomorrow.

9:15 P.M. My husband will be home in fifteen minutes, so I grab a towel and water bottle and leave him a note that I'm at the gym. Hopefully, by the time I get back, he will be asleep and then we don't have to pretend we are interested in each other's day or that we're even happy to see one another.

10:30 P.M. I get back home, and he isn't even home. I don't even call his job, because I know he's not there. I take a shower, grab my book, and read myself to sleep.

11:00 P.M. He's tiptoeing in the bedroom, trying not to wake me. I speak first. He mumbles something about overtime and dashes out of the bedroom for fear I will ask questions. I've gotten to the point where I really don't care anymore. I've caught him cheating twice, so most of the time my questioning, even simple inquiries of his whereabouts, turns into arguments. When I complete law school and begin to practice law, I'll be able to buy him out of our house and divorce him. I'm getting out of this relationship. I really am.

RESOLVE

10:00 P.M. Escaped Junior League meeting. During first thirty minutes two women cornered me and asked if I was planning to have children. I found myself making excuses and apologizing for the decisions I'd made in my life. Boy, was I on edge. Mad at myself for feeling defensive. It's my life! As I drove home, I realized that Junior League is a great organization with a good mission. It's just not for me. And, here's the great part . . . It's OK to resign and wish them well and find something more in line with my priorities. What a revelation!

MICHELLE BARNES, 39, *Morrison, Colorado*;
marketing executive, Outward Bound

6:00 A.M. Put the coffee on and make some toaster pop-ups, not a good breakfast but fast, need caffeine, need to move faster, get done quicker. If there were an Olympics for women, I could be a contender in the triathlon of life. How to do fifteen things at once. See, I'm getting better, not exaggerating as much, I would have said a million, 'cause that's what it feels like. My husband says, "You know you start about thirty things and finish two." I say, "You know, Dave, you are right." Can you hear that grit in my voice. It's very hard to come face to face with your own shortcomings, but face, here we are. You are fifty-two, overworked, overstressed, weigh a little too much, don't exercise enough, don't have the tolerance for people that you used to. And you know what, probably none of this is going to change so let's just throw on the purple hat and get moving.

SHARON E. LAMBERT, 52, *Bear, Delaware*; **payroll administrator**

6:05 A.M. Someone brings in Krispy Kreme donuts. I'm mad and glad at the same time. All I need is a few more calories. I immediately eat one and immediately regret it. A little later I'm eating Cheetos out of the machine. I really need to start planning my meals. Yeah, right . . . I've been saying that for years. I've been working out with a trainer since last February. I go three days a week and we do weight work for thirty minutes and I usually stay and do cardio for twenty to thirty minutes. Yesterday I commented on one of the ladies and how great she looks. Turns out she works out sixty minutes three times a week. I'm just not willing to do that much. I have good intentions of working out five to six days a week, but every day I'm so tired when I leave work at 1:00, that I talk myself out of it.

JANE ALEXANDER, 42, *Fargo, North Dakota*;
morning disc jockey, KVOX-FM Radio

9:00 A.M. Time to practice guitar so I'm ready for my lesson. Sometimes I wonder what on earth I'm doing taking electric guitar lessons at sixty-four years old. I started lessons in March, not knowing how to read notes or how to play an instrument. I'm just doing so-so but I'm determined not to quit. I have to prove to myself that I can do it. I'm good at starting things but not always finishing.

Ruth Joffrey, 64, *Glenview, Illinois*; **hospital volunteer**

7:15 A.M. I am getting up for the day, lying in bed with a broken arm. I am getting up for my AmeriCorps position at Minneapolis Public Schools. My name is Lisa Baron, I'm an AmeriCorps member and I get things done.

Lisa Baron, 35, *Minneapolis, Minnesota*; **AmeriCorps volunteer**

New York Times Reporter, Metro Desk, Night Shift

Wrote 115 "Portraits of Grief" about victims of the September 11 attacks. "With each interview, I learned a new version of sadness." Attracted to journalism by "its potential to fight the good fight." Married to her second ("and final!") husband, a software entrepreneur ten years her junior. ("As my ninety-eight-year-old friend once described him, 'he's everything except old.'") Requested the night shift to have days with her baby daughter and lunches with her husband. "I know the pain involved in having a marriage fail, so it's a priority to make it work." Needs a lot of interaction and conversation. "I communicate for a living and don't stop when I come home." She laughs, "Sometimes my husband wishes I did." Has kept a daily journal since age fourteen, inspired in part by growing up with a father with a heart condition. "This instilled in me the idea of how precious life is. It's part of my interest in preserving an accurate description of my life." A published poet drawn to nature, love, and questions of "what if." (As in, "What if my dog were human?") An obsessive knitter. A pet lover. Addicted to multitasking. "In order to get everything done, I have to do a couple things at once."

TINA KELLEY, 39, *Brooklyn, New York*

It's midnight and I am typing away at the metro desk of the *New York Times*, talking to former mayor Ed Koch, who has always been gracious when I have had to call him late at night. I can't imagine ever retiring fully if I left the helm of this city. I would want to keep my fingers in it, even if that means being wakened up just before midnight with bad news, in this case, that the man who took over his congressional seat has died. I hear from hizzoner how the late Bill Green was very shy as a campaigner, not the usual trait you see among politicians.

A few minutes later I see that Good Friend 1 is calling, upset about something at work, and I ask her to call me tomorrow from what we call the "mental health room" at her office, a waiting room with a phone, where one can have personal phone calls without colleagues overhearing.

Five minutes later I am talking to former state senator Roy Goodman, another of Mr. Green's colleagues. I knew he was awake when I called him, so I didn't have to dread the beginning of the call, as I usually do after midnight, when I get a sleepy wife who wants to know why a woman with a young voice is asking for her husband at this time of night. Then I hear that the obit won't run tomorrow, there isn't space, so I can relax a bit. I send in what I can get, to the obit queue, and one of the editors says, "So he'll die tomorrow."

My husband Pete calls to see if the guy I had talked to earlier in the evening, the one who had talked to the eyewitness of the most recent sniper attack, had said green van or cream van. Pete had heard me say green, though I had said cream. He didn't want all the authorities to be looking for cream if it should've been green. I love how he can be such a newsie. My twenty-month-old daughter Kate misses me, he reports.

In by 12:30, I have written the latest on that horrible story of the eleven bodies found in the grain-hopper car in Iowa, presumably immigrants who were being smuggled up from Mexico. They probably had been in the car since June. No word on ages, sexes, or who might have forgotten about them and never opened the doors to let them out into their new lives.

I am hungry and grab a chocolate bar. Doesn't that sound horrible, or uncaring, to go off to a Butterfinger after writing about such a tragedy?

I send Monica, the late editor, a message asking if she wants a brief about a man found stabbed in the chest in Manhattan. Usually they are interested in Manhattan murders, but there is no name, no suspect, no arrest, so she passes on it.

One of my former editors comes by and wonders aloud if he should give in to his kids, who have let a neighbor's Jack Russell terrier puppy sleep over. My friend Cheryl and I give him the pros and cons of dog ownership and of JRTs and of the opportunity vs. costs—get a pound puppy, save a life, this particular puppy will easily find a home, but then again, his son, who has been afraid of dogs, loves this particular one. He has left it up to his wife, and he leaves, wondering if a puppy awaits him at home.

It's not a very late close, and I get a ride home with Monica. I like nights that she works late, because she is good company and, besides, she's a much safer driver than your basic New York taxi driver. I am probably the only person in New York riding in a car at 2:30 A.M., knitting a pink ear for a stuffed kangaroo, but you never know. That's one of the best things about New York, it is so giant and varied that one is seldom truly alone in her eccentricities.

At home, I feel bad that Moose, the cat, has to be closed in the bathroom, but Pete's allergies seem to be getting worse, and she can no longer sleep with us. I sit on the floor with her, reading, hoping that my usual pattern of reading myself to sleep can work in the bathroom as well as in the bedroom. When I get too sleepy, I head to bed, and she yowls when I close the door. Lights out at 3:19.

Kate gets up at 8:30, near the time we had set the alarm, and we allow ourselves the luxury of lying in and listening to the radio for five minutes, like we used to. I'm wondering if that 3–10 shift might not be a good move eventually, even tho it would require Katecare for four hours. I wouldn't be missing out on that many hours of her presence, actually, if I were more wide awake in the mornings for her, and could push her nap back 'til after I went to work (but I would miss the free time her naps give me, that half hour or hour. . .). Getting home before 11:00 would be a luxury, and I could have more time awake together with Pete, and maybe her, because she often stays up later than that. We shall see. I haven't gotten to the point of wanting to let go of my illusion of being a full-time stay-at-home mom and a full-time reporter, with no day care. It's an accomplishment I'm proud of, but it is not necessarily sustainable, the 5.5 hours of sleep a night, the lack of time with Pete, especially when his business will be keeping him busier.

Nursed Kate 'til around 9:30, dozing, watching her half fall asleep, feeling a bit sore—I think she's teething. We sang some of the songs from her *Thomas the Tank Engine* book, and I read some of the paper. Pete and I talked about our immigration policy, with me asking why can't we just let everyone in, what would the harm be in that. I know it's terribly naive, but if people are willing to die to get here, and countless, uncountable people do, what would be so horrible about letting everyone in? Pete pointed out that the conditions in Mexico are so grim that people are willing to risk death to come here, so another solution would be to get Mexico's economy back on track.

Around 10:00 Kate was eating, but feeding Addie, our nine-year-old black Labrador, with her spoon, so I had to wash it. Kate is saying so many new phrases lately that it is hard to know, sometimes, what she is talking about. This morning she was saying "Susie Subway," which cracks me up. I got sick of the boys' club of the world of *Thomas the Tank Engine*, where the men get things done and the few females are mere receptacles, passive passenger cars. So we are telling Kate that it's Susie the Subway and Molly the Metro (when we were in D.C.), so she knows that women have important jobs, or, in her daily life, THE most important jobs.

I tried to call a bunch of people to keep me company while I tackled the pile of clutter that is my apartment, and found Dad home. We yacked a bit, and I told him about our adventure with the new car over the weekend, how we had parked it outside the house where our friends' wedding took place, and when we left at the end of the night, we saw nothing but an empty street, no parked cars, and TOW ZONE signs. We called the tow folks, and then the cops, and no one had any record of the car. We started filing a police report, and I drew a map of it for the officer, who called back about a half an hour later to say the car was right there, where we'd left it—we'd just come out of the house around the corner from where we'd entered. Geez that is embarrassing! And here I already had called four West Coast girlfriends to bemoan my fate! The cop was very nice and didn't arrest me for filing a false report. And Pete and I were glad we had had this misadventure together, because if either one of us had acted so goofily on our own, the other would never have let us live it down.

Pa really cracked up about this. Then I got a load of wash in, changed Kate, and continued trying to get the house in order while keeping the baby occupied while getting through my to-do list of calls to make.

Time to leash up the dog, put the baby in her sling, and find the car to move it. Ah, alternate-side-of-the-street-parking regulations! The things New Yorkers obsess about, at the expense of all the great literature we could be writing, or relationships we could be nurturing. No, instead, we have to set alarms so that we remember to move our cars for three hours a week, so the streets can be cleaned. We have to double park them, leave a note on the dashboard in case the person we're blocking in needs to get out, and then we have to remember to go back and find a new parking place, hopefully one that is good for an entire week, before we get ticketed, before the meter folk, the public servants who I think are statistically most likely to come to physical harm on their horrible jobs, slap us with tickets or put big neon stickers on our cars saying they are hazards to the sanitation of the city.

Kate and I went into the park to throw sticks for Addie. We saw the tap dancer man, and I finally decided to talk to him. He is usually perched on a little hill overlooking the park drive, the sun behind him, tall and lean and incredibly agile, dancing on a 3' x 3' wooden floor he carries with him. I want to try writing a column about him for the City Weekly section, though I didn't identify myself as a reporter. I will see him again and make sure it's OK. I don't know his name, but you never know, he might not want the publicity! You always have to think of the worst-case scenario in my profession—maybe he is on the lam, or homeless, or may have some other reason for not wanting his cover blown.

Back home, I reached my friend Frith, to tell her what happened with the car—the last she knew we had been the victims of grand theft auto. Kate spilled cereal all over the floor. I talked to my mother-in-law as well, and my roommate from college. By the time I finished these calls, the house was looking great, or as great as it tends to get around here. Not company-ready, but ready for the cleaning lady to come.

Then it was time to go cuddle with the dog, who was lying on the futon. I feel bad that she has gotten ignored a bit, understandably, since the baby's arrival. Soon Kate's existence on the planet will be worth it for Addie, as Kate gives Addie increasingly more love (and table scraps). Meanwhile, the cat is starved for love since we've stopped letting her sleep on the bed! I was kneeling down in front of the dog, sort of on all fours by the futon, and the poor cat jumped up on my back for the few minutes I was sitting still petting the dog. Especially since the weather has started getting colder, she is starved for warmth, both physical and emotional, and I am letting her down.

But then the baby started amusing herself with her books, and I had a chance to write in my journal, wahoo! Moose sat on my thighs as I worked at the kitchen table. That didn't last long, about three paragraphs, and Kate needed a diaper change. She was talking about who had tails (she pulls the cat's and dog's once in a while and gets in trouble for it). I figured out a way to give her a tail, by tucking a very fluffy scarf of mine into the back of her pants, and it made her laugh, but just briefly. Then she wanted to hear *Jamberry*, one of her favorite books, so I sat on the futon, with the dog and cat and baby, just us girls.

My friend Melissa called, and we talked a bit, about how fabulous her son is, how her abscess might be returning. Hung up some of my clothes while we talked, and then Kate wanted to use her potty, so it was time to take all of her clothes off, not just her bottoms, and she was successful, and very pleased with herself.

Back in the living room I discovered, while puttering around, that cereal had spilled all over one of the bags still to be unpacked from the trip to D.C., so I got Addie to eat it up. Tried to get a plate of nachos made and eaten before I had to move the car back to a legal spot at 2:00. Pete needed some quiet for his business calls, so I agreed to do some errands, to keep the baby out of the house. Dropped off some dry cleaning, dropped off the film, changed the laundry, all while nursing the baby in the sling, but trying to keep her awake. I hate it when she naps when I'm out doing errands, as I need this quiet time at home, near the keyboard. If she gets lulled by the motion of my walking, which often happens, I feel like I've missed out on that one half-hour or so a day when I can be with my thoughts and get some creative writing done, even if it's just my journal.

After I got home, she went down for a nap pretty easily, and I wrote in my journal until I bored myself. Got caught up to Saturday, which means I wasn't that far behind, but then I fell asleep with the pets. Moose is so good at stealing my consciousness! What a nap aid!

Kate woke up before too long, and I nursed her forever. Pete joined us on the futon for a bit of a cuddle, and he decided to make it official and take a nap. Just as he was settling down to sleep, Loren, our wedding photographer and friend, called. He's no longer engaged. He sounded so sad, and I sounded trite when I told him how he would definitely find someone great in the end, and at some point he would look back at this as a necessary step towards finding the right woman. It sounded so Pollyanna! I talked of my own experience, growing after the divorce, how I never would've been emotionally ready for or worthy of Pete if I hadn't been tempered by the bad times, but Loren didn't sound convinced.

As I talked to him, I sat on the futon and watched Kate try on her hats. I gave her the big mirror, so she could look at herself. It got so cute, so quickly, that I was compelled to finish off the roll of film, and get a good bit into the next one.

After Pete woke up, he wanted to go on a bike ride, so we hitched Cutty up in her seat, got her helmet on (bears! she loves the bears on it!) and took a spin around the park. (Cutty is Kate's nickname; it went from Katherine to Kate to Katelet, because she was so little, to the Cutlet, in a matter of days.) The weather wasn't great, but it always feels so good to be back in the saddle again. If we'd had longer, we would've done two loops. It felt good to get my heartbeat raised, even for such a short while.

Across from me on the subway an older man was fiddling around with a metal pipe he inserted into what looked like the handle of a tennis racket, covered with tape. The handle had six holes in it. He fitted a mouthpiece on the pipe and he started playing. At first I dreaded what I might hear, sure it would be too loud, but it wasn't. It sounded like the sounds the composer of "My Mama Done Told Me" would've made, improvising, before hitting on the melody. It was sort of sweet, sort of jazzy. I noticed the hospital bracelet on his wrist, his unscuffed red suede shoes, the ashy and damaged skin of his ankles. He wore a longshoreman's cap and a gold sweatshirt, and carried a luggage cart with a cane taped on it. I wondered about his story.

So I got into work at 7:15 P.M. and checked with Pete K. to see what there was to do—nothing. Left a message for my friend in Biz Day, Neela, "Hi honey, I'm at work," and read my messages, which included the address of the boy who fell down the elevator shaft at his school and was in critical condition, plus "the pager number for the flack from Jacobi," so I could check his condition. By 8:00 P.M. I had finished reading the list of stories that would appear tomorrow, the updates to that list, the briefs, and Good Friend 1's performance review, as she wanted a reality check.

Talked to Ma to find out what color yarn my college roommate had left for me as a present at Ma's house—she bought me a whole sweater's worth, wow. Ma said it was amethyst, a worsted weight. Pa said it was purple and kind of cord-y. Can't wait to see it!

I told Good Friend 1 that I thought her performance review was much more complimentary than she did, and told her she could meet the challenge they had put before her, to be more productive. She has always been able to meet any challenge, I said, and I meant it. I think she felt better.

At 8:35 read over my e-mails and asked Pete K. if he wanted a brief on the pedestrian killed by a car, but he said no. Then I left messages for all the remaining "Portraits of Grief" contacts, and I think some of those names will have to be crossed out. (If a family member doesn't return three messages, I'm not about to leave a fourth. I think that means they don't want to participate.) I have to say, I'm always sort of hoping the answering machine answers, so I don't have to go through the interviews, and put someone through all those hard questions. Even this long after the disaster, it is painful on both ends of the phone, though you can't compare the discomforts of course, as theirs is full-time, forever.

At 9:17 I got an e-mail from the cops saying a deliveryman had been shot, and it looked like he was going to die ("in critical condition, likely" is how they often word it). I got Ann, one of the Brooklyn stringers, to go out to the scene to get as much information as possible. I always feel lucky when people agree to go out to such places, it can't be pleasant, and I caught her during dinner. While I was waiting to hear back from her, I searched for Pa's war buddy's brother on the Internet, and read the Poynter.org Web site. Here's a headline from today: "Near Crime Scene, Geraldo Treats Hooters Waitresses to Butt Autographs." Things that don't make me proud to be a journalist.

It was time for the 10:00 P.M. news, which I watched, as I always have to, at least the first fifteen minutes. Ann called, and the deliveryman had died. Sad story. The news said he had only been in the States a few years and was sending money home to his family in China, so he could bring them over. At 10:22 I realize I haven't had coffee this shift, and it's too late—if I have it now, it'll just keep me up when I'm trying to fall asleep at 3:00. Come to think of it, I didn't do a great job of getting Kate fed, or myself either today. Watched the 11:00 P.M. news, the first ten minutes.

Ann didn't get much at the scene, although she was able to hear an interview between the dead man's roommate and TV news. I kept trying to find numbers for the owner of the restaurant, but the cops gave out the wrong name of the establishment at first. I hate calling people at midnight. Several wrong numbers. I didn't get as much as I had hoped for the midnight deadline.

ON THE JOB

JENNY KALES, 36
New York, New York
registered nurse in palliative care

9:30 A.M. Hit the floors with Doreen and Rebecca and start at 11 East to see the first of seven really sick patients. Sam is on a ventilator after suffering an MI and a catastrophic CVA and will most likely die. He has suffered quite a bit over the past few years, in any event, and we are planning on having a family meeting with his ex-wife and family today to discuss what to do in his best interest. He looks comfortable so we move on to 6 West where we have three patients. I go to see Mattie who is my favorite. She is a stout little black woman in her late seventies who had polio when she was two and has been blind and suffered right-sided weakness ever since. She thinks she is still in her thirties and that she has to get back to work taking care of peoples' children. She also used to sing in her church choir and it is quite evident because when she gets disturbed she sings to comfort herself. Even though her eyes are damaged they still sparkle and there is an aura around her that is indescribable. Topping it off, she is addicted to green apple Blow-Pops. I would never encounter someone as wonderful as Mattie if I was not a nurse.

Afghan American Comfortable in Both Cultures

"*I*'m tired of being portrayed as this tragic figure caught between two worlds. I love both cultures. I like being on the borderlines. Being a Muslim and Afghan doesn't get in the way of being American." An educator, pursuing her doctoral degree in literature. A watcher. "I was one of those odd kids who stared a lot." A healer. Her scholarship and work as a poet, film scholar, and editor reflect a common theme—"The point is to build bridges; to show Afghanistan is not so foreign, it's not so far away." And it's not all about war. "Before, Afghan Americans stayed low key, in part because of the political purgings in Afghanistan and because they were trying to figure out their own ethnic issues. After September 11, they realized they had to come out as Americans. And Americans reached out to them as well." When she finishes her dissertation, she plans to travel with her father to the country she left as a baby. She is excited about the growing dialogue between Afghan diaspora and homeland. "Now Kabul and New York are so close, you can hear the gossip going back and forth."

ZOHRA SAED, 27, *Brooklyn, New York*

12:30 A.M. I just completed grading a large load of papers for the Arab American Literature class. The students are so eager to learn about Arab culture and literature. They are confused by the combination of Arab American— for some it is an oxymoron, for others it is something that has been part of their lives since birth, so normal is this title for them that they don't have the words to articulate it. It just is. But despite this excitement for my students, I'm exhausted.

I am at my computer desk enjoying my fast Internet connection. I write e-mails to take a break from all the grading. I've got four piles of papers from four classes that I am teaching this semester. Now, I'm looking at the picture of myself for the Ping Chong *Undesirable Elements Reunion Show* and thinking, "Hey, I'm cute!" Chong is one of the top Asian American playwrights. I met him in 2000 when he was interviewing people for his play, which features the life stories of marginalized American voices. As an Afghan American in 2000, I was quite a marginalized voice. I wish I hadn't quit the show the way

I did last minute, but I couldn't revisit the lines I had said about my life in 2000. I couldn't return to that old skin, not after what has happened in my life in just the past two years.

In 2000 I was light and thought I was going to float away. My journal entries from that time are so happy and bubbly. My family was everything to me and I was going to finish my MFA in poetry. Everything was just peachy. I can't imagine myself being that same exuberant and naive person. Besides, I didn't want to go through talking about my mother. It makes me sick to my stomach to talk about her . . . and everything from 2000, even my poetry manuscript is about my family, about how my parents met. Since she ran off and abandoned us—and took my dad's life's savings and my money with her, so she could marry some guy who was my age—that kind of ruined the whole mother image I had of her. These past four months have been about putting my life together after my own mother sabotaged the very beginning of my career. My father was devastated and so was my brother. She left without telling anyone, only called me from a pay phone to tell me that it was up to me to take care of everyone and she didn't want to do it anymore. So I had to tell my dad and my brother. How heartbreaking . . . but no one's heart broke as profoundly as my father's, who never suspected and who trusted because she was his precious wife . . .

How can a mother do this? Aren't mothers and daughters supposed to be enveloped in one skin? But apparently she was the cannibalistic kind and did everything possible to get in the way of me trying to complete this Ph.D. in peace. Her dream for me was to be a businesswoman with nice clothes and a nice car. She thought writers were messy people who carried two book bags and never wore sharp clothes. She didn't feel that a writer or even a scholar was worth boasting about. So, I found out since she's left me with all this mess to clean up—her lies, her closet. She has been telling everyone that I was a pharmacist with a house in Manhattan Beach. And the neighbors believed her because I was barely home to vouch for myself. Goodness, what a deep hole I fell into and I just thought I was going to write about grading papers at midnight. Anyway, I'm too tired to deal with this betrayal stuff lodged inside my heart.

8:00 A.M. Wake up to alarm. Wake up my brother so he can get to his classes. Duty done, fall back asleep for another hour.

9:00 A.M. Alarm goes off again. Find out that my brother is just waking up now too! Guilt-trip him into hurrying up and going to his physics class.

10:00 A.M. After shower, grade papers as my hair dries. I'm too lazy to get the hair dryer out.

11:00 A.M. Rush to put on makeup. Surma swept across my eyes and smudged here and there for the smokey look. I'm dressed all in black to go with my overpriced leather jacket.

12:00 P.M. Stuck on the Q train to Manhattan. I have forty-five minutes to get to Midtown from Brooklyn and I'm praying that I get there on time. I teach an Arab American literature class at Hunter College. I've had the flu for a week so I had to cancel last week's classes. If I miss today, it will set us back a month!

1:00–2:00 P.M. Finished returning student papers. Half of the class is out today, I suppose expecting me to be sick again. This class is great. There is a good mixture of ethnic and religious backgrounds: Russian, Arab, Pakistani, Hispanic, Indian, Jewish, and Polish. This is enough of a mix to have healthy discussions, which allow them to make cross-cultural connections. Three students presented Kahlil Gibran's poem, "Dead Are My People," to the class. My Palestinian American student, who is on the panel, admitted that she did not like poetry until she read this poem. The poem was written for the Lebanese people who had starved during the WWI blockade of Lebanon's ports by the Allies. In the poem, Kahlil Gibran expresses how he would rather be an ear of corn to feed a dying child than live in the riches and comfort he is surrounded by now. He expresses how his role as a poet does nothing concrete to help his people. It can only carry the message for others to help his people. As a Palestinian, this student felt a deep connection with this poem and how she felt for Palestinians back in her homeland.

One of the questions that the panel had to think about was what made the poem they chose Arab American. The three Arab American panelists said that it was this political awareness of their people's struggle back home. Being Arab American meant more than preserving the food and language of their grandparents, it also meant remaining connected to the political issues of their ancestral land. This was particularly interesting because, up until now, we had been speaking about the importance of language in connecting a people to their culture. These women said that language or culture didn't matter—as long as they remained politically conscious of what was going on back home, this is what made one Arab American. This activist strain—to always bring attention to and be the voice for their people—is what made a person Arab American. These were very poignant remarks made by such young students.

A Russian American student said that she agreed because what made her mother Russian was her connection to the politics of what went on in her homeland. Then, I had them read out loud Etel Adnan's "Beirut Hell Express." They read the ranting poem of this lesbian Lebanese American poet, and what they expect from female poets and female Middle Eastern poets was shattered. They are not comfortable reading all of the gritty parts of the poem. But being uncomfortable is a good thing for a class. We must have busted at least some stereotypes in just one poem—not bad. OK, so the poem is six pages long and a mouthful with so many references to world history that the students need to footnote every other line, which is exactly what they had to do for their homework.

2:00–3:30 P.M. Teaching West Asian American Film and Literature. Race to the other side of the building and sneak a cookie from the office because I don't have time to eat between classes. As I zip through the halls, I go over my lesson plan in my head. Because this class is an upper level course and not an introduction like my earlier class, the students are always on top of the game and go through the material much quicker. Here they compare Adnan to Lawrence Joseph's "Sand Nigger" about racism shown towards Arabs, which he resists. In a sense, this poem is about his growing political consciousness and his connection to other minority groups. The class brings up the point that silence plays a large role in this poem. His father and grandfather expect him to stay quiet and passive despite the racism outside. He resists this kind of silencing that immigrants are known for. He rejects his family's insistence for him not to rock the boat. Then we compare D. H. Melhem's poetry about her mother to Naomi Shihab-Nye's poetry about her father. The students bring up the importance of seeds in exilic poetry to discuss how they feel scattered but also ready to grow in a new land. Shihab-Nye's father, after feeling nostalgic for figs, finally plants a fig tree in Texas to demonstrate his settling into this new country. Roots and seeds, they say, are important metaphors in many of these poems. This class always runs over the designated time and I enjoy their perspectives.

4:00–5:00 P.M. Ran to audiovisual to reserve a video projector and screen for the speaker I have invited to discuss and screen her experimental videos. She is Lebanese/Afghan American. This should cover all of my bases, since the West Asian American Film and Literature class encompasses the works of Arab, Iranian, and Afghan Americans. It is the first class to teach this combination of ethnic American communities in New York. This is what makes it exciting, but it also makes me nervous because I don't have too many people to ask for advice.

5:30 P.M. Met my friend, and former professor, Moustafa, for coffee in Park Slope. I asked him, since his area of research is migratory Islam, if there was such a thing as a Muslim aesthetics and he said that there was none because Islam no longer had a central civilization or artistic school as it had in medieval times. Now everything was scattered and it was only best to discuss regional Islam, so the Islam of Afghanistan would be different than Malaysian Islam. The notion that there is one cohesive system or that the Muslim world is monolithic is not accurate. This makes sense because so much of the Zoroastrian tradition has been interwoven into the Islam of Afghanistan and Iran. This was my important lesson for the day.

There is so much I need to learn, although I'm learning so much through teaching—more than I would have if I were just a student finishing up coursework for the Ph.D. Teaching really keeps me connected to the grassroots and keeps the mind on its toes, because my students are always surprising me with questions that I never had to face before. Academia is a sheltered place and everyone is politically correct. It is nice to be faced with non-PC questions, just to make sure I can handle questions from all angles. Teaching has also taught me the value of asking questions. Before I became a teacher, I remained very quiet in class. Now I've become quite vocal. I admire Moustafa because he is a public intellectual and balances the sheltering world of academia with the outside world and politics. He's been an important role model for me because his writing combines a creative voice with scholarly material. Because the topic of my research is so close to my heart, I am continually trying to strike this balance in my work.

7:00 P.M. On the way home from the train, I run into a Turkish lady who was friends with my mother. I tell her the truth about what happened. Somehow, her broken English and my broken Turkish help us communicate on a darkening street in Sheepshead Bay. She feels sad for me and tells me, "Don't worry, I'm mother." She gives me her number and I'm not sure how I feel. I'm embarrassed that my mother did this—left me a trail of lies and deceit, which I have to clean up. I told Moustafa what happened, too, and it wasn't as burdensome, the act of telling, as it was when I told this old friend of my mother's. When I told Moustafa it was between friends. When I told this lady, it was to clean up a big mess. Maybe, this is what made me feel so overburdened after speaking to her. Her pity for me was burdensome as well. All I wanted to do by coming down this street was to buy some bread for dinner. Now, I'm a mess again.

8:00 P.M. Michelle, my good friend and neighbor of twenty years (so we grew up together) came down for dinner. We made mac & cheese and read each other's fortunes. It is how we unwind after work. We communicate through cards, addressing topics that we may not have brought up had it not been for our divination toys.

9:00 P.M. My father comes home. Michelle and I are still playing with our tarot cards. We have gotten close like sisters. She has taken care of me through these difficult months and made sure I didn't feel lonely in a house which had always been too full, rather than as empty as it has been these past months.

10:00 P.M. Michelle goes upstairs to her apartment. I sit with my father and watch the news. During commercial breaks we process the past. I don't tell him about the Turkish lady I ran into. I don't tell him that I cried as I walked home, because these things make him feel helpless and he worries about me so much already. I put on a cheerful face and listen to him. Before he goes to sleep, I crawl in next to him on the couch and lean my head on his shoulders without saying a word. He doesn't ask me what is wrong. He pats my head and I am soothed by his big, soft hands. I loved my father so much as a little girl that I denied ever being born of a mother. I would put my hands on my hips and say in a bold voice that I had popped out of my father's mouth. So funny that I said this, now that I've come to a point where I've disowned my mother and my mother has disowned me. These things that I said as a joke when I was little now seem to carry a deeper meaning.

11:00 P.M. I grade papers for the Literature for Young People course I teach at Brooklyn College. We have been reading psychoanalytic criticism of fairy tales. This is what I come across in a student's paper: "Through the planting of a tree, she (Cinderella) keeps the good-mother's image within her." This is a striking sentence. When will I be able to plant a magical tree, which will allow me to keep alive the good-mother image within me?

FEEDBACK

5:45 P.M. I step into the Read Café, take a seat on one of the stools at the counter, and say hello to John, Maurice, and Lawrence. It's warm inside and smells of muffins and coffee. I love the fact that after a long day of working here, I leave smelling of coffee and sugar. John gives me a small cup of coffee and I lighten it with milk, then sit back down and flip through a copy of *Time Out New York* while I wait for the line at the counter to thin. When it does, I ask if I could leave a couple copies of a magazine I'm published in with the lit mags up front. Read is both a used bookstore and a café, with a large selection of art, fashion, and literary magazines for people to browse while they have their coffee. Lawrence says, "Can I read it?" and takes the magazine from my hand. After a few minutes of staring at the page he frowns and says, "I don't get it. I don't like it. I can't understand it," and throws it at me. My boss throws my magazine at my head. And then he adds, "and I hate Sylvia Plath" and turns and walks away.

JASMINE D. WAGNER, 24, *Brooklyn, New York*;
coffee barista

GIRL TALK

1:30 P.M. Finally leaving the house. I can't imagine how Perla (my best friend) manages with her two little girls. Perla's taking her first mommy vacation when we go to New York. She and Swarn (another girlfriend) have already arranged to sit together on the flight to JFK. Tommy (another girlfriend from high school) is getting married in upstate New York. I'm so excited! My husband Anthony says it's going to be one big estrogen fest on the plane and that he'd love to be a fly on the wall. This is how my husband imagines our conversation: "How's your uterus, honey?" "My breasts are big, girl!" Silly man.

PEI P. STEWART, 28, *Dallas, Texas*;
computer teacher

BUSTED!

6:16 P.M. Caught, eating dinner in front of the TV! When we lived in Greensboro, we got a lot of "crunchy" points just because we were vegetarian, but here in Asheville that doesn't carry much weight. I feel like everyone we meet here eats all organic, avoids all dairy foods and sugar, doesn't own a TV, breastfeeds their children 'til they go to kindergarten, goes to the acupuncture clinic, and has a well-defined spiritual path. I always make sure that people who visit our home understand that the 36-inch screen TV was a gift from Jay's parents (the same people who gave Flannery the life-size Barbie).

CHRISTINE ROKEBY-JACKSON, 40, *Asheville, North Carolina*;
speech transliterator

WABI-SABI

5:30 P.M. Mizuguchi-sensei, my *Shodo* teacher, waits for me at his desk in the school office. He is probably in his early forties, but carries the wild yet innocent look of a child. Hair in slight disarray, always speed walking from one place to the next, he remains in a state of calculated disorder. In the *Shodo* practice room, however, he is focused only on the strokes he makes with his brush. He moves the brush deliberately and without hesitation. A peacefulness comes over him as he lets everything else go. Today I am practicing the Japanese *Hiragana* characters for the syllables: *ka, ki, ku, ke,* and *ko*. First, *ka*. Holding my brush in midair and perpendicular to the page, I think, "*Wabi-sabi*. Peaceful thoughts, peaceful actions." I study Mizuguchi-sensei's *Shodo* for a few more seconds and imagine forming the same precise and fluid strokes. Finally I touch the tip of my brush to the paper and, for a brief moment, it becomes an extension of my arm, body, and mind. A window into Japanese culture cracks open and I catch a glimpse of understanding.

SARAH MERRILL, 28, *Yawatahama, Ehime, Japan*; **English teacher**

IT'S ONLY ROCK 'N ROLL

11:45 A.M. Was just in the copy room and asked one of the lawyers whether he knew of any connection for tickets to see the Stones at the Hard Rock in Las Vegas. I really want to go. This other lawyer was in there, and he goes, "Wow, I never would have figured you for a rock 'n roller." When I asked what he WOULD have figured me for, he said, "Barry Manilow." Yowch. I must be doing something wrong. I gotta change my image or something. That's harsh.

JUDI EHRLICH, 45, *Santa Monica, California*; **insolvency administrator**

PROGRESS

As I work I see my grandbaby Patrick's beautiful face in my mind's eye. So hard to live away from him; already miss him from the weekend and won't see him 'til Thanksgiving. By then, I will have passed papers on the condo and they can see it. My son is a bit sad about my selling his childhood home but, then again, he's not there when I'm shoveling the dreaded driveway by myself. But I understand how he feels because I feel it myself. A kind of pain in losing a bit of one's history and having it only in one's memory. But hell, isn't that what progress is about!!!

LUCILLE A. MAGLIOZZI, 63, *Lexington, Massachusetts*;
world-music booking agent and teacher

ℱAITH

Up at 1:39. My seven-year-old daughter, Sara, is restless. I hear her rolling around in bed. It is hard to not get up and check her every ten minutes. It is hard to believe the results from the sleep study we received. How does she survive? How does anyone stop breathing for anywhere from 157–211 seconds three to four times an hour? It seems unreal. I can see her from my bed, so I know she is breathing. I want to check on her but I resist. If I am to show my faith I need to believe that my prayers will be answered. I pray each night when she goes to bed that the right thing will happen. The right thing would be to continue to breathe and break out of the obstructive sleep apnea. Hers is just so much more dangerous because of her heart defect. I need to stop thinking about this because it just makes me worry. I love her so much. She shouldn't have to suffer.

BRAILEE SMITH, 42, *American Fork, Utah*;
Mormon and mother of two special-needs children

Inmate #193053

*H*er crime: second degree murder. Her routine for the past six years: 6:00 A.M., wake up. 6:30, breakfast. 7:00–3:00, work as a data entry clerk. 5:00, dinner. 5:30–9:00, college classes towards an associate's degree. 10:00 P.M., locked in her cell. Her day is punctuated by mandatory counts. "Nobody moves until the count clears." The prison offers counseling sessions. She went to grief counseling, but also attended groups on abuse and other issues. "I had never been abused so at first I thought, why would I take a course on that. Then I started thinking, if I took a group that had nothing to do with me, if I wanted people to understand me, then I needed to be more empathetic." She grew up in a family of five children. Raised in a small Midwestern town by middle-class parents. She's always loved crafts—now she's the "Martha Stewart of Shakopee," making cards for her fellow inmates, and blankets to donate to charity. When she's forty-seven, she'll be released from prison and would like to work as a mental health advocate. Shakopee is a minimum security facility that houses maximum security offenders. There are no barbed wire fences. "There are people who say this isn't a real prison . . . but if you're taken away from those you love, it's punishment."

JANET R. OLSON, 35, *Shakopee, Minnesota*

Here it is October 15. I should be at home preparing a birthday celebration for Jordyn's seventh birthday next Tuesday. Instead, I am sitting in my prison cell remembering the day I gave birth to her and how I'd give anything to hold her in my arms again. If only. .

If only I had realized I needed help.

If only David had stayed home from work that day.

"If only's" just don't matter anymore. I can't go back to that fateful day. So June 1, 1996 will forever be the last day of the life I dreamed of. The last day I spent with my two precious daughters, Hannah and Jordyn. Not only did I defy nature by outliving my children, I betrayed my children when they needed me most. While suffering from undiagnosed post-partum psychosis, I attempted suicide and was responsible for my children's deaths. This is my reality.

Six years have passed and not a single day goes by when I don't think of them. Not just at my loss. But what I took from them. The years they had ahead of them and the lives they should have lived. The joy they brought to all who met them. They say that when you lose a parent, you lose your past; when you lose a child, you lose your future. How incredibly profound.

I had to ask forgiveness and truly believe it was granted. My entire family has stood by me with so much love and support that there are times when I have to wonder where I'd be at in my life if not for them. I often wonder where my strength comes from. With the parents I had growing up, I knew I already had a strong foundation to build on; and that made all the difference. My parents' love not only gave me life at birth, but again during those first months at the mental facility when I had lost all hope of ever living again.

I made it through my divorce. I even made it through my sentencing. When the prosecutor suggested I had taken their lives as a way of ending a financial burden, I was speechless. I did not understand myself how it could happen. I loved both my children more than life. The only words I could find the courage to say on my behalf was a sob-filled "I loved my children." I did not take my case to a hearing. I could not put my family through any more pain. Although I accepted a plea bargain which charged me with Second Degree Intentional Murder, it was not done because I was guilty of murder or even intended it. It was because I had to take responsibility for my actions even when they occurred during a psychotic break. My parents taught me to believe in justice. They taught me right from wrong. If there is truly any justice in sentencing me to twenty-five years in prison, then I hope that the memory of my children is never forgotten by those who stand in judgment.

I adored my children. I know that prior to June 1, I had done everything I possibly could to make sure that they were safe, happy, and healthy, and more importantly, loved. If this could happen to me, then I know it can and will happen again. That to me is unjust. I pray that one day society acknowledges that mental illness is not separate from physical illness. Just as there is physical health, there is mental health as well. Mental illness is not simply a term concocted by a defense attorney as a way to deny their client's guilt or excuse their behavior. I do not deny responsibility. I do not want an excuse. I just want to help prevent this needless tragedy from ever destroying another mother's dreams.

With all that said, I now begin this day as I have done for the past five years. I will go to work. I will go to school. I will take time to remember my beautiful girls. And I will remember that it is through my thoughts that I create the experiences in my life, moment by moment. I alone have the ability to experience freedom as if I were not confined to a prison cell. The freedom to create and to live again. The ability to make a difference even from a prison cell.

HUSBANDS

7:40 P.M. I broach the idea of quitting my job with my husband, whose first question to me is, "What would we do without your salary?" Way to be supportive, thanks hon. I know he can't help it. He worries a lot about money so it's tops on his mind. I just wish he would have said, "Whatever you need to do is fine, we'll find a way to make it work." I'd like to think I would have said that to him if he were so depressed about his job.

ALYSON M. MAGLIOZZI, 27, *Chelmsford, Massachusetts* (MARRIED TWO YEARS); **e-mail marketing program manager**

My husband calls again and asks if I'm ready for him to come home. What does that mean? Oh yeah, he wants SEX! What else could it be? I love to make love to my husband but please . . . He offered me a massage but what does he want from me? Men. Gotta love them for their simplicity. Give them sex and you can get anything you want right after. Love you, honey. Luckily, he's a great father, amazing husband, and terrific at many other things. OK, I'm harsh at times, he's had a hard day, a quickie will do. Ha ha. I'm in trouble for this one.

JACQUELYN PRUSSING, 34, *Staten Island, New York* (MARRIED FIVE YEARS); **children's portrait photographer**

1:30 A.M. Lily wakes up crying. I mumble to Dave to go give her a bottle of milk. Last night I did it and she wanted to be rocked for half an hour. He reaches for his glasses and they fall off the nightstand. I place the bottle on his chest. It sits there for a minute and I have to wake him again. By this time I am awake and think I should have done it myself.

KRISTIN MARTINSON, 32, *Portland, Oregon* (MARRIED NINE YEARS); **at-home mom and elementary school teacher**

8:15 P.M. Home. Laundry. Home again, then heating up leftovers and getting ready for my nightly ritual of calling my husband, who lives three states away in Vermont. We talked about my job and reviewed the cat's daily ritual. I worry my husband isn't eating right, and I feel sad that I'm not with him to share in the ups and downs of his job. We know that this working arrangement is only temporary. At first, it was easier to be away from him while I was getting used to the hardest job I have had. I don't feel that way now, and I miss his being next to me when I go about my chores at night.

I don't feel lonely so much as lonesome. I know that my husband is by my side at all times.

LINDA LEE LANDRIGAN, 42, *Hartford, Vermont and New York, New York* (MARRIED TWELVE YEARS); **editor of** *Alfred Hitchcock's Mystery Magazine*

9:20 A.M. Milt (my significant other) just came in to the living room and was so surprised to see me sewing. He said he'd never seen me sew before. He went and got his camera and took several pictures for me to give to Evan, showing his grandmother sewing his "piddow" cases. Milt *has* seen me sew before. I've made little things for his great grandson! He's just forgotten. Why do men want to take pictures of people doing tasks? Milt will call me to come take his picture sawing a tree or painting or building something . . . so funny. I'm literally giggling out loud all alone here, remembering the time he wanted his picture taken when he was using his chain saw. The shot is from the back as he's hunched over the offending tree stump and the smoke is billowing out behind him from between his legs! I post it on the fridge from time to time. It always makes me laugh!

JONEAL SCULLY, 63, *Charlottesville, Virginia* (TOGETHER BY CHOICE FOR EIGHTEEN YEARS); **personality profiler and handwriting analyst**

7:00 P.M. Tomorrow is the seventh anniversary of my husband's death. I'm remembering Bob and what those last days of his illness were like and it still hurts. Yet I have a new life with a good man and days filled with love and laughter. It's a bit of a wonder to me that one thing doesn't erase the other. They exist side by side.

ALYCE HEMAN, 66, *Skokie, Illinois* (MARRIED TO FIRST HUSBAND THIRTY-SEVEN YEARS; MARRIED TO CURRENT HUSBAND FOUR YEARS); **retired schoolteacher**

5:00 P.M. Feed the dog and get dinner ready. Barbecue. Gives hubby something to do. He sometimes gets on my nerves. Retirement is great for the guy but not for the woman who has had the run of the house all her life and all of a sudden there is this guy who tells her what to do! Maybe I should tell him more what to do! He needs another hobby besides me.

MARION MAHN, 67, *Franklin Lakes, New Jersey* (MARRIED FORTY-FOUR YEARS); **homemaker**

Lawyer for MTV Networks Latin America

One of those kids who was always at the top of her class, she saw law as the most practical path to success. Loves the rush of fighting for the upper hand, closing the deal. The job brings out her adversarial side but she tries to turn it off with friends. "People who know me socially have a hard time imagining me as a lawyer. People who know me as an attorney can't see me as easygoing. It's an issue with women lawyers; you have to have a split personality." Raised in a conservative Cuban American community in Miami, she wanted to party, travel, get away. "My parents called me *pata caliente* and *caballito ensillado*, literally 'hot foot' and 'saddled horse.' I was always ready to go!" She attended Duke, then returned briefly to Miami to help run the family business. After Columbia Law School, even the considerable allure of NYC couldn't keep her from moving back home. Time and distance gave her a new appreciation of family and familiar things. "I didn't realize how different we were. I missed the Cuban coffee, and people speaking Spanish in the background." A recovering perfectionist. Loving, but also moody. ("That's your warning.") Still single, but always looking for a good man . . . "even if it's only *para pasar el tiempo*."

SIRA VECIANA-MUIÑO, 29, *Miami Beach, Florida*

12:02 A.M. Return movie to Blockbuster.

12:07 A.M. Arrive home. Don't even take the laptop out of the trunk, there's no way I'm doing any work at this time. I don't know why I even bother sometimes. Home is home, and I should keep it that way, but sometimes, there's just so much that I feel guilty . . .

Pick up mail, haven't picked up mail in a couple of days. *No es por nada,* but why the hell do I get so much junk mail? I can't afford to get any more credit cards! No wonder there are so many people declaring bankruptcy. It's like they freaking shove them down your throat.

In elevator: Why is it so difficult for people to make eye contact? I mean, why do people go out of the way to not look you in the eye when in the elevator. Like, how difficult is it to be, "Good evening . . . eighth floor . . . have a good night." Like what the fuck, we live in the same building, why go through so much trouble just to avoid eye contact? Are we that consumed with ourselves that we can't even take the time to be polite, as if we regret the time and energy that it takes to maintain a relationship, even if it's just a superficial neighborly relationship—or is it that we just fear the consequences of letting someone else into our lives?

Remove medieval torture device (strapless bra). Can't believe I've gone fifteen, sixteen hours all day wearing that thing.

Pick up dumbbells and do some quick reps. Check out if *Daily Show* is on at 12 or 12:30.

12:29 A.M. Finished doing dumbbells. Take a really quick shower to catch the end of *Daily Show*.

12:31 A.M. Wow, I really need to start doing some situps. I'm getting so freaking flabby. I haven't had a gut like this since the Freshmen 15.

I need a pedicure. Mental note: Call Sonia (best friend) tomorrow so I can get Alicia's (the manicurist's) number and make an appointment for a pedicure and manicure before the Video Music Awards Latin America (VMALA) show.

12:44 A.M. Sit down to fold laundry and watch *Daily Show*. OK, I really need to stop being so cheap and get rid of some of these underwear and socks . . . *dan vergüenza* . . . but who has the time or the desire to go underwear shopping?

I'm so disappointed . . . what the hell happened to Jon Stewart? You can't have a whole episode w/o him in it?!? This guy is so funny, and he's a hottie too. If the men in Miami had that kind of wit and personality, I probably would not still be single.

1:00 A.M. See what else there is to watch . . . I guess I'll leave the *Drew Carey* reruns on. Not much else on.

1:16 A.M. Put away laundry.

1:30 A.M. Get ready for bed, set alarm for 7:15. Put some hardener on my nails.

1:44 A.M. Lights off.

7:15 A.M. Wake up!!! Ah fuck it, just ten more minutes, snooze alarm.

8:09 A.M. Actually get out of bed . . . so much for just ten minutes. Heat up *café con leche* and get stuff ready for work.

8:27 A.M. Fix hair, help straighten it, take out frizz. As Sonia would say, what an optimist. Sometimes I'm not sure why I insist on going against nature. If the hair is curly why must we have it straight . . . you're never happy with what you have. Ain't that the truth!?! The grass is always greener on the other side.

OK, why is it that these balcony repair guys every day ride up that little elevator thing at the exact time that I'm getting dressed. It's like a freaking free peep show. I swear they must be timing me. If it weren't for the idiot repair guys I had in here last month, I would actually be able to close my blinds and not have to worry about flashing the balcony repair guys.

8:49 A.M. Get ready to leave and go to work.

8:55 A.M. I'm in the car and on my way to work! *Ay* Mami, (sigh) . . . damn I miss you. Hanging from my rearview mirror is this cute little pair of *alpargatas*, I believe they're called espadrilles in English, striped in yellow and red, the colors of the Spanish flag (and the flag of Catalunya, the region of Spain my mother was from). They're like a little miniature replica of traditional Spanish shoes. They used to hang from the rearview mirror of Mami's car. The little charm had been given to her by an old childhood friend in her hometown, back in 1999. She had met up with me there as I was ending a two-month backpacking trip in Europe. We had had so much fun. After Mami passed away two and a half months ago, and after Papi managed to total her car, I had swiped this little charm from her rearview mirror before any of my siblings or father could. None of them really knew what its origin was, but I did. Papi was crazy jealous of this old childhood friend, so my mom never told him (nor did he really ever ask). It was like our little secret. It's funny how the days go on and life just kind of continues and you start to forget . . . Every day I get in my car and I glance at it and I think of her and I remember her and sometimes I miss her and sometimes I cry and sometimes I laugh out loud and sometimes I wonder how she could be gone.

No es por nada, pero mira que hay gente estúpida en este mundo. If you're blocking the driveway, why don't you move your freaking car instead of just standing there and smiling as you perfectly see that I can't get through? *No, no, te digo* . . . the future of this country is bleak . . .

As I'm driving to work: I live in this beautiful apartment on the beach w/ an amazing panoramic view of the ocean, and I didn't even notice it this morning. I get so caught up in getting ready and out for another long day at work that I don't even get a chance to look out the window and admire the view.

Put on some medication for those pimples (thank you stress) and some moisturizer for those bags and wrinkles I'm getting under my eyes.

9:17 A.M. Arrived at work. That took a little longer than usual. I wonder what was causing all that extra traffic. Ahh, the usual smokers already outside. They've barely started their day! There must be a lot of stress going around the office.

Into the elevator . . . fifth floor . . . Damn, where's my security card to get into the office? I'm going to have to wait for someone to come in or out. Thank God, someone's coming out. That was quick.

Say hi to Ana, my boss's assistant, on the way into my little cubbyhole. She sometimes greets me with an amazing cup of *café con leche*. (She makes it from scratch, not from instant coffee the way I do. What can I say? Sometimes you gotta take some short cuts!) Ana usually comes in to chat, but today there's no coffee and no chat. She must be busy. I guess I'll make my own coffee.

9:25 A.M. Weave through the maze of cubicles into our brightly decorated kitchen. No offense, but I think the office decor is growing old. They've got these bright colors, orange, red, yellow, lime green, tons of pictures of kids, on the floor, walls, everywhere. It's the Nickelodeon floor, but sometimes it's just a little too cheerful.

Take out the espresso packet, add the water to the machine, break out the sugar packets, heat up the milk. Make myself another *café con leche*. I know, I'm addicted, but it's just so yummy . . .

Back into the cubbyhole. Close the door so I can get some quiet.

My office looks like I'm drowning in a sea of paper! I really need to clean up these stacks of papers and periodicals. If this mess is a reflection of my life right now, it is one scary reality.

Sit down and get through those million-and-one work e-mails and reply.

10:15 A.M. Still reviewing work e-mails. Muted the TV (I guess at some point I turned it on, just as I turned on the computer) and put in my Bruce CD—live from NY.

11:10 A.M. Reading and reviewing business and industry news—*NY Times, FindLaw, GigaLaw, Broadcasting & Cable, Multichannel News International.* Gotta stay on top of what's going on. You never know when it will give you that extra edge. I really try to get through all these daily e-mails, but sometimes they just pile up. It's funny b/c when I'm swamped I just read the headlines and move the e-mails into a folder titled "Pending Reading" under the faulty notion that I will actually go back and read some of the articles. Don't know who I'm kidding.

Damn, amazing how much incompetence there is in this world, even w/in my own department. I'm crazy looking for this one file, and it's not in the cabinet nor in the file index, so you'd think it may be in those boxes of files sent to storage earlier in the year, but no . . . there's no way of telling. How can you send boxes of files to storage and not keep an index of which files you sent, or some kind of guide to which boxes contain which files. UGH! And not to mention that we've got lawyers that don't question things and make mistakes and overlook things although that's what they're being paid for. OK. Sira, some patience. We're all under a lot of stress . . . cut everyone, including yourself, some slack. It's only 11:27 in the morning and it's been a long two to three weeks and we still have nine days to the show. Patience.

11:32 A.M.–12:45 P.M. Reviewed further work e-mails and responded re: VMALA issues. Limo agreements, music clearance, guest releases, synch licenses, venue agreements, grant applications, guest shuttles, caterers, Red Bull—Ahha, gotta love that Red Bull—talent contracts, Shakira, Avril Lavigne, Maná, Santana, Anastasia . . . It'd be nice if some of their attorneys and managers actually returned calls or replied to e-mails. (Who the hell is Anastasia anyways?) Oh, and my favorite . . . hotel barters!!! Agh!?! Move ten rooms to this night, move four rooms to this other night . . . Four years of college and three years of law school, and I'm trying to make sure hotel rooms are being booked properly.

12:40–12:45 P.M. Prepare for conference call at 1 w/ employment attorney in Brazil, to go over our standard employment contracts and provisions for executives and high-level employees in Brazil.

1:15 P.M. Stepping out for lunch (well, technically, not stepping out, just going upstairs to the sixth floor kitchen) since the conference call got postponed 'til 2. Funny, we've got a kitchen on the fifth floor, but we all go up and use the sixth floor kitchen. I guess we all prefer the windows with a view.

Quickly heat up sandwich in kitchen and chitchat w/ coworkers. Just the usual suspects. Talk about the sniper. Who the hell is he and why is he doing this? War on Iraq—no doubt that we've become a nation of followers. Nobody even questions why we need to attack them.

Mental note: Things to do. Call Alicia and set up manicure and pedicure appointment for Saturday. Meet up w/ Sonia at Barnes & Noble to research and discuss four-year plan. Set up dinner plans w/ Papi for b-day on Saturday, coordinate w/ Anita, Vicki, and all to meet up for dinner.

Heating up leftover half of a *croqueta preparada* sandwich. How old is this anyways? A couple of old kiwis and a bag of chips. Not so bad.

2:15 P.M. Conference call w/ Brazilian counsel . . . Nothing I didn't already know. No real change in the law, but I guess it never hurts to check and double-check w/ local counsel. Kinda like an insurance policy on my work.

3:00 P.M. Trying to decide whether to have weekly Tuesday pool nights. Just spoke to Sonia, found out her mom is not doing well. They think her hepatitis B might have complicated to something else, but of course she hasn't been going to the doctor regularly for checkups. Why are people so scared of going to the doctor? If they only went on time they could prevent a lot of problems. *Pero, bueno* . . . funny how irrational fear can be. I guess maybe they fear the news they may get. Or maybe they're just trying to avoid the inevitable . . . Mental note: do some research on the Web and see if you can find anything on hepatitis B.

3:35 P.M. Just got the great news that TOPA signed the contract. Unbelievable considering they bitched and complained to me yesterday for sending them a new draft of the contract to review and sign.

3:45 P.M. Finished my cover-your-ass e-mail to file on employment contracts in Brazil. It's truly amazing how you can get many things done so much quicker by just orally communicating your findings or your questions, or, more importantly, your advice, to the pertinent individuals, but you end up spending three times as long by putting it into writing so that you can have some backup. It seems I spend lots of my time writing "c-ya" e-mails, or memo to files. Setting up and preparing for 4 P.M. VMALA meeting.

3:47 P.M. Made manicure and pedicure appointment for Saturday.

Ay dios mio, more barter deals. Talk about running around with our heads cut off. Ten days before show and we are all crazy. Trying to do as many barter deals as we possibly can to keep costs down. Hotel rooms, limos, drinks, food, you name it . . . we can come up with something to barter for it. It's a good thing our brand is such a great thing to associate your brand with . . . makes closing a barter agreement so much easier.

4:28 P.M. Just finished sending e-mail to Papke. Running late for VMALA meeting. Oh, just twenty-eight minutes late.

5:17 P.M. VMALA meeting is over. This show is going to be awesome! The stage design is amazing—it's like this tunnel into the Milky Way, the lineup is awesome, the statuette—a tongue w/ an MTV pierce is just awesome!!! Everyone is so impressive!

5:24 P.M. Back to work. Review more contracts, send more e-mails, remind more people to do what they should have already done. Everyone is so overworked. Gotta make sure things don't fall through the cracks.

7:50 P.M. Trying to decide whether I should just order in food or get the hell out of here.

7:55 P.M. Doing some really quick research on hepatitis B on the Web.

8:15 P.M. Damn, it's freezing in here. I'm going to go get coffee to warm up a bit and walk around a little to *despejarme* and start to move on to another item.

8:40 P.M. Call Papi and make sure he's OK. Make sure he's not completely bored since there's no baseball on TV tonight. Set up a date for his birthday on Saturday, take him out to eat at a real nice restaurant.

9:00 P.M. The rest of the legal department is now out of the office. I'm still stuck here. Can't leave until I really get this shit out and off my desk. Maybe once I'm done, around 9:30 or 10, I'll give Sonia a call and see if she wants to go get a drink.

9:40 P.M. Meeting up w/ Sonia at Segafredo's, a fashionable loungy outdoor bar/restaurant w/ lite fare on Lincoln Road (a long pedestrian mall full of shops and restaurants and people-watching). It's just around the corner from work. It's nice to finally get out of the office and have all these neat places just outside the office to hang and chill. Sometimes I don't take enough advantage of it. I order a Peroni beer and a ham, cheese, and artichoke sandwich on American white bread.

Sonia bitches about her boyfriend, not without reason. Nothing unusual . . . wet towel on the bed, splashing outside the sink, leaving his socks all over the place, drinking too much and acting stupid when he is with his buddies. You know, general immaturity. What can you expect from most men, anyways? Mental note: Don't get yourself a boyfriend like Sonia's. I say this out loud and it cracks Sonia up. He's really not so bad. She's just a little too harsh on him sometimes. But why shouldn't she be? I mean, don't we deserve better? What's wrong w/ being demanding? It's like we hold ourselves to the highest of standards and everyone else benefits from it—our families, our friends, our employers—and we kill ourselves in trying to achieve all these goals and trying to be perfect in any and every way and in making everyone happy with our work and with us, and it's almost as if we're these superwomen. We do it all, and do almost all of it well, so why should we accept anything less from anyone else? Why can't we find a partner who is just as ambitious and as hard working and as "super" human? One who cleans up after himself and can cook and excels in every way possible? Why should the bar for them be any lower than the bar we set for ourselves?

10:32 P.M. What the fuck, I'm finally out of the office and it's now raining. You gotta love Miami. Unexpected downpours when you least want them. And, of course, we're sitting at a table outside.

10:45 P.M. I'm actually finally eating. (Completely ecstatic and belated!) Sonia's nursing her Bacardi O and tonic. I'm going to be so happy when next Friday rolls around and this freaking show is finally over! I'm gonna do the dance . . . I order a little espresso. (Yes, I'm still quite the coffee addict that I can have one this late in the evening.)

The espresso comes out quickly. Yuck, Yuck, Yuck, *azucar en almivar*? It's like pure sugar in syrup. Damn bad espresso considering the place is named for an Italian espresso brand, Segafredo.

Just had the most sad conversation with Sonia about marriage and pre-nups and husbands and children. I mean, I can't believe she thinks that way. She's going to be very disappointed by Life. She's so busy thinking about every contingent or possible evil a man could impose on her, putting up walls to protect herself from any possible attack or injury, that she never really risks or takes the big gambles that give you the bigger payoff.

I don't know . . . maybe, I'm too naive, maybe I'm too trusting b/c I've never experienced anything horrible, and maybe someone will trample all over me one day.

12:15 A.M. Ask for the check.

OLD FRIENDS

11:30 A.M. I turn into Bel Air and slowly drive up to my friend's house. She was the beloved mother in the TV series *Father Knows Best*, Jane Wyatt Ward. The houses here are beautiful and fall is in the air and in the gardens, but unlike years gone by the area is full of construction sites. Everyone seems to be remodeling. I can see into gardens that are normally concealed behind high hedges.

I have not seen Jane since my husband's funeral eleven years ago. She is now ninety-two years old, and both a contemporary and old friend of my husband, James Roosevelt. Her mother was a friend of my mother-in-law, Eleanor Roosevelt. Jane married Edgar Ward, my husband's roommate at Harvard. Edgar died a few years after my husband.

I turn into Jane's circular driveway. The front door has a little porch area that reminds me of homes in the countryside. The exterior is dotted with little flower pots. Jane's housekeeper takes me in and the familiar voice calls me into her breakfast room. Jane is still very pretty. In fact she is ageless, until she stands up to go out to lunch with me. Then I see the challenges she faces, following a broken hip and a stroke, but her magical laugh dismisses her frailty.

We arrive at the Bel Air Hotel. We make several attempts to find a ramp into the restaurant, but with her lovely chuckle she says, "I can manage the steps if you help me." She is warmly welcomed by the staff who greet her by name, and show us to her favorite table. We decide to have a pre-lunch drink. Jane orders sherry and I order a glass of Chardonnay. We look at the other lunch guests. One of them is the star of *The Capital Gang* but we cannot remember his name.

Our lunch is delicious. I love my ginger carrot soup and tea sandwiches, with a Cobb salad. She has tortilla soup and a Chinese chicken salad. We both chat nonstop to close an eleven-year gap. We talk about our years of involvement with the March of Dimes. She tells me wonderful stories about her mother and my mother-in-law at social events that took place before World War II in the old houses up and down the Hudson River, when they were both young.

She tearfully tells me war stories about my husband. My husband was a Marine Raider and served with Evans Carlson in the South Pacific in World War II. He was awarded the Navy Cross and the Silver Star for his leadership in the Makin Island Raid. Jane remembered his dedication and that of his brothers, who served in Europe in the Air Force and the Navy. Jane thought that they were all so brave.

Jane also tells me my husband's funeral was the best funeral that she ever attended, except that there were so many people she had to sit in the back of the Methodist Church. It is only then that I realize how frail she is. Seconds later she whips out her lipstick, and soon looks gorgeous again. It is mid-afternoon, and we wend our way slowly back to the car. She is exhausted by the time that I pull up by her front door, and falls into the arms of her housekeeper. I kiss her goodbye, with the promise of another lunch after the holidays. I had a wonderful time with a remarkable lady, so full of life, and humor. I drive away with memories of her on stage at many events, introducing other celebrities, like Jack Benny, and Beverly Sills. She always wore beautiful, brightly colored chiffon gowns, and was eloquent and elegant. Another era gone!

MARY ROOSEVELT, 63, *Corona del Mar, California*; **retired educator**

Actress-Comedian, Currently Multihyphenating into Comedian-Actress-Singer-Writer-Producer

"I'm going for a Chris Rock meets J. Lo kind of thing." Her big break, the first woman and African American to host *Talk Soup*. Recent gigs: a guest star on *Friends* and Mother Nature in *The Santa Clause 2*. Has a book deal with Dutton to write a "modern girl's guide to life, or, as one of my guy friends put it, 'how to be a badass.'" Once, she wanted to be an environmental lawyer... until she tried standup. "I wanted to save the world. I hope I'm providing a similar service now, albeit with slightly lower stakes." Current favorite bits: her addiction to bikini waxes; finding a pair of abandoned underwear in a Mombasa hotel room; a trip to Montreal to see male strippers. "My show is for grownups. No babies or grandparents allowed." Favorite professional moment: the ninety seconds backstage before her first appearance on the *Tonight Show*, the "Holy Grail for any comedian. I almost peed my pants." Married nine years to an attorney turned real estate developer. Loves kids, but also loves late nights, sleeping in, and drinking on school nights. "I have to leap onto planes at a moment's notice. A kid probably wouldn't appreciate that without hours of psychological therapy." Focused. Open-minded. A hugger. "The other day I hugged one of my attorneys. I don't think you're supposed to do that."

AISHA TYLER, "AGE ARRESTED AROUND THE FIFTH GRADE,"
Los Angeles, California

9:32 A.M. Woke up two minutes ago, when I got my wake-up call. It was a totally restless night—typical—I can never sleep in hotel rooms. Woke up at 3, 4, and 5, worried about how late I had eaten and how my stomach was staging an internal retaliation for my thoughtlessness. Drank water, adjusted my pillows, fell asleep, woke up again. Room was too hot, but I hate how hotels are usually so cold (they always turn the a/c up to "tomb").

A little hungover from dinner and drinks with Amy, my brand new publisher from Dutton. It was a proper girls' night out—me, Amy, and Lisa, my publicist. I don't think Amy knew what she was in for—thought she was just going to have a nice little drinks date, and instead we dragged her all over Manhattan, doing silly things and drinking too much champagne until one in the morning. I definitely should have come back to the hotel sooner. I'm going to be feeling it later.

I'm going to the VH1/*Vogue* Fashion Awards tonight, a fête of music, fashion, and excess, and I have nothing to wear. I chose something last week, tried it on on Friday and had a mild panic attack because it just did not work. I know that considering the times we're living in, my fashion crises are about as relevant as the McRib, but this is a part of the gig, and I take the gig pretty seriously. Went out last night and chose an amazing outfit from New York designer Cynthia Rose, a beautiful vintage wool coat that I was planning to wear as a dress, but it's vintage, and women were apparently Ewok-size back then. The three-quarter sleeves cut into me like a blood-pressure bracelet, so I've got to find something else. It won't help the designer or me to be caught on TV worrying at my cuffs like a fourth grader. It is a beautiful outfit, so I'm planning on changing into it for the afterparty, where I can fidget a bit in the shadows without anyone noticing.

It's the morning of an awards show and I have nothing to wear.

Good Lord, my job is weird.

9:50 A.M. Working feverishly on a press release re: the book—probably should've done it on the plane. Coming up with a thinky-yet-funny quote is the bane of my existence, especially on no sleep. It's times like this I long for coffee. I hate being all healthy 'n stuff.

10:45 A.M. Forty-five minutes late for my spa appointment at Oasis on Park. Considered canceling but I need the work done—and I'll be so much happier tonight when I'm relaxed and not self-conscious about my gravedigger fingernails. Walked from the hotel, about a half-mile. NYC is "brisk" right now, which means, for me, nose-runningly cold. And I take a kind of perverse enjoyment in walking here, as if I am defying my California girl by humping it around on foot, sans valet or nice, dry trunk.

I have nothing to wear tonight. I've got about six hours to find an incredible, one-of-a-kind couture outfit for tonight, by myself, in Manhattan, on foot.

Today is going to be crazy.

1:57 P.M. Left the spa and rushed across town on foot, totally bewildered about where I was going. Getting a taxi in this town takes some kind of mysterious ninja skill that I clearly haven't learned yet. I ended up hopping on the back of one of those bicycle rickshaws that was steered by a crazed French exchange student. He was quite cute and flirting with me, and I was fielding his little sidelong questions—"are yoo verry afrayed?" he cooed in his Depardieu accent—until he told me the ride cost $20. He totally suckered me and I knew it, but I was too tired and late and sweaty to bother arguing with him and his broken goofy sexy English.

2:47 P.M. Vivienne Tam was a bust. Found one thing I liked, and as I was signing it out, some crazed fashionista ran out of the back room and yelled at the girl helping me that she couldn't loan it out. She didn't even look at me, just issued fashion orders and stomped back into her cave. Some lovely ladies in the fashion industry, I must say. Still nothing to wear. Off to get sunglasses.

3:45 P.M. Leaving Solstice sunglasses, bags full of killer shades. Brand new store, very cool, and they took great care of me. Still have nothing to wear, but at least my eyes will look good.

The designer Cynthia Rose gave me this killer baby-blue Kangol-style hat, and it matches the sweatsuit I have on, and I got a pair of gigantic blue rock star shades at Solstice. People would think I was a rap star, if I wasn't hoofing it around the island in flip flops, weighed down with my own freight.

4:58 P.M. Oh, thank heavens! Found not one, but two (!) incredibly gorgeous dresses at Donna Karan. Genius dresses. Perfect dresses. So great I couldn't decide. I like one a little better for tonight, but I don't have the right underwear, so now I've got to walk (Walk! The very idea! I have truly become an Angeleno) to the Macy's, fifteen blocks south, to try to find some underwear that don't show through what is a very sexy and only slightly transparent fabric. If there are panty gods, I am praying to them now.

5:42 P.M. I bought every nude pair of tap pants that store had. No time to try any of them on. I am sweaty, my blue hat is making my head hot, I haven't eaten all day, and I have to drag my big bag of underwear back to the East Side. But I can finally, finally, get dressed.

8:17 P.M. Running very late. Fabulous dress rebelling against me. Carefully placed tape, intended to keep breasts from leaping out at inopportune time, proving weak and ineffectual. Pre–red carpet panic setting in. Running very, very late.

We had a little flap with some nutty fashionista who was sitting in my seat (which had my name clearly printed on it). When informed by the usher she would have to move, she gave me a "who the hell are you" eye roll that almost severed her optic nerve. I tried not to laugh out loud. Some people take this stuff a bit too seriously.

The show was good—kind of a surreal grand spectacle. Debra Messing did a great job—being funny while carrying seventy pounds of couture on spaghetti straps ain't easy. Saw David Bowie perform live, sat in the same row as Ralph Lauren, drank champagne in the bathroom, and watched Paris and Nicky Hilton wobble about like baby deer in stilettos while silently wishing they would eat a bit more protein. Spent much of the show adjusting fabulous dress to prevent nationwide viewing of my bosom. Instead may have induced nationwide opinion that I am the most fidgety woman in the world.

12:15 A.M. Jumped back to the hotel to change for the afterparty at the Hudson Hotel. Fabulous dress was a big hit, despite a reporter who not-so-gingerly pointed out that it was slightly transparent. "Hey," I sauced, "Good enough for J. Lo, good enough for me." Lisa almost fainted. Cracked a joke with Steven Tyler. I told him people often asked me if we're related (me being black and all, you can see the crisp witticism) and he laughed and pursed back "Of course, baby, it's all in the lips!" I tittered away, thinking that not only are my lips rock-n-roll, but I made Steven Tyler laugh.

Went to P. Diddy's after-after-party at Lotus. The VIP section was jam-packed with people, some VIP, some not-so-much. The heaving mass of tipsy humanity eventually swept my five-foot-two publicist off the dais and onto the bouncing dance floor, not to be seen for many hours. I tried to follow, but was blocked by the biggest bouncer in the entire world, who picked me up and deposited me into a booth next to a dancing Hugh Grant and Naomi Campbell, who was merrily putting holes in the leather seat with her Blahniks. Glamorous.

The job is weird, yes, but I'm not complaining.

LITTLE THINGS

This morning when we were in the checkout line at Target, I was looking for a York Peppermint Patty but couldn't see one. My husband Jim said, "What are you looking for?" I told him and he said, "Sorry." Then as we were in line at the last store he saw them and put one in our cart. He is considerate like that.
ANITA MATCUK, 64, *St. Louis, Missouri*; **homemaker**

5:00 P.M. Picked up my dry cleaning. I don't know what I'd do without my black pants. They are so thinning and stylish. The lady who checked me out was nice. We exchanged "How are you?"s and I said, "Pretty good, for a Tuesday." She chuckled and said thanks to me by name. It's nice to hear your own name in positive cheer. Megan!
MEGAN MILLER, 28, *Cheyenne, Wyoming*; **teacher**

7:30 A.M. My husband has done it up big—our kitchen is a birthday explosion. A banner on the wall, balloons, presents, cards. My presents are wrapped in a way that only a (heterosexual) man can: excessive tape, crumpled corners, a wrapped blob. I love it because I know he did it on his own. My presents are also subliminal displays of love—a new kitchen faucet and a cheese grater! I admit, this may sound depressing to some people, but I'm genuinely excited.
JENNIFER JACKSON, 33, *Birmingham, Alabama*; **advertising account executive**

6:30 P.M. I pick up Jordan at Jane's house. Jane lives a block from me and her daughter Hannah goes to the same school. As I'm putting on Jordan's shoes, Jane asks if I like pot roast. She cooked a huge dinner and gives me a delicious meal to take home. I feel such gratitude. I am so moved by the ways, both large and small, that women take care of each other.
JENNIFER ALLYN, 34, *Hoboken, New Jersey*; **senior director, Catalyst (nonprofit organization working to advance women in business)**

11:30 A.M. always comes faster than I want. Rush out the door at work, not saying anything to anyone, but giving my assistant and friend Karen a little squeeze on her shoulder on my way by. She knows where I am going. In the car I am blasting Celine Dion, brush my hair, and put on lip gloss. As I get to the hospital's little check-in booth, the security guard, John, is asking people, "Are you a patient or a visitor?" As he sees me, he says, "How are you today? It's nice to see you." I drive up to the main hospital entrance. The parking attendants are smiling! Boy, I am almost happy to see them! They have become my buddies over the past few weeks of treatment. Henry, Albert, or John always have my sign-in card ready. They know my license plate number: VALAIS. Albert even knows where this is. He had gone to the Valais for hiking, had stopped in Sion, my hometown. What an extraordinary thing, a parking attendant so engaging, sophisticated, caring, and knowing where I come from. They make my day.

HÉLÈNE ROTHERMUND, 53, *Hanover, New Hampshire*;
retirement community admissions director

Professor of Gross Anatomy

She tells her medical students, "It's OK to feel bad or grossed out . . . but it's a gift, and you honor the donor by doing the job well." She came to teaching after being in a solo private practice, "not enough hours in the day." Two years ago, she and her partner—both activists in the Freedom to Marry movement—exchanged vows in a civil union. She has a good relationship with her two stepchildren, "They have a mother and a father. I thought they had plenty of parents and so did they." Did she ever think about kids of her own? "For about five minutes." Loves gag gifts, "toilet golf!" Her favorite holiday is Halloween, "the only expectation is that you get candy and have fun." She had an idyllic suburban childhood ("the whole neighborhood was our backyard") . . . to a point. "When I left for college, my mom said, 'if I don't ask, I don't want to know.'" She and her father still don't communicate. On the job, she's fighting for changes in the med school curriculum. "Students teaching students. Less facts, more learning. Heresy!" Resistance from the powers that be have got her seriously thinking about leaving teaching and doing a pathology residency. "I love the idea of getting paid for learning."

JEAN SZILVA, 51, *Winooski, Vermont*

4:20 A.M. I awaken before the alarm. Dreams? Pee? Stress? Hot flash? Probably all of the above. Thinking, thinking, thinking. Will we invade Iraq? Will my stepchildren be drafted? Will I bomb when I give my lecture today? You know, the important issues.

5:30 A.M. Alarm goes off at our usual time and, after a hug and a kiss, we spring into our morning routine. Bridget, my spouse by civil union, checks for dog poops and takes Griffin, our geriatric dog, out. I start the coffee (my priority) and get out the dog food. Dry, some wet, crushed pill. We give the other pills in a peanut butter sandwich. I put last night's dishes away and we are ready for breakfast. We both have cereal. Bridget goes off to her "office" to write and I to mine. Our offices are actually nooks in bedrooms that are not in use when Bridget's children aren't with us. I rehearse my lecture. PowerPoint you know. I research some birth defects quickly on the Web and take a quick look at the news. Another victim falls to the sniper in Virginia. I read Senator Leahy's speech on why he voted against the resolution giving so much power to George Bush to invade Iraq. Very moving.

7:00 A.M. I cease my peripatetic activity, jump in the shower, dress, and head off to work. Of course, I have my own pill routine. Both the dog and I have those little plastic boxes for meds organized by the day of the week. The dog has one such case. I have two. The dog is old and feeble. Hmmm.

8:10 A.M. It's brisk out (20°). The thirty-minute walk to the University of Vermont where I work refreshes and settles my nerves. My mind wanders somewhat like that state when you are not asleep but not awake. I can wrest control over where my head goes but I'd rather not. I usually hit my office before anyone else. I like the quiet. My routine is to power up the "'puter" while I start more coffee (did I say I was addicted?). I remember to stick my lunch from home into the fridge most of the time. I answer phone messages and e-mails before I head down to the infamous Hall A where we make doctors.

9:00 A.M. I give my lecture on the Development of the Head and Neck to ninety-seven first-year medical students. I talk as if I understand this miracle, but I don't. Not really. I can tell you what happens when and I can tell you the consequences of the usual course of events not happening, but I cannot even imagine why all the tissues move to form a face. We all look like monsters at the start. Some of us grow out of it. The pictures are alarming enough that fewer students than usual are sleeping. Victory!

10:00 A.M.–12:00 P.M. Lab. Gross Lab that is. Very gross. Eighteen tables of the donated remains of local citizens and each table has six students at it. I teach Gross Medical Anatomy. Today, the students are dissecting the pharynx (where you get sore throats). I help them bisect the heads. Fascinating. Necessary. Very weird. Sometimes I still get bad dreams. These dreams take the form of my loved ones interacting with me but they are in various stages of the dissection process. Their bodies are being peeled off layer by layer as we talk, play, make love. It's a very bad dream. I talk nerves, arteries, and muscles with the students. We poke wires through holes in skulls trying to help them visualize why an injury at the base of your skull would cause your eye to pulsate.

12:00–1:00 P.M. Lunch with my coworkers Bruce and Betsy who also teach gross anatomy. I bring leftovers from home. We talk about students, changes in the curriculum, and the state of the world. Betsy and I continue our almost daily attempts to "enlighten" Bruce's political views. By enlighten, we mean bring around to our own point of view. Bruce makes no efforts to enlighten us.

1:00–2:30 P.M. Two medical students come in for some extra help. These are very smart people having a very hard time. Their medical education is strikingly similar to my own, thirty years before. I used so little of what was shoved down my throat. Now, I appear to be on the other side. Yet, change is in the air. Medical school curriculums are changing all over the nation in an attempt to have these students start thinking and reasoning like physicians right out of the gate instead of the information binge-and-purge routine that I trained under. I have been placed in charge of eleven weeks of the new curriculum. It's a huge responsibility. The changes I am pushing for are enormous. The hardest thing to do is to get people to change and especially people who have been "successful." Yet, success is relative. You can always do better. We need to incorporate the new resources into our teaching.

2:30–5:00 P.M. I'm trying to write examination questions. It's so hard. If they are straightforward, they are boring. If they are interesting, they are more open to misinterpretation. No matter how careful we are (six people review each question), students always find a way to look at a question in an unanticipated fashion. I know the students care for us. I know the students trust us to be interested in their welfare. I also know that they think we want to trick them. We had a question once which asked how many cranial nerves would you be using if I asked you to smile and you did it. About six students came down to the front of the room to ask if the person in the question could lip-read.

While I am writing my questions, the computer-help people come up to give me back my computer, which has been in the shop. The hard drive crashed. I know not why. I know nothing about computers except that I have become dependent upon them at work. I even think on them. It feels like I'm always trying to catch up with the technology. Do the young people just accept that as normative? Is it such an everyday occurrence that they have no angst about it? It feels like my pencil is constantly developing new features that everyone knows about except me. I never master it. Humiliation is my constant companion.

5:15 P.M. Bridget picks me up at work and drives me home. Before she moved here in September, I walked. Now, I'm so glad to be living with her after five years of a long-distance weekend relationship, that I want to take advantage of every opportunity to be with her. Her graciousness of driving me to and from work (and my acceptance) has added five pounds. I'm trying to get back into the walking routine.

5:30 P.M. Arriving home is interesting. Griffin has defecated and trod in it. He's Bridget's dog and she accepts the task of cleaning up after him. I open the mail and get some more bad news about my retirement funds. Bummer. Yet, I have money to spare on gag gifts that also have arrived. Toilet golf, funny tee shirts purchased for friends, and a baseball cap from the Human Rights Commission (received for sending in a donation) remind me that, compared to most of the world's people, I am obscenely wealthy.

6:30 P.M. Joanne and Taylor (friends and neighbors, which is handy) come over for dinner. It's vegetarian fare, which is what we mostly eat. We talk of friends and relationships starting and ending. Dyke drama. The world situation obsesses me. I know I'm beginning to sound like a crank but I can't help it. I cannot believe that my generation (early baby boomer) wants to take this country to war. I can't believe that the initiators of Earth Day will be willing to kill people to keep their SUVs. I can't believe that we who said, "Don't trust anyone over thirty," would forget why we said that. I told you I was cranky.

8:30 P.M. Our guests leave and it's just Bridget and me. I calm down with light fiction. Bridget rubs my feet as she often does. I am so blessed by the love and respect of this amazing human being. She likes the parts of me I like best. This is a very good thing. I wish everyone could have all that I have.

9:30 P.M. We are in bed. I fall asleep in Bridget's arms. Goodnight moon.

COLLECTIVE GLIMPSES ───────────────

64% of day diarists felt stressed out

47% worried about money

57% didn't get enough sleep

22% cried

55% prayed

12:50 P.M. Arrive early at Jones and get seated. Dad said he would help me pay for getting my car fixed but I feel like such a loser . . . thirty-two and asking for financial help?!! I don't know what I'm doing. I'm not focused enough to write a screenplay. I'm not confident enough to direct anything. Of course, I'm sitting here waiting to meet with some producer who tracked ME down after seeing my film—there's a little hope. Waitress just thought I was my sister, "Did you change your hair?" Poor Monica. She gets this too. I need to take some of these nutriceuticals that help you focus and give you endurance naturally, no caffeine. Meredith told me "they" have some studies that antidepressants cause you to have little holes in your head. I guess that's preferable to the giant hole I would have if I blew my head off.

LEANNA CREEL, 32, *Los Angeles, California*;
film producer/developer (and identical triplet)

Asdzáán, Asdzání, Amá
(Woman, Wife, Mother in the Navajo Way)

She grew up in a federal Indian boarding school where her mom was the caretaker and her father a teacher—part of a sheltered, close-knit community in Navajo Mountain, Utah. Received degrees from Dartmouth and Harvard. She married a white classmate right after college. Had a career recruiting American Indian students for California State, and teaching American Indian history. Misses the energy of the classroom, "when they get it for the first time," but not the misconceptions she sometimes encountered in the state school system ("Ooh! Ivy League!"). Now an at-home mom balancing two teenagers, two toddlers, and "a husband who doesn't always get it." She wanted to teach their oldest kids the Diné language; he worried it would hinder their ability to learn English. She lost that one ("He's an Assistant U.S. Attorney who's been arguing all his life") . . . but he's come around. She teaches the little ones her language, while "he reminds them that they're half him, too." Not "Miss Perfect" in a mom-competitive community. "We aren't the norm, so we don't even try to fit in." She would love to move home to Navajo Mountain, but that would mean divorce or a dead husband. "It's gotten better. I don't think about it every day now."

MABELLE DRAKE HUESTON, 38, *Corona del Mar, California*

12:59 A.M. Two-year-old Kinsale calls out: "My sheet, my blankie." I say menacingly, "I don't play this game, go back to sleep."

1:15 A.M. I'm sleeping on the couch. Someone's playing with a padlock, loud gnawing, under house, hear it in vent go *boom*, and silence. I immediately think about the morsels of Simply Fiber cereal that Kinsale had spilled all over her floor just before she went to bed. Because I was intent on getting Kinsale to bed at her rigid bedtime (7:30 P.M.), I had decided not to clean it up until morning. I could picture the rats scurrying from the vents in the hallway, scampering through her possibly open door, and eating the cereal morsels strewn across her carpet. Where are my goddamn glasses? Turn on lights, I sound like an elephant. Get up, turn on lights, shut her door, go to kitchen. Hear noise, turn on outside light. Should I wake my husband, John? Now,

I don't see anything, only hear. What's there to do anyway? Go back to couch, pull blanket up. A noise. That's it, "John, you HAVE to get up!" We put trash can and stack of newspapers on vents. Still annoyed, "Get your glasses on! I can't find mine." Go in the bedroom near desk, realize computer is on, I'm annoyed. I'm the only one who turns it off when it's in standby. No more noises, I finally find my glasses.

1:39 A.M. Go back to bed.

2:30 A.M. Rat noise again, in the vents. John's out setting traps. I'm still in on the couch. I get up, shut off computer.

6:30 A.M. Tara, my fifteen-year-old, is up. Her room is in the garage behind the house so she has to come into the front house to eat breakfast. She doesn't know about the rat traps on the ground in the backyard. John rushes out the back door to warn her. He has to save the dog, Patsy, too, who stays with Tara in her room at night. Baby Shea hears the commotion and cries. I snuggle deeper in covers. John always gets babies up. Kinsale wakes up, "Mom?" She immediately takes off diaper in middle of living room. Baby is at my breast. I'm in my Queen's chair—an oversized armchair that I use to breastfeed. If anyone else is already in the Queen's chair when I have to feed, they have to give it up. Daddy dresses Kinsale, buttons up her back. Kinsale demands being buttoned. John says, "Yes, your highness." Tara comes over and covers my exposed breast as baby eats. "Lovely," she says sarcastically. I'm thinking, "John's great." John's thinking about rats. "Will they eat meat, Tara?" he asks. Breastfeeding discomfort, feeling like I don't want to be touched.

7:00 A.M. I have gas. Ryan's up early to get his contacts in. He has to leave to catch the carpool for GATE, the pull-out Gifted and Talented Education program. Usually he just has to walk across the street and up about three hundred yards to get to school. I have to try to get the contacts in his eyes. I went into my room and couldn't remember what I came in for.

7:36 A.M. Calm. Kinsale is watching *Sesame Street*. John asks me what I'm writing. I tell him about the diary. I get cynicism from John, "It's nothing but blackmail. It's a threat that you'll write down things." I warn, "Be good today." I notice the laundry basket is full again! How does it do that? I hear *Sesame Street*. Mr. Noodle's annoying. Elmo's voice is annoying.

7:55 A.M. *Sesame* Street is over, TV goes off. Kinsale spotted the new Princess fruit snacks in the high cupboard. She asks Dad for it. He inadvertently brings the box down because he doesn't know what they are. He realizes his mistake. I roll my eyes. Now he has to give her one. Boy, is she happy. She then says, "My dad is so lucky to give that to me!"

8:15 A.M. Rat conference with neighbors. They tell me to use Cheetos as bait. I call John at work to tell him.

8:30 A.M. Is it only 8:30? I showered, hearing the babies' cries for help. None there. I get dressed choosing warm-ups and a white shirt. My nipples show and they're crooked. I fix them. I don't want people to think that it's a bad boob job.

9:05 A.M. Cheetos snack with milk. A bribe to get Kinsale to sleep. I want a nap too. Forget the mess, just get some rest.

9:12 A.M. Both kids are in for a nap. Some whimpering from Shea but she was silenced with a tap on the door and a "Go to sleep!" Ah, cozy Navajo blanket on couch. Wonder what John's doing. (John is chief of the United States Attorney's office in Santa Ana, California.)

10:19 A.M. Shea up! Patsy barks loud. Shea crying. Gotta get Kinsale up. Gotta sneak in a piss first.

10:38 A.M. It's cold. Get sweater for Shea with matching hat/cap. Kinsale's on autopilot. She's already dressed herself: purple hat, jacket, pink socks, black shoes, yellow dress. I still have to get diaper bag, bottle, keys, and Shea. I was actually proud that I saw the deodorant and put some on. There's either bird crap or very dirty raindrops on the car. I move a bottle out of Shea's car seat. The nipple on the bottle has been pushed in and milk spills out on the unprotected carpet in the car. Hate that! Carpet looks like shit and I don't want to pay anyone to clean it. All buckled in, Kinsale wants to do her own buckle. Wow! She did it. Surprise! Uh oh, hope she doesn't try to learn how to unbuckle, especially while I'm driving! The same tape is in the car, *Wee Sing*. "Down by the ocean, down by the sea."

10:42 a.m. Wish I had my makeup bag just to put on some powder. I see people in the restaurants as I'm driving along and notice drivers in their work vehicles. It occurs to me how strange it is that people think it's normal that only white people are in restaurants or driving nice cars and living in nice homes. How's that OK? I know, I live in a very wealthy area but that just seems to amplify something wrong with the picture. Why are most of the people white and wealthy, and don't people wonder if there is something wrong with that outcome? It's not just in the U.S. but I noticed it also in Germany, Austria, and Switzerland this summer.

10:47 A.M. Park in tight spot on street to ferry. Scary, push in the side mirror so it lies flat against the car door. At Mommy and Me. Am looking frumpy. Only Shea's cute sweater is nice. I hate parents who can't control their awfully behaved kids. Well, it's my turn today. Kinsale is usually so great. She listens, plays, shares, etc. But today she kicks toys (just to be an imp). She tries to tear away Sophie's hand while Sophie is sitting on the rocking horse. I silently threaten her that we're going. Later, she asks, "Is it time for a nap?" I realize that she must not have slept when Shea and I did. I'll be glad when the group ends.

In Mommy and Me, I worry that Kinsale will ask another little girl about her birth defect and I won't know what to say. I notice Kinsale staring and trying to take a closer look. I think the mom's really great and I would like to get to know her better. I'm not bold enough to try. The talk at Mommy and Me varies. First it's about Bali and Al Qaeda. I don't watch news or read the newspaper so I don't know. It was a "one-up-on-you" type of conversation. "I know someone who died in terrorist stuff." "Well, I know someone closer to me that died in the terrorist stuff." I don't say anything. Outside during snack time, the moms and I talk about how cold it is. I mention the rat under the house. I don't tell them that I suspect we have more than one rat, and that they are in the walls and ceiling too. I thought they'd think that I was a real loser or something. No one else has rat problems. Oh well. Thinking about my lost wallet. Where else could it be? Last I remember I gave Misha, our ten-year-old neighbor who walked our dog, $2.00. Got the kids in the car and drove Ryan to swimming yesterday. It has to be in the car.

12:46 P.M. Back home, I find a bag of Cheetos, almost empty and throw it away so I won't eat any. On a sort of restricted diet. Any eating that cuts out snacking, fat, sugar, and extra carbohydrates is a restricted diet to me. I gained so much weight after the baby was born that I need to lose at least forty lbs. John has said that I am overweight and that I have to eliminate my bad eating habits so I am . . . trying. I make myself and Kinsale lunch: no-fat bologna and cheese sandwich. Having Diet Snapple. I take the bag of Cheetos back out of trash because I know it's right on the top of the can and not contaminated.

I can sneak some into my mouth. Kinsale went to bed after purposely spilling her juice on the table and floor.

This is my favorite time. Babies are asleep and/or going to sleep. I want to get on my family Web site to check what my siblings have written. We started this Web site a year ago to keep in touch with each other and then we invited our mom's extended family, the Natoh Dine'e Tachiini clan (Tobacco Red Rocks on the Shore clan). My mom's clan is originally from the Teesto/Jeddito area of the Navajo Reservation in Arizona. We share pictures, news, recipes, a family tree, plan reunions, and reviews. We have another site to talk about serious family issues, usually about our mom.

1:00 P.M. Look in car, no wallet. I notice there's snack evidence, an empty candy wrapper, in glove compartment. I take it and throw it away.

1:06 P.M. Call John. Hopefully he's seen my wallet. He says to call Albertsons, the neighborhood grocery store, a.k.a. Albie's. I explain last steps preceding lost wallet. Sense he's not listening. "Listen, I'm jammed," he says. I quickly ask if he's teaching tonight and he says yes. That tells me that I have to pick up Ryan. John's good about not beating around the bush when he doesn't have time to chit-chat. We could talk at length about inane things if he wasn't busy. I don't really know what his schedule is like during the day but I always try to find out the parts that affect me and the babies. I do know he cherishes his time in the mornings with the kids, because sometimes his work takes him in the evenings and he may not be guaranteed time with them before bed.

I call Albie's, no black wallet. I check the trash cans. Anyone filthy enough to take out a bag of Cheetos from the garbage can dig through trash bags. I give up after one bag. Baby's fussy. I changed her and am now feeding her. Jeff Garrett from Dartmouth College admissions called. He blabbed on the answering machine while Shea babbled right along. Didn't hear a word he said. He's coming out here on a recruitment trip in a couple of weeks and wants to discuss ways to recruit more Native Americans from the L.A. area. I'll wait until Shea is in bed to hear message or call him.

2:05 P.M. Found wallet! Ryan put it in the side compartment in back of the van. Call Discovery Toys lady to order kitchen chef toys for Kinsale's Christmas present. House still a mess. I have to vacuum up the *twosh chiine* (a blue cornmeal that Navajos use to make a breakfast mush or porridge) off the carpet in Ryan's room and my room. My Navajo stuff—an assortment of Navajo rugs with designs from various areas on the reservation, Pendleton blankets, wedding baskets, pottery, traditional stirring sticks, brush, rug dress, concho belt, sash belt, various turquoise jewelry—is still piled by the window in my room. Ryan's friends may come home with him after GATE. Gotta clean up a bit, just in case.

2:07 P.M. Logging on to check MyFamily.com site. Computer slow. Love picture of our family in Germany in front of castle from vacation this summer. Wish it weren't so fuzzy. I'm reading a book while I wait for the page to load. *Your Child At Play: Birth to One Year* by Marilyn Segal. It says that Shea may not know what I'm saying but she knows full well whether I am pleased, excited, cross, or indifferent.

My family Web page has finally loaded. Roxie, my niece, is coming back with a vengeance. She was self-exiled after she disliked a comment made on the site a month ago. Now she's commenting on everything. Her spelling is atrocious. She spelled mosquito, "musquitio." I am urging my family to buy a book to learn how to write in Navajo. I asked my siblings and their kids for assistance in helping Mom through her current financial crisis. I can't do it alone because of the two babies.

3:09 P.M. Am checking e-mail now. Ryan's home. Oh my God, is it really 3:00 P.M.? Have to balance Kinsale on knee while she asks questions and I type.

3:50 P.M. My friend Adriana calls. She's neat, doesn't brag, just so matter-of-fact. I'm more baby-competitive than she is. I don't brag about my kids but I observe and compare quietly. I absolutely love to hear surprise or praise that my babies are precocious, walking, and talking earlier than other kids their age or older. I work so hard to stimulate them that it's fun when it pays off. I think the kids also benefit from the verbal praise from another person other than their parent. Whenever I say to Tara, "Did I ever tell you how smart and beautiful you are?" she always answers, "Thanks Mom, but you're just saying that because you're my mother."

4:02 P.M. I have to get Tara from school. Saw my reflection in car window, saw my big belly. I sucked it in but not a flattering outfit. Almost drove off without Kinsale's belt on and mine too. Luckily she said, "I'm not ready yet." Sometimes I wonder who's the mom. My car needs cleaning. Ryan leaves back window open. Have to close it. The noise distracts me while I'm driving. Stopped at light. Staring off, singing song on CD and trying to remember things to do. Can't concentrate. "Hi ho the Dairy-O, the cheese stands alone." Tara says she's the second fastest runner today. Zari came in first because she didn't stop at the light. I'm so proud of her. She said she's inspired by the movie *Iron Will*. She saw it in fourth or fifth grade. I feel very happy for her and she made a huge effort to mention that she's wearing her Dartmouth t-shirt. I sarcastically say no one at CDM (Corona del Mar High School, where she's a sophomore) would know about Dartmouth. She notes the X-country coach has caps from all schools except Dartmouth. I told her that maybe none of the CDM X-country kids has made it into Dartmouth.

Get home. Chaos again. Get the mail, listen to Tara chatter. Kinsale needs attention while I'm on the phone. She wants fruit snacks (the ones John showed her by accident this A.M.). Tara's already started making popcorn before I could stop her. I told Ryan he could make the lemonade. He asks me repeatedly for stuff: "Where's the sugar? Where are the measuring cups? Where's the pitcher?" I finally cry out, "I asked you to make the lemonade and I end up making it myself!"

We're all in the kitchen, Tara yells, "Yay, the *Science Times*!" She notes that element 118 is a fake. She's in chemistry this semester. I ask what they do to scientists who fake their theories. "Do they go to jail?" She says, "Oh, they fire them, I guess." I heard her cuss today, she said, "What the hell?" Time to take Ryan's contacts out. Gotta go, Kinsale's crying. She wants her juice now instead of when I first asked her.

4:44 P.M. We are swarming out to the car. See neighbor, the one we call "The Grandma," but don't make eye contact because she's a chronic braggart. Once you get sucked in, it's hard to break away. Ryan teasing Kinsale. Kinsale just crying. Wants jacket on. Neighbor in front of her house, I can't see what she's doing. I'm just nosey like that, don't stop me to talk when I'm in a hurry, but I still want to know what you're doing.

Ask Kinsale if I can listen to news. If I don't, then she acts like the two-year-old that she is and screams that she wants her music on. NPR 89.9 is a treat! "That noise hurts my ears," Kinsale says. The story is about a man who takes photos, one is of an electrocution in Florida. I wonder what the title of his book is, then realize I might be weird. "Mom?" Shh! Where's the news? Next is sports injuries you don't want to brag about. Next the traffic report, thank God, it's not for me.

4:55 P.M. Ryan is out of the car. Shea's fussy. Lady crossing street has very small eyes. Good thing I looked over my shoulder before I moved over, black car in my blind spot.

5:01 P.M. I'm back at home now in my Queen's chair, breastfeeding, remote control's on TV. Shea's playing with my hair. Kinsale's asking if the Diaper Genie's for ants or diapers. She's trying to use it to get higher to get the remote. She's talking to herself, "We're trying to help our mom." She sounds like Gollum (the deformed hobbit in Tolkien's *The Lord of the Rings*). John has been reading the second book to the bigger kids before they go to bed.

5:11 P.M. BBC *World* is on, Bali again. Oh my God, twenty-five years ago Korea kidnapped Japanese and they are coming home. I listen as I trace letters with Kinsale and breastfeed Shea. I take extra time to show Kinsale how to trace the "X" correctly. Saddam Hussein election. Mark ballots in blood. Seven more years in power. What's Kinsale been doing? I think she's OK. Shove frozen chicken in microwave.

Pam calls, she is the mom of Tara's friend, Whitney. Fortunately, I can tell her that I can't do a Navajo presentation in her class this year. The babies are too young and it is a pain to prepare for a presentation. After we talk, she says that she needs to ask Tara about Whitney, who took off with some friends, and needs to be tracked down. I told Tara I'd kill her if she did that. Can't help but look into my neighbor's backyard when I'm at kitchen sink.

Loaded dishes in dishwasher. Microwave's very dirty, get Windex and paper towels. Baby hits forehead on table leg. I say, "Baboom!" She is fine. When she knocks her chin on the shelf, I say, "Oops" instead and she cries. I tickle her and she loves it. Nuisance fly on food. Can't get it. "Baboom!" Oh no! She hit her head again! Goodness gracious! Come here, let's rub, rub, rub. I want some wine for dinner but already had beer last night. I'll wait for John, maybe have beer after run.

6:06 P.M. Gotta get Ryan. Gotta go potty first. Shea on floor, Kinsale coming in. Wonder how many dads have to do this to go potty? Notice milk on floor again.

6:14 P.M. We're all getting back in the car again to pick up Ryan from swimming. Grandma out in front of house again. Shea has bottle. NPR news again. Shea screaming, bottle fell out of her mouth. Kinsale has bottle and is trying to push in the nipple again. I honk horn by accident, Oops, but try not to act guilty. My left-turn signal still on again. Shea still crying. Lots of cars. I don't see Ryan. He saw me. He's reporting: "Day became horrible." His coach let him out earlier. He had to wait forty-five minutes instead of his usual thirty. He's in charge in back now. I change volume up front. I can hear the news again. "Ryan, stop yelling! And close the window back there!" Can't stand Arianna Huffington's voice. "Kinsale, no yelling please, it hurts my ears." Screaming in the van's deafening. I yell, "STOP YELLING!"

Two women are sitting on the ground in front of our gate. Ryan's afraid of them. He thinks they're beggars. I try to act brave and say, "It's OK, it's Corona del Mar, not Eastern Europe." They realize we need to pass so they move. They ask to use our phone and I say, I am sorry, no. Everyone is hungry. I say another thirty minutes. Still haven't cooked dinner. Basmati rice could have made this dinner easier and quicker. Instead, I am grilling pork ribs and chicken! Trying to save money sucks! I would have bought take-out but I'm trying to save money to pay taxes on house. Ate pork, with veggies and pasta. Kids ate well except for Kinsale.

7:28 P.M. Kinsale's in bed early. Harder to do when John's not around. Kinsale had a BM and I didn't know it, I ripped off her diaper only to see the surprise. I rushed her into the bathroom yelling, "Don't touch. Don't sit down." I cleaned her off and put on a diaper. Next was Shea. I was trying to change her diaper and it had a BM too. A double whammy. Ryan asks if I've done the wash. He has no pants he says. I tell him to go out to the garage and get Tara. "Get the clothes out of the dryer and put the wet ones in the dryer." They dump out the clothes on the sofa. The living room looks like a war zone. They help put away the clothes. Tara's almost hopeless and can't tell the difference between Kinsale's and Shea's clothes. Breastfeeding again. Watching the Learning Channel, *Medical Detectives*. Shea in bed.

Left at 8 P.M. to run. Slow jog. Toenail hurts. Listen to *The First Eagle* by Tony Hillerman on tape. It's cold out and no runners out. Came back to find babies sleeping alone in front house. I go to Tara's room in the garage to tell her to stay with babies next time especially if they're sleeping.

8:34 P.M. Have to go to store. I go alone in the van. Took forever to choose liquor. I chose Kahlua and vodka for various drink choices. Got John his Guinness. Thought of getting flowers to celebrate John's two years as chief of the Santa Ana office, but they were too puny. Just as well, he's gonna be late.

I'm standing by the counter in the kitchen. Big black ants on me. Tried to step on them with my running shoes but the treads are too bumpy. Gotta put away groceries and dishes. I'll wait for John to do Cheetos and traps. I hear jazz on radio and change it. Lady singing sounds too much like Yoko Ono. I hear a Jesus station, skip, some other station, OK, Motown, "Jimmy Mack." Cleaned up, wow! Called John. He's coming home soon. My vaginal area itchy, nothing serious, probably just need a shower after my run.

9:43 P.M. I sign into my family Web site. My sister-in-law, Mitzi, has arrived in Hawaii. There's a photo of her with her new granddaughter at the airport. We're still trying to figure out Mom's possible forgery situation. Mom is on a fixed income so she has to watch her money very closely. She noticed that the check that she had given to Mitzi (to help with her brother's funeral) was cashed for four hundred dollars more than the original amount. I am checking into what may have happened. Annie, my eldest sister, seems to be helping Mom out a lot, probably out of guilt.

10:25 P.M. John's home. Needs envelope and stamps. He's going to the post office tonight. I explain that Tara is second fastest. Asks about Ryan's contacts. We talk about Mr. Drama, Ryan's name when he exaggerates his disappointments. I wanted to see the recorded final episode of HBO's *The Wire* with him but I waited up for nothing. I'll just wash up and go to bed. He says, "I thought you were waiting up for me." We both then fake hearty chuckles, Ha, Ha, Ha, Ha. I sleep on couch again. I snore and don't like to sleep with John, only to have him wake me up to tell me I'm snoring.

10:32 P.M. John's angry because the machine at the post office wasn't working. He says he'd like it better if the machine said, "Fuck you!" instead of "Out of order." I ask about Bali, he says he hopes my lack of geography and knowledge motivates me to read the newspaper and to keep up with news so I don't sound like I'm ignorant. I say that I don't care to keep up because it doesn't affect me or my babies. We whisper about the neighbors on the other side of us and the rat tree. He doesn't know what the guy, our neighbor, does at night. He's up at all hours. His wife is about to have her baby. "What's she going to do?" he asks. I say, "Fuck it up, just like the first two." We laugh.

John's cussing at the rats. He's now talking about possible partnership plans with law firms. My glasses are off and all's fuzzy.

I hear Grandma's TV. John says, "Now that I'm wired, I want to watch *The Wire. Yaadila!* (Navajo expression of exasperation.) I smile with my eyes closed, remembering the way Tara says it, *Yaa di la ni!* She uses the form often used by frustrated moms when their kids are begging them for something for the umpteenth time. John asks, "Are you sure you don't want to go in the other bed?" I reply, "Rat doesn't bother me enough to chance snoring and getting awakened and told I'm snoring." Love that man. I get three toothpaste kisses. My lips were still puckered for more. Never enough.

10:57 P.M. Good night.

ON THE JOB

TEJINDER K. GREWAL, 30

Royal Oak, Michigan

**General Motors manager providing support to global team of senior executives
(every three months she switches to a new GMC car)**

7:25 A.M. Waiting in the lobby for an executive. Pray that I don't trip and fall flat on my face while we are walking. Hang out with the two other support people waiting to receive their executives. Today is the release of corporate third-quarter business results to employees by our senior leadership. We broadcast the results throughout the corporation, live, globally, at the end of each quarter.

This is the strangest job I have ever had. I spend most of my time focused on what can go wrong and how to head it off before it can be noticed or do any damage. My job used to be assessing impacts to engineering operations, the plant, and the customer. Now, it's about avoiding the faux pas (who has the wrong meeting material, who doesn't have ANY meeting material, who is sitting in the wrong seat and how do you ask them to move).

One executive arrived; his support staffer gone. Two of us left. Both of us holding coffees, waiting for our executives like parents waiting for their children, or children waiting for their parents. (Why was my mother always late picking me up after school events?) Second executive arrives, his assistant goes outside to meet him and I think that he must be insane as it is less than 40 degrees outside. No way am I going out there in a short skirt. Oh horror!!! The coffee the staffer was holding was for the executive!!! Ack! Was I supposed to get coffee for my executive??? It doesn't seem like something he would have us do, plus I don't know how he takes his coffee. But still, I didn't anticipate that potential faux pas. (Imagine, if you will, me meeting my executive and him mistaking my coffee as an offering. There is no easy, clean way out of that situation. Better to have him think I'm a slacker that didn't get his coffee.) I run back into the auditorium after getting by the gate-keepers (Really, I belong here, I do!!!) and set my coffee down under my chair.

7:30 A.M. So deep in thought about crisis narrowly averted and so happy when I finally see his truck that I (being the idiot I told myself I would never be) head straight outside. Of course the wind whips through my suit jacket, up my skirt, through my hair. COLD, COLD. The day gets brighter as he steps out of the truck holding . . . his own coffee!!! The brilliant man stopped at Starbucks on his way in! Depressing as it is, it doesn't take much to make me happy. Usher him into the auditorium, hand him off to my boss. They disappear behind the curtain at the back of the stage to get ready for the report.

From Three Generations
of Master Luthiers

She continues the family tradition. At age eleven, she began crafting her first violin. At sixteen, she came to work full time for her family's business, the Chicago-based Carl Becker and Son, world-renowned makers and restorers of stringed musical instruments. When she married and moved to Minneapolis, she opened a new shop, but maintains the centuries-old standards of Stradivarius and Guarnerius. She's mum on the family's "secret recipe" for varnish. The work takes time. "What's two years in the making when the instrument will last for centuries?" She can hear inside sounds, her ear automatically picks apart tones. "It can be a curse. I'll go to a concert and my husband will see the scowl on my face. He thinks the music sounds wonderful, but it is easy for me to get sidetracked and all I hear are the two or three sick instruments." They have three kids, ages twenty, seventeen, and ten. It's music versus sports in their household. She plays the cello in a community orchestra. Loves to put her creativity to use in school plays, sewing costumes, making puppets, designing sets. "I feel if you've been given a gift like I have, you should use it to add something, to better this world."

JENNIFER BECKER JUREWICZ, 47, *Minneapolis, Minnesota*

Midnight at my mom and dad's house: I'm tired but can't sleep. Tomorrow will be a deciding day for me. Can I really adjust the tone of a whole orchestra? Will the Chicago Symphony Orchestra really let me touch their instruments if they don't know me? I wouldn't if I were them! I know I can do a good job but they don't know that. I'll try a cup of tea. NO TEA IN THE HOUSE! Mom and Dad haven't lived in this house for a while. How frustrating. They should sell this place and stay in Wisconsin year-round. Got to get to sleep, I must talk to Scott before he leaves on his sales trip to Wisconsin tomorrow morning. He wanted me to look at some work he was doing in the shop.

9:30 A.M. OH NO I'm late! Scott must already be gone! My brother Paul is here, I wonder what he will say about the CSO? I hope no one comes while I'm getting dressed.

10:20 A.M. Paul is offended that I am going to work on the CSO instruments when he has a shop in town. Why don't the players come to him now? Maybe they don't know he does adjusting and not just sales. They asked me to come so I don't care what he thinks. Even if I don't get to do anything, at least I tried to help. Why does my brother still have to be so competitive?

11:00 A.M. I have an hour to kill before Joe comes. I'll go upstairs and do something in the shop and make myself useful. Robin, the new bow person, needs help with rehairing bows. I'll show her how to do one.

11:05 A.M. Can't concentrate on this rehair. Don't goof it up; you are supposed to be showing Robin how to do it right! What if I make a fool of myself at the Hall? What if nobody remembers me working in the shop with Dad? It's been over twenty years since I worked in Chicago. I wonder if any of the same people are still playing? OK, comb the hair straight now, get the length right. Her setup is all wrong! I'll have to make a new clamp for the frog.

11:50 A.M. There, perfect job and ten minutes to go before Joe gets here. That should be fun! I've known Joe since 1972, when he bought a Becker violin my first year working full time in the shop. He plays professionally, but in the last year he's been taking my instruments on trips and showing them for me. He used to work for Paul so this could be strange.

12:00 P.M. Joe is here, Paul is polite and we leave. Joe is nervous too. I forgot breakfast! Great, a headache is all I need right now. Maybe there will be time to eat or have a cup of coffee before I get started with the CSO.

12:40 P.M. There's the garage. My God where did we park? We must be eight blocks from Orchestra Hall! There's no time to get coffee now. Man, that smells good passing a Starbucks. I'm getting a headache. I hope it isn't a bad one, I don't need a migraine today. This walk feels good, relaxing; I need to get more exercise.

12:55 P.M. Gary Stucka, one of the cellists, is supposed to meet us at 1:00 or was it 1:30? Joe is outside having a smoke. What a smelly habit. My clothes are going to stink. The guard can see Gary in the Hall on his camera; why isn't he coming to get us? This was a harebrained idea to think I can do anything constructive on the CSO instruments.

1:30 P.M. Finally! Gary shows us into the main floor. We have to stay halfway back during rehearsal! Now what am I going to do? I'll be damned if I just sit passively for six hours after driving from Minneapolis to do this! I'm going to the stage! Otto Strobek is here! I haven't seen him for twenty years. What a joy to see him still playing and looking so good! Several of the older musicians send their regards to my father. They recognize me! The guys I had appointments with this past Sunday and Monday come in and give me a glowing report of the work I did on their cellos. What a rush!

1:40 P.M. Rehearsal is starting, I have to get off the stage and go sit down. I'm going to take notes on which instruments to fix. Probably won't get near any of them but it can't hurt.

1:50 P.M. I can't believe this is the CSO! They sound so BAD!!! The musicians are perfect and working so hard but the instruments sound terrible! I wonder if they know how bad this sounds? This is going to be a LOOONG rehearsal.

2:15 P.M. The singers are wonderful. German opera singers rehearsing a Wagner opera. My mom would enjoy this. It's so sad she had to give up her dream to be an opera singer when she had kids. I hope she has a chance to see an opera this year. She enjoys that so much.

2:20 P.M. OH NO, my cell phone just went off!!! I can't believe I forgot to turn it off! It's my sister Marilyn wanting to know how it is going. If she only knew! I hope the conductor didn't notice. We could get thrown out of here!

3:00 P.M. There might be a break where I can go to the stage again and talk or work on the instruments. I better not miss it. Joe looks nervous but also is enjoying the music. He questions why I look so uncomfortable. He hears the few violins that sound too bright but not the rest of the problems with the instruments. It just sounds fuzzy to him and he thinks it's the Hall.

3:30 P.M. They are stopping. Quick get up there before everyone leaves. It's amazing how fast eighty musicians can disappear! Only one cellist, Ron, comes up to me and wants help with his cello. It's not responding right on the lower strings. Maybe I'll get another chance to do more during the next rehearsal.

4:00 P.M. Ron is a nice person to work with. He has a nice cello too. This is easy, it is so obvious what to do. The bridge is way off where it belongs. I know this will help a lot. He is so thankful. Ron comments that no one in town knows how to adjust an instrument so successfully. What kind of idiotic workers are in this town anyway? Why don't the musicians go to Paul? He does a good job. This isn't rocket science, you just have to be willing to listen to the person and do what is needed to get it right.

4:05 P.M. Rick from the violin section comes up to me in the aisle and asks me to say hi to my dad. Evidently he went to the shop a few years ago and had some work done by my dad. I talk him into having me look at his violin even though he doesn't think it sounds bad. It was one of the fuzzy ones I heard. It doesn't need much but he is amazed anyway how much better it sounds. If only I could take care of the rest of the section, this orchestra could sound great.

4:15 P.M. Joe is going to get me a sandwich, I hope it is soon enough. I won't be able to see if I get a migraine. I have to go to the bathroom quick. Oops, I'll have to wait. One of the musicians who missed his appointment with me yesterday comes up! I thought he might have changed his mind about having anything done. Fantastic! We work on his cello on stage. This is more like it!

4:25 P.M. Everyone is coming back on stage. Maybe I can talk to the violinists now. Wow, talk about a cold shoulder! I just asked a few of the younger violinists if I could look at their violins. Most of them wouldn't even look at me! I wonder what is going on. Out of time, rehearsal is starting and it is time to go sit down again.

4:30 P.M. Rehearsal is with the choir this time. I better go eat quickly and take a bathroom break. Joe comes with me. Maybe we can talk about his sales trip to Florida next month. I hope that goes well. He tells me about David Taylor, the associate concertmaster. Joe says that all the violinists respect David and listen to what he has to say, he certainly has earned that respect! We have been invited to go to his house after supper. That's so cool. Oh man, was I hungry! That was the best Schlotzsky's sandwich! Just in time too, no headache now.

4:45 P.M. Back in the Hall. Wow what music! Don't focus on the bad tone, just enjoy where you are and what you are listening to. I must get autographs from the singers for Mom.

5:00 P.M. This is so relaxing. I did enough with the cellos, word will spread and the next time I come, the rest of the orchestra will be ready to have me work on their instruments. I hope.

5:15 P.M. I can't believe I fell asleep. I hope no one noticed. I always fall asleep in concerts. It's like dreaming listening to music, the images the music creates are different every time.

5:30 P.M. Break time, more chat. This isn't so bad. The cellos sound better and I fixed one of the problems in the second violins. Too bad the bright nasty one in the firsts wouldn't let me touch her instrument. I can't believe that the concertmaster is playing a Strad! It sounds terrible with only half the tone it should have, only bright edge and no depth. This is so frustrating.

7:00 P.M. Rehearsal is over. Gary brings his other cello for me to look at. David, the associate concertmaster, doubts if I can play well enough to judge it! There, I hope he is impressed with that bit of playing.

7:15 P.M. David, Gary, Joe, and I walk to Berghoff's for dinner. I hope I have enough money. Still haven't had time to go to a cash machine. I don't think Joe will have enough to cover it.

7:30 P.M. What a great place! This is the best German restaurant in Chicago! I think I'll order the veal sautéed in garlic. I know Mom's sauerbraten is still better than what they have here.

8:00 P.M. Can I please eat? Do you mind if I take a bite or two? How many questions is this guy going to ask me about adjusting? This is endless! At least he is not asking dumb questions.

8:30 P.M. I'll tell them about Antonius Stradivarius and his ten kids and maybe he will stop asking questions about tone and adjusting. I just can't go into enough detail to explain everything correctly. Setting up an instrument can be very complicated. It is hard to condense it into a few answers.

9:00 P.M. Dessert: YUM, apple strudel. I better leave a little to not look like a pig, even though I want to eat it all. Thank you Lord for your help today, I couldn't have done it alone.

9:30 P.M. I am going with David on the train to his house. I think I'll take my tool bag, at least Joe won't have to lug it to the car. I don't think it is very nice to split up like this.

9:40 P.M. Riding the train in Chicago. Boy, this brings back childhood memories. I should have given my tool bag to Joe. This is heavy and awkward to hold on my lap. There is no way I'm going to put it on the floor! YUK! David just said something but I couldn't catch it, it's too noisy on the train. Walking again. I need more exercise. I thought he said it was five minutes to his apartment. Whew!

9:55 P.M. What a place! Beautiful house with oriental rugs on the oak floors. It's so clean and neat! Lots of glass cabinets and huge paintings. I can see David is a collector of other art objects too. I have got to clean up the house when I get home. What are the kids doing right now? Are they in bed? I wonder who made the paintings. I feel like the girl in the scene in *Risky Business* when she is casing the house. David's wife comes downstairs. She is pretty, looks a little put out that I am here. I'll bet she wants to get back to practicing her violin. She gets us all coffee and goes back upstairs to practice. David explains that she is preparing for a competition coming up in one month.

10:10 P.M. Joe arrives. It's about time! I don't know what to say to David anymore. The questions have been a constant stream. How do you determine when a soundpost fits? Why is it bad for a post to be at an angle? What do you do when the E-string squeaks? How do you determine what style to make a bridge? I feel pumped dry.

10:30 P.M. David has a few very nice bows and two nice Guadagninis. Value? Maybe 1 to 1.5 mill. Piacenza: harder varnish, pinched f-holes, deep trough around edges, oval lower holes, check the purfling—Yep, the corners are right. Nice scroll, has the dots too. Turin: what happened to the varnish? This doesn't look right, better not say anything, David might not appreciate it. The arching is right, purfling, wood, f-holes, linings, all OK. I'll have to remember this one.

11:00 P.M. David asks me to listen to his violins. What do you know, maybe I'll get a chance to work with him.

11:20 P.M. Yep, I fixed them both. Wow, much better tone. Next to making a violin, this is what I want to do most of all, getting instruments to sound right. David says nobody else could get his violins to sound so good. Can't other people hear what to do?

11:25 P.M. I can't believe David dragged his wife downstairs and is making her have me do an adjustment. She is the most reluctant one yet! She has a death grip on her violin and is glaring at me. Understandable too, she is in a competition in one month. This is not the time to change anything! Dear Lord please guide my hands to do the right thing! I need to make one very small move on the post . . .

11:45 P.M. His wife is glowing! What a difference! Joe just let out the breath he has been holding all this time. David says I should adjust the whole CSO to make them sound better. Now I get it. This is the guy who didn't think I could do anything in such a short time. He must have told everyone in the violin sections to ignore me, that I couldn't make a difference. That's why he was so nosy and asked so many questions before letting me look at his violins. I don't blame him for wanting to know if I knew what I was doing. Well, thank you Lord for the convert! I'll be back in February and I'll be ready to really go to town on the CSO!

Midnight. David breaks open some Schnapps and I finally totally relax. I know I will sleep well tonight.

BUBBA

Started my coffee and the cat Bubba was crying for his food and medicine. He gets Valium morning and night. Can you believe that, the cat gets the good drugs, I get coffee. No justice. Bubba—rescued by my daughter Sachi from the neighborhood bullies as a kitten—was adopted the same time we adopted Sachi. So when Bubba got really neurotic living at our new house, destroying the furniture, spraying everywhere, it was either kill the cat or get the good drugs. Not wanting to scar my dear sweet adopted daughter more, I opted for the drugs. I pick up the prescription at the neighborhood grocery store, since my insurance plan does not cover animals. The pharmacist reminds me that Bubba shouldn't operate any heavy machinery or drive, and don't mix with alcohol.

LETHA SUNDQUIST DeCAIRES, 43, *Kailua, Hawaii*;
Crime Stoppers coordinator, Honolulu Police Department

THE PRICE YOU PAY

Corey and I went to Marshalls which SUCKED big time. I thought I could find some long-sleeved shirts for under $10 but not even close. They didn't have any clothes I would have worn, but I would have bought a yoga mat. Maybe still will when I start it at home. So now I have to check UGHmart for shirts. It sucks being so poor that you can't stick to your principles. Bah.

SØREN MASON TEMPLE, 28, *South Deerfield, Massachusetts*;
artist currently on disability

SLASH, SLASH

3:30 A.M. This has been happening to me, lately. If I have a particularly exciting day of editing, it takes a long while for my mind to shut down. Today I discovered I could eliminate a scene that I thought was necessary to the movie: the character Alison confessing that she called the cops at the kid's party. That was never in the script, but when the actress playing Alison came up with that during an improvisation (she had actually called the cops once, during a high school drinking party), I thought, wow, let's put that in the film. The problem is that it's too momentous an action—that could be a story in and of itself. A kid's betrayal that leads to a death. And Alison isn't even the main character. So it clutters the story with yet another twist that intellectually I could justify but, in this two-hour container which is the absolute longest this film should be, it just muddies the basic paradigm of the movie. It was really liberating to cut that scene. Slash, slash. The form of the film begins to emerge from the bulk of footage.

NORA JACOBSON, 49, *Norwich, Vermont*;
independent filmmaker

LABOR DAY

9:15 A.M. I leave for work and walk to the train. As I cross the street to cut through the park, I realize that I am wearing the wrong shoes. I had planned to wear my black boots, since I am wearing my black stretch pants and green sweater, but I threw on the brown ones out of habit. I feel like a dork, and I know this is going to bother me all day. Then I feel stupid for knowing it's going to bother me. I hate the fact that I am so fixated on my shoes and the color of my shoes. I wonder where it comes from. Probably my mother or my grandmother. They were both obsessed with the whole Labor Day rule thing—no white shoes after Labor Day? Something like that. I can't even remember the rule, and yet I know I was highly conscious of it all the way through college.

GENEVRA GALLO, 29, *Chicago, Illinois*;
staff writer, Planned Parenthood

BUREAUCRACY

2:00 P.M. I now have time to call Social Security about my aging parents. I don't feel like doing it. I'm always calling people who are associated with the world of old people like insurance companies, social workers, and the Department of Housing Services. These calls usually entail talking to someone who gives me a piece of information (or misinformation, however you want to look at it) that wasn't given to me the last time I called. This causes delay in fixing a problem because now I will have to get a document/fill out a form that didn't exist before, since no one knew or told me about it, but now is mandatory if I am going to solve my dilemma. Or sometimes they'll tell me I have to call someone else first who then won't return my calls. Or stand in line somewhere. Or pay for something. Or wait. Then I will be so frustrated by this new barrier to resolution that I will go into a bathroom or hallway to cry. Then I will wipe my tears and go back to my desk and work.

MEGAN WEINERMAN, 33, *San Francisco, California*;
co-creative director of Simply She notecards

POLO

I have a lesson this morning with my new polo students, two divorcees and a middle-aged man. We scrimmage. Today is a breakthrough day. They have been taking only a month's worth of lessons and were at the stage where everything seemed confusing. Nearside, offside, hook, bump. Last week their eyes were staring back at me with blank looks. Now, after the scrimmage, I could see it click. Victory! I think. Last week, even though I know that it is always like this, I wondered if it was me, if I wasn't explaining things properly or was giving them too much to digest. But today made all the hard work and worrying worthwhile. They actually looked like they knew what they were doing.

KRIS BOWMAN, 38, *Vero Beach, Florida*; **polo instructor**

NEUROLOGY

9:00 A.M. I'm eating breakfast before going to work. Ooh, this hot Korean sweet potato tastes so good. So I guess Dad didn't go to work today because he has another funeral to go to. Dad is sixty-six or sixty-seven. It seems like every other week he is going to a friend's funeral. Dad says he saw my father-in-law at the wake last night. He says that he gave such a wonderful neurology. I say, What? Neurology, he gave a very nice neurology. Uh, Dad, I think you mean eulogy. Oh, yeah. Sigh. Foreigners.

BONITA B. HWANG CHO, 32, *Glenview, Illinois*; **attorney**

Documentary Filmmaker

*C*urrently producing a documentary on men who lost brothers in the World Trade Center attacks. She worked nine years in L.A, then five years as assistant to director Phillip Noyce (*Clear and Present Danger, The Saint*). Half the time they were on location—Mexico, London, Moscow. "When the exhaustion started to catch up with me, I'd wake up in the middle of the night and wait to focus on a wall to figure out where I was." Loved the job but it was relentless. She came home to family, to New York City. Learned to set healthy boundaries, learned to say no. "I was living essentially an unconscious life, not aware of things being somewhat out of control." Finally, a life more in balance. Then came 9/11. Worked for months at the headquarters for disaster relief. A caseworker, she advocated for displaced workers and homeowners. "One woman called me her guardian angel. We all were." After volunteering at Ground Zero, the images still linger. "It's difficult to fit the memory of that war zone into the rest of my life's memories." Single in NYC. "To quote Sarah Jessica Parker in *Sex and the City*, 'New York is my boyfriend'... and I helped him heal."

STEPHANIE ZESSOS, 38, *New York, New York*

11:59 P.M. Signed off computer in guest room at Susanna's house in Nyack. Susanna and I did 9/11 casework and Ground Zero volunteering together. I love coming up here to visit her and her great family. My eyes hurt. Desktop is multiple images of Kurt Cobain—reminding me of my old, unhealthy saving fantasies—"He wouldn't have died if I loved him."

12:04 A.M. Hot-water bottle on my stomach will help me fall asleep. I can't sleep if I'm cold. Catching up on stack of sections from the *New York Times*. Wonder where in the world James Nachtwey is tonight. Saw documentary about him, *War Photographer*, for second time at arts cinema in Pleasantville tonight. First time I saw it at the Film Forum with my friend, just before he left for Ingushetia, Cambodia, and Sudan to shoot for *National Geographic*. There are compassionate photographers, yet we still only see their images framed, contained, edited. We'll never know the whole story. What is it like to be there? Do I really want to know? I have never been around so much loss in my entire life as I have this year. London in 1996, a friend from Sarajevo told us in a taxi on the way to a party,

"I would go to a party and the next day, ten of those friends would be dead."
I remember feeling sympathetic and distant. Today I am empathetic and closer.

12:14 A.M. Good night?

12:30 A.M. Still awake. Forgot to watch *Nightline* piece on Nadia Comaneci.
I was a bit interested in where she is now. Hear train in the distance.

7:50 A.M. Clear cold fall day. Sun shining on Hudson River. Another reason I
moved back East from L.A.

9:25 A.M. Fellow Ground Zero volunteer just e-mailed me a photo taken by a
Verizon employee a few days after the attack. The shot is at night from Verizon's windows overlooking the destruction. There are winged, glowing figures
all over the image rising to the sky. They look like angels, or Emmy Awards.
Don't know. I'm a bit skeptical about this one. I remember hearing about this
photo early on. What struck me often was the vast emptiness of the site. One
night, ghostly fog moved through the light memorial for hours, while body
parts were being brought up the ramp in red hazmat bags and traveling by me
on the FDNY ATV units.

10:03 A.M. In taxi on Tapan Zee Bridge. Eyes heavy. Need more sleep.

10:45 A.M. On train. Looking at river. Thinking of rowing on Charles River in
college. One of my favorite sounds was the click and echo of the oars as we
rowed under the bridges. One of my least favorite smells was when a couple of
guys on the men's team were having a contest to see who could go the longest
without washing his shirt. Boathouse stunk when these guys came in. Smell lingered long after they left.

11:00 A.M. Still on train. Saturday, Sean and I are interviewing a brother, Jose
Quintana, who lost his two younger brothers, Felix and Ivan Vale. Both worked
for Cantor. Jose works for the NASDAQ in 1 Liberty Plaza, which faces the
World Trade Center. He saw the whole thing unfold as he emerged from the subway—asked a stranger if he could borrow a cell phone to try to reach his brothers up there. Person said no.
    Still trying to get two Dominican brothers who worked at Windows on the
World. They were out that day. Their other two brothers were working. All four
usually worked the same morning shift together. Arriving each day at 4 A.M.

they'd make coffee and look out at the mountaintop view of sleeping Manhattan. They don't speak English. Waiting for caseworker to return my most recent calls. Been trying to get food service workers in the documentary for months.

Want to sleep but can't. Metro North seats are so uncomfortable. Last thing I need today is a pinched nerve in my neck.

11:15 A.M. Windows on the World brothers' caseworker just called! They're interested in participating. She'll call me back to confirm but this is good. I'll tell Sean when I see him.

11:30 A.M. Aging Goth-woman with long jet black hair drove taxi back to East Village.

1:21 P.M. Man on radio just said, "We're approaching the World Series, and probably war with Iraq."

2:30 P.M. In apartment on hold with FDNY HQ. Need permission to film at a firehouse next week. Looking at photo of Mikhail Baryshnikov taken during moment of pause in a rehearsal studio. Some ballet dancers appear to be channeling an otherworldly force. I think Jacques d'Amboise calls it "the demon-goddess." Wish I could have seen Suzanne Farrell and Allegra Kent dance. Wendy Whelan of NYCB appears not so much to be channeling the demon-goddess as providing an almost extreme vessel for the art. When she is on stage, I can't look at anyone else. A ballet I have thought about a lot this year is *In Memory of . . .*, about a young woman who is deteriorating and finally dies. At the end of the ballet two men lift her and her legs move through the air, weightless and free towards heaven. Cried in that one. Also cried when Damian Woetzel crawled across the stage into his father's open arms in *Prodigal Son*. Wished they hadn't brought up the lights so quickly because I wanted to bawl my eyes out. I've been going to ballets at Lincoln Center since I was a little girl. THANKS Mom and Dad. Still on hold. Going to have to call back, I gotta go.

3:00 P.M. Sean's picking me up soon. Sean McGinly is directing this documentary about men who lost brothers on 9/11. His younger brother Mark worked for Carr Futures on the ninety-second floor of Tower 1. Sean said everyone below them, from ninety-first floor down, got out. Mark was twenty-six years old. In January, Sean e-mailed me saying he wanted to make this documentary. And here we are—two dozen brothers and counting. The brothers have all been so brave, honest, and open, and of course they relate to Sean. I don't know where Sean gets the strength to do this. This project is emotionally draining for me. I hope someday it might help someone, perhaps someone who might feel isolated in their feelings, or just forgotten.

3:44 P.M. In Sean's Jeep now on way to Jackson Heights, Queens for follow-up interview with John Cartier, our long-haired, Harley-riding, deer-hunting, local 3 electrician/foreman whose younger brother James was killed on 9/11. John has become a victims' families advocate and activist with Give Your Voice. Sean handed me the paper to get some show times for *Bowling for Columbine* tonight. My old boss, Sam Shepard, is on cover of "Arts and Leisure" section with his new book. Loved working for Sam. He'd rather talk to a ranchhand than an executive producer.

4:29 P.M. Sitting in brother's house. Ray is making last adjustments on the camera. Interview starting. Turned phone off. Sean and John are comparing their recent visits with psychics. These guys are the least likely candidates for this kind of thing. Even though Sean lives in L.A., he's just not the "candles and crystals" type—and John looks like he could make a call and a hundred Hells Angels would be at your door in five minutes. But I have found that many victims' families and friends just want information—anything—about how their loved one died, if they're OK now. As John just said, the living are "chasing that last bit of breath they expelled."

5:12 P.M. Have to begin healing from all these months of working and giving to the aftermath of this tragedy, including listening to these brothers. John is talking about his work in the recovery effort at Ground Zero. He worked there with intense devotion, trying to find his brother. They found some remains eventually. There are things I heard and saw down there that still haunt me—watching the guys raking carefully and respectfully, looking for any trace of what used to be a human being—in between getting the workers eye drops, gloves, coffee.

Back listening to the interview. In regards to dealing with life after something like this, John just said, "get busy livin' or get busy dyin'."

6:00 P.M. Sean, John Cartier, Ray, and I are at Jackson Hole diner on Astoria Blvd. I'm off to the restroom. What is that woman doing in there? She just came out saying, "Sorry, I was putting my hair up." Poster of Marilyn Monroe on wall when she was still Norma Jean.

7:40 P.M. Checked message on cell phone. Melanie is safely back from business trip in Europe. Thank God. Love my sister. Our secret, silly language—well, sounds really. Our communicating has become so abbreviated, we call each other and make weird sounds.

Speeding on BQE listening to the White Stripes, good, hard music. City sure looks pretty tonight.

7:50 P.M. Walking north on Thompson Street. So quiet.

9:33 P.M. Sean and I are at Union Square theater about to see *Punch Drunk Love*. We're both tired. After this it's off to bed. I can't take in any more information today.

11:30 P.M. In video store on Broadway using coupon that expires tomorrow. Got Michael Moore's film *The Big One*. Wanted to see this before *Bowling for Columbine* to catch up on his work. In line with kids (probably ages sixteen to eighteen?) chirping, laughing, telling stories:

"I'm like . . . then she was like . . ."

"She's like . . . what da fuck?"

"So I'd be like . . . touchin' all dem bitches."

11:58 P.M. Walking past gorgeous flowers on 9th and 1st, keeping up with the Bridget Jones's. Still a Singleton.

11:59 P.M. Halfway to Avenue A. Looking into Bolivar Arellano gallery—photographs of firemen's faces, falling bodies, the collapse, that skeletal piece of the tower, Father Mychal Judge. Also a small shrine of flowers and candles underneath the poster of the 343 firemen who perished. Sometimes I'll keep walking but sort of reach my hand out for a moment towards the pictures. Sometimes I stop and look. Sometimes I walk on the other side of the street.

AMERICA THE BEAUTIFUL

We take the exit to the Badlands. It is a drive through Badlands Loop. We use my lifetime pass to get in the park for free. My husband Colby just loves it 'cause parks are not cheap to get into. When we were in Hawaii and we went to visit a volcano park, the ranger and Colby somehow got to talking and the ranger found out I was legally blind so he gave me a lifetime free park pass. Colby LOVED that! And he always smiles when we get into a park for FREE! And I always say, "Aren't you happy to have a blind wife?" and we laugh. My in-laws, Mim and Vern, got in free too 'cause we gave Vern a birthday present the other day for a yearly park pass. He got in FREE. He really was so pumped about that too.

ANIKÓ SAMU-KUSCHATKA, 36, *Walla Walla, Washington*;
bakery owner and coordinator of Deaf Camps, Inc.

I get a call at 4:30 that gets me really excited. The hotel tells me I have mail and I am sure it will be my transfer paperwork. I have been having a problem getting my unit administrator's work accomplished in time. I will have to re-enlist in thirty days and if my transfer is not complete I may be discharged accidentally. I wouldn't have said this when I was younger, but I do love being an Army Reservist. It is just enough army without it becoming a dreadful chore. There is nothing that can compare to the fraternity between soldiers. It is a bond that is lifelong. It is something I am glad to share with my husband. It is one of the only places where I can go to work with no makeup, comfortable clothes, and get paid the same as a man.

HEIDI GRISA, 30, *Chicago, Illinois*; **U.S. Army Reservist**

I arrive at the meeting in Oakland about The Precautionary Principle. The room is full of people who hate corporations, like me. I'm pleased and settle in to listen to a very smart woman who talks about poisons, carcinogens, mutagens, teratogens, and Big Corp Pharma-Chem-Co turning them loose with no testing because they are presumed innocent because it's good for bloody business. There are nurses and doctors there, whom the system has spat out. I love them instantly. I find out the speaker is married to a militant New Hampshire organic farmer. A power couple for the twenty-first century. He farms, she sues. There's to be a meeting tomorrow in Berkeley (alternative healthcare) at City Hall. The same people will be there. Only in Berkeley, and that's why I live there. On purpose. The meeting ends. We eat lots of food like guacamole and brie and talk and exchange stories, outrage, phones and e-mails, and drift away.

CHRISTINE VIDA, 55, *Berkeley, California*;
home health nurse and Spanish/French film voiceover talent

At the post office we discuss the weather for a few minutes and touch on local politics. The post office and our local restaurant/bar are our community gathering centers. School closed sixteen years ago and it has been over twenty-five years since Seneca has had a grocery store. Our entire community is needed to keep our town alive. Only the registered village voters will be able to decide the outcome of the board members. Two of the current members have totally taken control of the village business. These two women are the most vindictive and hostile women I've ever known. So far on their term, they've spent their efforts controlling the people and establishing their territory. No improvements have been done. Their actions have cost the village a great deal in lost revenue and progress. We have to remove them somehow. Hopefully the election will take care of the problem. I don't remember the people being so united for our community.

JACKIE SEVIER, 49, *Seneca, Nebraska*;
Northern Arapaho tribal member and mixed media artist

I was determined to walk today. I start out thinking I'll do lazy, just around the neighborhood then to CVS to drop off photos. Instead, once I get into the wind, I walk up 16th Street and through Malcolm X Park and back, which puts me at CVS at 8:10, exactly forty minutes after I started, an acceptable walk. I love walking the neighborhood, so much to notice, so much madness. The gentrification just about slaps you in the face, the white folks with big dogs that they don't bother to control, the folks who speed up and turn when they see you crossing the street. The chocolate in the district still makes you smile, the lady with the little boy she could have spit out holding hands and crossing the street, the brothers cleaning up the park who stop to say hello. Even the crazies. A man sitting on a bench in the park offering commentary on the problems of government, every other word is W. I don't hear him at first and just experience his voice as background noise, but when I focus on the W, I realize that the man is saying something and I listen.

JULIANNE MALVEAUX, 49, *Washington, D.C.*;
syndicated journalist and president of Last Word Productions

What is this world coming to (or at least American TV)? A woman suing another woman for the first getting pregnant because a car accident made her forget to take her birth control pills. What a crazy lawsuit. Does she really expect child support? The crazy things we do in America!

MALINDA BOYD, 22, *Durham, North Carolina*;
M.D./Ph.D. student, Duke University

One of America's Leading Spiritual Teachers

$\mathcal{A}$ Buddhist whose work is based on the ancient practices of mind-fulness and *metta* (loving kindness). Thirty years ago, she was seeking resolution to a fragmented life. The quest led her to India and a life-altering discovery—with meditation comes clarity and peace. Cofounder of the Insight Meditation Society in Barre, Massachusetts, her way of bringing her discovery home. A meditation hindrance? "If I had one, it would be sleepiness rather than excitement." She was inspired to write her latest book, *Faith*, because of concerns about her public persona—an image based more on her skills as a teacher rather than her essence. "I don't want to be a fragmented person . . . what I felt when I first went to India." At first she disliked the descriptor "beloved" on her book jacket. Then she realized that it is indeed a mark of her life, "people love me and love me as a teacher." The cover also labeled her as "renowned." "That strikes me as funny. The bedrock of my life is meditation, so I'm famous for being quiet."

SHARON SALZBERG, 50, *Barre, Massachusetts*

7:30 A.M. I woke up, grabbed my pad of paper, and made my first day diary entry, "meditated and did yoga." Then I reminded myself I was still in bed—and that a diary wasn't an idealistic document, but a truthful description. Sometimes a theme for the whole day arises right away, and I wondered if it would be truthfulness, or lack of pretense . . .

I meditated for about forty minutes. I am staying at my friend Amy's apartment in New York. She has already left for work so I am alone. I had been on the road since August 5th when my latest book, *Faith: Trusting Your Own Deepest Experience*, had come out (and which, coincidentally, was my fiftieth birthday). I often needed a lot of determination to incorporate my usual routines, such as meditating, into my life when I was on the road. August had been the most difficult—ten cities in fourteen days, eventually waking up in the morning, like in a joke, not knowing where I was or what I had to do next. By now my schedule had slowed down, so it felt relatively luxurious. Still, it was easy to overlook my practice, to just get up and get down to work, and I had to be careful not to.

10:00 A.M.–12:00 P.M. Someone had interviewed me for the *Shambhala Sun* magazine during one of my rare trips home while on my book tour. It would run a cover story about my spiritual path. I checked my e-mail and saw that I'd received the rough draft, then spent much of the morning reviewing it. I was intrigued to see how I was seen by someone else. She describes me basically as a mirror—"If you were angry you might think she was angry, if you were sad, you might think she was sad; if you were lonely or bored or tired or scared or feeling above it all or deeply, deeply depressed or very happy, you might think she was that." I wondered if she understood me, since I might function as a mirror while teaching, but in my personal life I am a human being with feelings of my own, like anybody else. I wondered if I wanted to be understood to any real depth, so publicly. My teaching is my service to others, after all, and I don't feel it is fair to depend on my students or readers to be my good friends and confidantes.

It was strange to be looking at "me" from the outside—I'd spent so many years cultivating the feeling of being at home within myself. I probably would have written it differently, choosing different things to emphasize, such as work I do to help in the promotion of other people's books, in aid of the democracy movement in Burma and its leader, Aung San Suu Kyi, and in support of the work of the Dalai Lama. Trish concentrated pretty exclusively on my path of meditation, rather than the expansive ramifications of that path. Is this how the whole world sees me? I wondered. I have a public persona—it's not a pretense, but most people know me through my teachings or my writing. I felt immensely grateful that the author of the piece skipped over the phenomenal messiness of my kitchen, with mail piled up everywhere, since I'd been traveling too much for too long. And I felt just where the writer and I met most genuinely—in a keen love of meditation practice and the joys of spiritual aspiration, not wanting to settle for an unconscious life.

2:00 P.M. I walked into a nearby Indian restaurant for lunch. I'd organized a gathering of people from different parts of my life who had wanted to meet each other. I care about people realizing they have an interest they share, or a bond they can appreciate, or a way they can help each other through a source of sorrow. The first person I saw was Daphne, whom I had met three months earlier when I was leading a retreat in California. We had Krishna Das as a mutual friend, but had missed each other at a couple of his appearances. He had given her one of my books to read, and suggested she do the July retreat. Daphne and I formed an immediate friendship at the retreat, solidified later at my L.A. book appearances in August.

At the lunch, I'd known one person for thirty years, one for twenty-eight, a couple for two years, and Daphne, whom I'd known for three months. There was a psychiatrist present, an artist, a real estate developer, two actresses, my assistant, and Krishna Das who travels everywhere doing devotional chanting and world music. Krishna Das was the person I had known the longest, and I consider him a remarkably sensitive and generous friend. He is the kind of person who literally would give someone the shirt off his back. Trish, the person writing the article about me for the *Shambhala Sun*, commented on how many different worlds I entered. I was startled by the comment, and replied, "Lots of different people enter my world—I only inhabit the one." I feel that is true, and I'm grateful for it; from the very beginning of my spiritual practice I had wanted to become a more integrated person, simply being who I was in any situation, instead of feeling so fragmented all the time. I think my years of meditation practice have accomplished that.

It was great to see people bonding over the latest technology, over music, over love for a spiritual perspective, over love. One couple spoke of the new house they'd bought in Woodstock; another of their trip to Bali, and a comment by a Balinese healer about the wondrous nature of Krishna Das's music (they'd never met, and Krishna Das was surprised and moved). We all played with a gizmo that was a combination of cell phone and e-mail device complete with keyboard.

5:00 P.M. I tried and tried to get a taxi uptown. Finally, a baby blue limo pulled over, and I got uptown. Krishna Das and I were teaching together that night about faith (the logic, and title, of my latest book), and meditation and chanting. It was a benefit for the local meditation group. Many events on my book tour had been benefits for different meditation centers and groups, and this organization, New York Insight, was one I was particularly close to since I spend so much time teaching in New York City. Krishna Das caught me on my cell phone, saying there was nothing to sit on but the bare wooden stage.

I ran in—he was doing a sound check—ran around a bit trying to get us something to sit on. I saw two of the organizers, but they didn't know anything about the stage. I was irritated especially since Krishna Das was doing this as a favor to me and I wanted him to at least have something to sit on. Finally, someone ran in with cushions she happened to have in her car.

5:45 P.M. I went to a nearby restaurant to meet someone, a woman I didn't know very well but whom I liked. We had missed each other several times in NYC, so even though this was an inconvenient time for me just before teaching, it was the time that worked so we did it. She had wanted to meet with me about setting up a series of women's conferences. It's a topic that has come up a lot; as the nation seems to be marching toward war, as the things we thought we could count on—a robust economy, a safe trip to get gas in D.C—were shaken, a lot of people have begun wondering what might come out of women gathering. I promised to introduce her to other women organizing those kinds of conferences. I wished I wasn't so busy; that I could pay more full attention to things that particularly inspired me without fearing I'd soon get overwhelmed.

7:00–10:00 P.M. I don't usually prepare before speaking these days, but try to be quiet and feel the room. I haven't been nervous in years about public speaking, though basically I'm quite shy. Somehow, in teaching, something notable comes through me as long as I can step out of the way. There were lots of friends there and joy at seeing them. Also, Krishna Das and I had been teaching together in a variety of venues for a month. This evening (with three hundred attendees) was the last thing we had scheduled until next April, so the transitions between us—singing, meditation, speaking—were very smooth. We've been friends for thirty years and there wasn't any egoic wrangling between us. In fact, I wish he'd sing more; he wishes I'd speak more. The conversation turned to our lives in India thirty years ago, where illness, adversity, and uncertainty were met with energy, courage, and lightness of heart because we all felt we were on an amazing adventure of discovery.

I told the story of a friend who had recounted to the doctors at the local clinic in Barre, Massachusetts, the terrible ordeal of the heat during the hot season in India. She talked about 110-degree heat, and of how she had suffered in it because she was in New Delhi going from government office to government office trying to renew her visa. She said she was particularly sensitive to the heat because she was weakened from hepatitis, worms, and amoebic dysentery. One of the doctors in Barre looked at her in horror and exclaimed, "You had hepatitis, worms, and amoebic dysentery and you were trying to renew your visa! What were you doing, holding out for leprosy?" Of course, I was careful to say, staying and simply enduring terrible conditions isn't always the right thing to do. But it was extraordinary to look back and see how our love for what we were doing, for the friendships we were forming, and for the sense that our lives were opening up gave us the strength to work through difficulties. How can that translate to now, I wondered? If we could have some of that sense of adventure, of aspiration, of loving community, of learning all the time, today's challenges would seem so much more workable.

We had a fabulous evening together, sharing. People came up to have me sign my new book and talk. Many were having a sense of helplessness about affecting the world, trying to make it a better place. I pointed out various people in the audience I knew were doing different kinds of work. One person was organizing a peace movement in response to the threat of war in Iraq; one was affiliated with socially responsible businesses; one was a documentary film-maker who had done remarkable films, most recently a film called *Fierce Grace* on the spiritual leader Ram Dass; one was a writer who had charted the paths of courageous and innovative spiritual leaders. Maybe, I mused, the theme of the day was coming together, connecting.

10:30 P.M. Dinner outside at a nearby café, even though it was chilly. A group of people associated with my retreat center, the Insight Meditation Society, had come down from Massachusetts for the event, and we had dinner together. It was particularly gratifying to have people travel so far to the event. Several friends walked by who had been at the talk, people I knew quite well from my classes and retreats. It was like we had taken over the neighborhood. Here, again, different elements of my life had come together—NYC, Massachusetts. I though, just felt like . . . me.

Acknowledgments

$\mathcal{W}$e would like to thank the 529 women who generously contributed day diaries to this book project (a complete list follows these acknowledgments). Forty-one of the day diarists also participated in a trial run of this book; their early faith and contributions helped us to find a publisher.

A special thanks goes to the following individuals: Melinda Blanchard, Tracy Comeau, Nancy Fontaine, Fran Ginestet, Jeanette Heinz, Kim Keating, Deborah McKew, Cornelia Purcell, John Raven, Judith Seime, and Matt Swett.

Additional thanks to Michelle Barnes, Outward Bound USA; Duane Bates, Habitat for Humanity International; Sharon Becker, The Miss America Organization; Robert B. Buckley, Jr., legal services; Terry Galindo, tour manager for Anoushka Shankar; Barbara Goodell, Anderson Valley Adult School; Karen Miller, Minnesota Correctional Facility, Shakopee; Martin Needham, Brea Police Department; Dina Pappas, Women's National Basketball Association (WNBA); Barbara Pflughaupt, Feld Entertainment; Carol Pierson, Stave Puzzles; Edith Robles, the Office of Congresswoman Hilda Solis; Sally Rovirosa, Stahmann's Country Store; Wendy Thomajan, Ford Models, Inc.; Theresa Tirella, United South End Settlements; Wendy Weil, The Wendy Weil Agency; AmeriCorps*VISTA; Beyond Words Publishing; Guide Dog Foundation for the Blind; KVOX-FM Radio, Fargo, North Dakota; National Funeral Directors Association; National Organization for Women; Rod and Staff Publishing; Rosie's Place; Royal Caribbean Cruise Lines; Sharp & Associates Public Relations; Starbucks Corporation; Thunder Valley Racing; Tuck School of Business, Dartmouth College; United States Olympic Committee; and United States Polo Association.

For more information about *This Day: Diaries from American Women*, visit **www.thisdayinthelife.com**.

List of Participants

Anna Adachi-Mejia, NH
Bridget Ahrens, VT
Emily A. Alaimo, PA, 92
Jane Alexander, ND, 200
Jennifer Allyn, NJ, 238
Deborah Anapol, CA
Susan C. Anderson, AL, 92
Jenefer Angell, OR, 38
Mary M. Anker, ME
Aubrey Aquino, CA
Lupita M. Armendariz, TX
Katherine Armstrong, NH
Harjit K. Arora, NY
Mary Atkins, GA
Mary Jane Auker, PA
Anjali Austin, FL
Kendra M. Ayers, CA
Tara Bahrampour, NY
Kari Baker, MT
Kim Baker, MT
Peggy Baldwin, NC
Virginia Ballou, VT
Nancy Parent Bancroft, MI
Michelle Barnes, CO, 200
Lisa Baron, MN, 201
Geraldine Mercedes Barrutia, TX
Marlene Battle, IL
Emily Bean, ME
Judith A. Beers, NC
Rose Benson, CA
Julie Benz, CA, 78
Pamela Berelson, CA
Kathryn Berkowitz, AK
Aleksandra Bieńkowska, IL
Mary Kay Binder, NJ
Jennifer Bixby, MA*
Evie Black, HI

Michelle Blair-Weeks, CA
Betty Blockus, FL
Linda Blockus, MO
Lisa M. Blockus, NY
Alison Boden, IL, 145
Lake Boggan, OR, 86
Judith Bolton-Fasman, MA, 54
Marisa Bono, MI, 175
Gwendolyn M. Bookman, NC
Milica Z. Bookman, FL
Noelle Bortfeld, WA
Rochelle A. Bourgault, NH, 61
Sara P. Boutwell, VA
Kris Bowman, FL, 265
Holly Bowyer, CA
Jenifer Boyce, ID
Malinda Boyd, NC, 272
Peggy Brady-Ross, IL
Faith P. Brickman, KY
L. Kristen Brown, SC
Sharon A. Browne, MI
Jennifer Bruder, NY
Shannon E. Buckels, CA, 107
Goldie F. Bulgatz, IL
Nancy J. Bullock, NC
Vilasinee Bunnag, NY
Heidi Burg, CA
Cheryl Bush, NH,* 114
Alice V. Butler, CA
Devon K. Byers, VT
Chezia Thompson Cager, MD, 8
Robin Cantor-Cooke, VA, 146
Janet Carl, IA
Kay Carpenter, NC
Laurie Y. Carrillo, TX
Lucia Cascio, CA
Leigh Ann Castellanos, KY

Natalie J. Goldring, VA
Donna Goodwin, MA
Tejinder K. Grewal, MI,* 255
Susan E. Griesmaier, NC
Heidi Grisa, IL,* 271
Heather Gustafson, PA
Kathryn Haber, NY
Rebecca L. Hall, WV
Shannon K. Hall, CA*
Judy A. Hall-Griswold, ID
Ayun Halliday, NY, 140
Lisa Hammer, NH
Lori Hampton, VT
Barbara Handelman, VT
Erika Harold, IL, 39
Cindi Harrison, CA, 53
Jennifer Harrison, NJ
Lisa Harrow, VT*
Cheryl B. Hartsoe, NJ
Donna Hastings, NY
Lillian Kerr Haversat, ME, 192
Kari J. Hayes, CA
Alyce Heman, IL, 223
Anne Hendrickson, MA
Maria Henson, IL, 70
Taraji P. Henson, CA, 140
Kerry Henwood, CA*
Teresa M. Herbert, NC
Susan Heslep, VA, 30
April L. Holmes, NJ
Kathleen Holmes, MO
Rene Holtzman, TX
Trina A. Hosmer, MA
Marilyn Hough, CO, 14
Linda C. Howard, MS
Shelly Howell, CA
Anna Hubbard, AR
Mabelle Drake Hueston, CA
Feona Sharhran Huff, NY
Joyce Hughes, AZ, 21
Anna M. Humphrey, VT*
Mary Anne Huntington, NY, 115
Jennifer Hurst, FL
Ellen Hwang, NY, 14
Sharon Im-Lee, WA
Lanier Scott Isom, AL

Quietness Israel, WA
Jennifer Jackson, AL, 238
Nora Jacobson, VT,* 263
Vallary Jefferson, NC, 60
Penny Jessop, LA, 107
Ruth Joffrey, IL, 201
Christine Toy Johnson, NY
Gaye G. Johnson, GA, 100
Hannah Johnson, IL
Jacqueline A. Johnson, WA, 169
Jean Johnson, MA
Lisa Johnson, VT
Carrie Jokiel, AK
Angela Jones, NY
Meg Jones, WI
Tracey E. Jones, DE
Wanda S. Jones, GA
Diana P. Jordan, OR
Jami Joyner, MO, 145
Heather Juergensen, CA
Jennifer Becker Jurewicz, MN, 256
Lea Kachadorian, VT
Jenny Kales, NY, 210
Eva Kaminsky, NY,* 69
Irene C. Kassorla, CA
Joelle Gropper Kaufman, CA
Manmeet Kaur, NH
Tina Kelley, NY, 202
Mary Olsen Kelly, HI
Judith L. Kendig, HI, 133
Bonnie Kenyon, VT*
Rebecca K. Killian, NC
Julia Kim-Byun, CA
Ellen Kitchel, VT
Katharine Kitchel, VT, 108
Kimberly C. Knott, AL, 85
Susan L. Koester, MS, 14
Myrna L. Koonce, ME
Marianne E. Kosty, NY
Wendy Swartz Kotsakis, IL*
Tanya Kozlowski, IL
Lynne A. Kraemer, NJ
Karen S. Kramer, CA
Karen Krase, NY
Linda K. Krog, IA
Marcia Brumit Kropf, NY

Rachelle LaBarge, IA

Monica Lacy, CA

Lisa Lagasse, MA

Sanoe Lake, CA

Munira A. Lalmohamed, PA

Sharon E. Lambert, DE, 200

Linda Lee Landrigan, VT and NY, 222

Juleyka Lantigua, NY

Cynthia K. Larive, KS

Kathy Leffler, AZ

Anne Marie Lemal-Brown, MA, 146

Deana Lewis, HI

Joyce Butts Lewis, IL

Marigold Linton, KS

Ellen Lippmann, NY

Rebecca Lobo, CT, 95

Marcella J. Logue, OK

Bonnie Long, NM

Linda LoRe, CA, 126

Joann S. Lublin, NY

Kathy Lee Luger, NH

Shari Lynch, NJ

Susan Matcuk Maden, KS*

Maria Theresa Maggi, ID

Alyson M. Magliozzi, MA, 222

Lucille A. Magliozzi, MA, 218

Monique Magliozzi, MA

Patricia Maguire, AK

Marion Mahn, NJ, 223

Meg Houston Maker, NH, 60

Julianne Malveaux, DC, 272

Bobbie Mandel, CA

Gayle Seminara Mandel, IL, 14

Barbara E. Manger, WI

Jean Marcley, FL

Margaret E. Marder, MA

Linda Marks, MA

Irene Marshall, CA

Judy Martin, IA

Kristin Martinson, OR, 222

I. Joanna Massey, NC

Anita Matcuk, MO, 238

Roberta A. Mathieu, VT*

Christina R. Mautz, MT, 191

Betsey M. Mayer, MA

Nancy M. McFarlane, OR

Leah M. McGinley, MN

Deborah McGonigle, MA

Shannon Hope McInerney, AL

Sarah McKereghan, CA

Llewellyn McKernan, WV

Deborah A. McKew, NH,* 93

Katherine M. McShane, DC

Elisa Medhus, TX

Barbara Mellert, NH

Andrea S. Méndez, NH

Esperanza Padilla Méndez, TX

Sharon Mercer, SD

Jennifer C. Merrill, WY

Sarah Merrill, Japan, 218

Edith Merwin, GA

Megan Miller, WY, 238

Renée F. Miller, IL

Sharon L. Miller, NC, 62

Heather A. Hathaway Miranda, MI

Ramona D. Mitchell, IA

Betty F. Moffett, IA, 7

Emily M. Moler, AL

Angela Monson, OK

Gaye Moorhead, NM

Lisa Morita, CA

Valerie Mount, FL

Betsy Moyer, MA, 116

Marion Nassau, NY*

Michelle Nasser, LA

Carol Joy Nelson, NC

Hayley Nelson, NY

Robin Nelson, IL

Jean Nesser, TX, 92

Laura B. Newmark, NY*

Carolyn C. Newsom, PA

Honey Nichols, MA

Leslie Nichols, CO

Lyn Nierva, GA, 114, 158

Chris Niethold, MA, 77

Diane Norman, IL, 22

Lindsey Norman, WY, 38

Anne Nydam, MA, 8

Debbie J. Nylund, AZ

Kati Oakes, PA*

Meredith Oakes, NY, 60

Caroline M. O'Brien, FL

Helen C. O'Donnell, MA
Michael O'Grady-Leaver, CA
Therese Ojibway, NJ, 93
Janet R. Olson, MN, 220
April Jeanette Omoth, WA
Parminder K. Padgett, VT
Nancy A. Pageau, NH*
Janet E. Painter, IL
Patricia Palmiotto, NH*
Zoe JoAnna Papadakos, FL, 7
Carrie Patterson, VA
Rose S. Patterson, NE
Ellen Patton, LA
Kate N. Pearson, CO
Janice L. Peterson, SD
Judy A. Pich, MA
Nicole Pichard, MD
Sally Pinkas, MA
Jacquelyn Prussing, NY, 222
Cornelia Purcell, NH*
Kathryn E. Pursch, WA,* 141
Claire Marie Quinlan, CA*
Ann Moon Rabb, AL
Dorothy A. Rakhra, KY
Paula Raven, VA,* 61
Susan S. Reckford, NJ
Glenis Redmond, NC
Ann Reichsman, OH
Joan Reid, NY
Maryellen H. Reid, NJ
Hunter Reno, FL
Brenda J. Rescott, NY
Lizette Rettig, TX
Dyan Rey, ND
Ellie Richard, NC, 141
Marge M. Richards, PA
Carrie L. Richmond, OH*
Linda Riviera, TX
Beverly G. Roberts, TN
Debra Roberts, NC
Leslie Robinson, WA, 43
Tracy M. Robison, IN
Michaela Rock, CA
Lois A. Roelofs, IL, 107
Christine Rokeby-Jackson, NC, 217
Mary Roosevelt, CA, 232

Ann Rosen, IN
Kelly L. Ross-Davis, AL
Hélène Rothermund, NH, 238
Lillian Rubenstein, IL
Anna Rubin, MA
Trisha Souders Rubin, MD
June Rydholm, MI*
Shelley G. Sabga, OH
Zohra Saed, NY
Rita D. Salomon, CO
Sharon Salzberg, MA, 273
Anikó Samu-Kuschatka, WA, 271
Brinna Sands, VT
Tracey Sang, CA, 1
Amy J. Sanger, CA
Rhenita Satterfield, GA
Carole Saunders, VT*
Lynda Savard, MN, 191
Mary B. Schaefer, MA, 174
Ema Scheidel, VA
Wendy Scherer, MD, 145
Lenora S. Schur, IL, 85
Julia H. Schuster, FL
Yolanda M. Scott, PA, 160
Robyn Scott-McMillen, CO
JoNeal Scully, VA, 223
DeLores Seime, MN
Judith Seime, CT*
Michele R. Self, NM
Vicki Sengele, TX
Chessney Sevier, WY
Jackie Sevier, NE, 272
Anoushka Shankar, CA and India, 16
Robyn Sharpe, CA, 194
Arleen M. Shippey, CA
Jo-Jo Shutty-MacGregor, MI
Rachel Silverman, NY
Doris L. Simon, IL
Wendy L. Sims, MO
Merle J. Slack, DE
Brailee Smith, UT, 219
Cheryl L. Smith, TX, 37
Julie Dolan Smith, Russia
Marta L. Smith, NE
Deborah Soffel, NY
Hilda L. Solis, CA and VA, 124

Gail Somers, ID, 7
Karen A. Spengler, MO
Elizabeth T. Spiers, MD
Giulietta Spudich, England, 52
Nicole St. Pierre, NJ, 52
Sherry Stamback, VT
Cid Stanford, CA
Alice Steuerwald, KS
Pei P. Stewart, TX, 217
Mary Anne Vance Stillman, NH
Sheila S. Stover (Firehair), NC*
Anne E. Stuart, MA, 181
Kelly Stuart, MA, 60
J. Arliss Sturgulewski, AK
Maite Suarez-Rivas, MA
Rosa Sugrañes, FL
E. Jean Sutherland, FL
Teri L. Sutton, NC
Clara Swan, ME
Jean Szilva, VT, 240
Nahid Tabatabai, NH
Barbara A. Tallberg, CA
Katherine Tanney, TX
Gail Taylor, OH
Jacquelyn S. Taylor, MA
Linda Taylor, CA, 54
Søren Mason Temple, MA, 263
Janine Terrano, WA
Marisa Thalberg, NY, 182
Kadidia Thiero, DC
Dorothy Thomas, MA, 170
Johnnie Lockett Thomas, MT*
Suzanna Thomas, RI*
Beth L. Thorneycroft, TN, 159
Holly Tippett, DC
Linda Titus-Ernstoff, NH
Anupam S. Trombino, AZ
Michele T. Trujillo, CO
Stephanie Tuxill, MA, 86
Aisha Tyler, CA*
Helen Ubiñas, CT, 61
Michaelene Upton, WY
Mai Vang, MN
Gita Vasudeva, WA
Sira Veciana-Muiño, FL, 224
Ana Veciana-Suarez, FL

Emiliana Vegas, DC
Robin Vess, GA
Christine Vida, CA, 271
Laurel Viera, MN
Kristen E. vonHentschel, MA
Katherine Wadsworth, CT
Jasmine D. Wagner, NY, 217
Lynne Walker, NH
Marjorie G. Walker, WV
Sara Walker, IA
Christina Wang, CA*
Molly A. Watkins, MA
Nora Q. Waystack, MA
Tanya A. Weaver, Hungary, 115
Wanita Webb, NH, 192
Megan Weinerman, CA, 264
Peg Ghost Dancer Wene, NJ
Tina Weymouth, CT, 15
Kathy Whitehead, OR
Stephanie White Thorn, MO
Janice Whittemore (on-air name
    Anne Phibian), ND
Cheryl K. Wilde, UT
Ramona Willcox, MN
Karen L. Williams, SC, 107
Jennifer W. Wilson, CA*
Kris Winter, CA
Melaura Wittemyer, OR
Ruth Wolf, PA
Marsha Brown Woodard, PA
Valerie L. Wood-Lewis, VT, 52
Danielle Worthen, CO
Ally Wray-Kirk, CA
Sharon Shutty Wright, IL
Tina Wright, TN
Sarah A. Wuornos, MN
Sel Erder Yackley, IL, 38
Catherine A. Young, FL
Meg Young, MA
Agnes Anna Zephyr, VT, 158
Stephanie Zessos, NY, 266
Daphne Zuniga, CA*

Note: Diaries and excerpts appearing in the text are indicated by page numbers next to the participants' names; asterisks denotes participants in the "trial run" of the project.

About the Editors of This Day

This Day: *Diaries from American Women* was conceived, compiled, and edited by Joni B. Cole, Rebecca Joffrey, and B. K. Rakhra. Joni works as a freelance writer/editor and mom (often at the same time—such is life with a home office), and also teaches community fiction writing workshops. Rebecca is a marketing executive, and founder of The LookOut, a company that develops corporate online mentoring programs. Bindi is a fiction writer who left the nine-to-five world of steady paychecks and affordable insurance to write short stories and screenplays. The three partners and friends live and work in Vermont, where a day in the life is enhanced by their connectedness.

Beyond Words Publishing, Inc.

OUR CORPORATE MISSION
Inspire to Integrity

OUR DECLARED VALUES
We give to all of life as life has given us.
We honor all relationships.
Trust and stewardship are integral to fulfilling dreams.
Collaboration is essential to create miracles.
Creativity and aesthetics nourish the soul.
Unlimited thinking is fundamental.
Living your passion is vital.
Joy and humor open our hearts to growth.
It is important to remind ourselves of love.

To order or to request a catalog, contact

Beyond Words Publishing, Inc.
20827 N.W. Cornell Road, Suite 500
Hillsboro, OR 97124-9808
503-531-8700

You can also visit our Web site at *www.beyondword.com*
or e-mail us at *info@beyondword.com*.